I0123955

The Sordid Hypocrisy of TO PROTECT AND TO SERVE:

Police Brutality, Corruption and Oppression in America

Also by Thomas Fensch:

*At the Dangerous Edge of Social Justice:
Race, Violence and Death in America*

*Steinbeck's Bitter Fruit: from The Grapes of Wrath to
Occupy Wall Street*

Steinbeck and Covici: The Story of a Friendship

Conversations with John Steinbeck

Essential Elements of Steinbeck

The FBI Files on Steinbeck

*The Man Who Changed His Skin: The Life and Work of
John Howard Griffin*

*The Man Who Was Dr. Seuss: The Life and Work of
Theodor Geisel*

*Of Sneetches and Whos and the Good Dr. Seuss:
Essays on the Life and Work of Theodor Geisel*

*The Man Who Was Walter Mitty: The Life and Work of
James Thurber*

Conversations with James Thurber

*Behind Islands in the Stream: Hemingway, Cuba,
the FBI and the crook factory*

*Oskar Schindler and His List: The Man, the Book, the
Film, the Holocaust and Its Survivors*

The Kennedy-Khrushchev Letters

... and others

The Sordid Hypocrisy of
TO PROTECT AND TO SERVE:

Police Brutality, Corruption and Oppression in America

Thomas Fensch

New Century Books

Copyright 2015 Thomas Fensch

paperback ISBN: 978-0-9963154-5-6
e-book ISBN: 978-0-9963154-4-9

New Century Books
8821 Rockdale Rd
N. Chesterfield, VA 23236-2150
e-mail: newcentbks@gmail.com

Book design by Jill Ronsley, suneditwrite.com
Ebook formatting by Sun Editing & Book Design

Contents

Prologue:

To Protect and to Serve ...

... According to *Beat* magazine, the departmental magazine for the Los Angeles Police Department, the Police Department conducted a contest in February, 1955, for a motto for the Police Academy. The conditions of the contest stated that the "the motto should be one that in a few words would express some or all of the ideals to which the Los Angeles police service is dedicated. It is possible that the winning motto might someday be adopted as the official motto of the Department."

The winning entry was the motto "To Protect and to Serve," submitted by Officer Joseph S. Dorobek.

The motto *was* eventually used throughout the Los Angeles Police Department and in December, 1963, by official ordinance, was placed alongside the City Seal on the Department's patrol cars.

Since those years the motto has been accepted by countless police departments throughout the United States, and displayed just as prominently on patrol cars and on official documents. (Some police departments changed the motto from "To Protect and to Serve" to "To Serve and Protect"—as shown on the badge on the cover of this book.)

Those were the years before video cameras were available for civilian use; and years before bystanders could use cellphones to record police transgressions and outright illegal behavior toward citizen-victims.

During those years, claims against police departments—Los Angeles and elsewhere—by citizens who had been mistreated or illegally arrested by police officers—often simply could not be proven.

The watershed year was 1991—when the Department which first began using "To Protect and to Serve," found itself in a maelstrom of police misconduct charges, which became an on-going national scandal; and which led to the biggest and deadliest riots in recent history, damage to the LAPD's reputation (which to this day may not have been fully repaired) and which ultimately led to criminal trials and convictions of LAPD officers involved.

It began with one incident which was partially caught on videotape by a bystander ...

one

March 3, 1991, Los Angeles:
The LAPD and the Rodney King Videotape

WHILE THE VIDEOTAPES OF Bull Conner's southern brutalities—1961-1963—during the Civil Rights decade of the 1960s have largely faded into the past, the 1991 Rodney King videotape and riots have remained etched in the American psyche ...

Rodney King was born in Sacramento April 2, 1965; he grew up in Altadena, California. In November, 1989, he robbed a store in Monterey Park, wielding an iron bar. He threatened a Korean store owner with the iron bar; he was caught, convicted and sentenced to two years in prison. He was paroled after one year.

In the evening of March 3, 1991, he and two companions, Bryant Allen and Freddie Helms, were driving west on the Foothill Freeway (Interstate 210) in the San Fernando Valley area of Los Angeles.

At 12:30 a.m., officers Tim and Melanie Singer, husband-and-wife team members of the California Highway Patrol, noticed King's car speeding. They pursued King, but he refused to pull over; King later stated that he refused to pull over because a charge of driving under the influence (of alcohol) would violate his parole for his earlier robbery conviction.

King left the Freeway and the high-speed pursuit continued. After about eight miles, officers cornered King in his car. The LAPD arrived—officer Stacey Koon, Laurence Powell, Timothy Wind, Theodore Briseno and Rolando Solano.

Officer Tim Singer ordered King and his passengers to leave the car—the two others, Allen and Helms, did so and were arrested without incident. King got out, acted in a bizarre manner and waved to a police helicopter now hovering overhead. He grabbed his buttocks, which officer Melanie Singer believed to mean he was reaching for a weapon. She drew her weapon and approached him, preparing to arrest him.

At this point, Stacey Koon, the ranking member of the LAPD announced that the LAPD would be in charge. He ordered the other LAPD officers to holster their weapons; LAPD officers are instructed not to approach a suspect with weapons drawn, as a suspect may attempt to grab an officer's weapon. Koon then ordered the LAPD officers to "swarm" King.

King was able to throw Powell and Briseno off his back; LAPD officers then believed that King has taken the drug phencyclidine (PCP)—common street name Angel Dust—although a toxicology test later proved negative for that drug.

King was then hit by high-voltage Taser weapons *twice* and overcame both electrical charges.

At this point, George Holliday watching from nearby, began videotaping the incident. He eventually had nine minutes of black-and-white videotape.

King is shown in the tape, rising, and moving to attack officer Powell or to escape. King and Powell collide; Powell hits King with his baton and King falls to the ground. Powell hits him several more times; Briseno moves in attempting to stop Powell from hitting King

4

again. Koon apparently says "that's enough," but Powell and Wind are seen on the tape, continuing to hit King.

Koon then ordered the continuing use of the batons—ordering Powell and Wind to hit King with "power strokes."

Koon ordered the officers to "hit his joints, hit his wrists, hit his elbows, hit his knees, hit his ankles."

Holliday continued videotaping the assault.

The officers miss occasionally, but hit King 33 blows, plus six kicks. They again "swarm" him, this time with eight officers, and finally subdue his arms and legs. King is dragged on his stomach to the side of the road to await the arrival of an EMS van.

Two days later George Holliday told the LAPD about his videotape and then took it to Los Angeles television station KTLA which broadcast it immediately.

The tape was broadcast again and again, over and over and over and over. And nationally, again and again, over and over. And internationally again and again, over and over.

It became an example of "people power"—individuals with video cams (and now cellphones), which can record and transmit events as they are happening. And with video cams and cellphones, citizens can now disprove fraudulent, self-serving, contradictory statements or outright lies by officials.

King was taken to Pacifica Hospital. When he was examined, he had suffered a fractured facial bone, a broken right ankle, and multiple bruises and lacerations, King sued the City of Los Angeles and claimed he suffered "11 skull fractures, permanent brain damage, broken (bones and teeth), kidney damage and emotional and physical stress." Tests indicated he was intoxicated under California law. The tests also showed a minor amount of marijuana in his system, but nothing else.

Pacifica nurses reported that officers who took King to the hospital bragged about the number of times King had been hit.

A jury awarded him $3.8 million and an additional $1.7 million in legal fees.

The Los Angeles District Attorney charged officers Koon, Powell, Briseno and Wind with use of excessive force. Koon had not hit King, but had used a Taser. The trial was moved out of Los Angeles to Simi Valley, a largely white enclave -suburb of Los Angeles, where some white LAPD officers lived. The jury consisted of nine white members, one black, one Latino and one Asian.

Despite the Holliday tape, which Los Angeles television continued to replay, on April 29, 1992, the jury **acquitted all four officers** of assault and could not agree on an excessive force charge against Powell.

Rioting began the same day as the Simi Valley verdicts.

The verdicts were announced at 3:15 p,m. By 3:45 more than 300 protestors had gathered at the Los Angeles County Courthouse building. Others gathered at the intersection of Florence and Normandie in south central Los Angeles. More appeared at the Police Department headquarters at Parker Center.

They were quickly named the Rodney King riots and also, the South Central riots.

On the second day, April 30, violence, looting and destruction was apparent throughout Los Angeles County. There were open gun battles in the Koreatown area, between store owners and looters, Fire crews began being escorted by police; California Highway Patrol units were airlifted to the city. The California National Guard loaned equipment to other law enforcement units and 2,000 members of the National Guard were called into service, but were delayed for 24 hours by a lack of equipment and available ammunition.

On the third day, May 1, Rodney King made an appeal in front of his attorney's office. "People, I just want to say, you know, can we all get along?" The "Can we all get along?" statement was allegedly supplied by his attorney; King was apparently too inarticulate to ad-lib even a short speech.

National Guard troops were doubled to 4,000 and eventually to 10,000. A variety of 1,700 federal law enforcement officers from different agencies began to arrive to protect federal facilities. President George H.W. Bush addressed the nation, condemning "random terror and lawlessness." He ordered the Justice Department to review the case.

Professional games involving the Los Angeles Lakers and the L.A. Clippers were postponed. The baseball Dodgers also postponed games. A curfew in San Francisco caused a game with the San Francisco Giants and the Phillies to be postponed. Horse racing was not held; a Van Halen concert was cancelled. Bus service halted. Some freeways closed. The World Wrestling Federation cancelled events in Long Beach and Fresno.

On the fourth day (Saturday, May 2), 2,000 members of the 7th Infantry Division, from Fort Ord arrived, as did 1,500 Marines from Camp Pendleton. A total of 13,500 U.S. military forces were now helping support law enforcement. The Justice Department announced it would begin an investigation.

The sum total: 53 died during the riots, including 10 who were shot dead by police or military forces; over 2,383 were injured. The total estimates in property damage ranged from $800 million to $ 1 billion.

There were more than 7,000 fires; 3,767 buildings were set on fire. Korean and Asian immigrants seemed to be widely targeted. Some buildings were never rebuilt. Half of those arrested and more than half killed were Hispanic.

Although the Rodney King videotape and the not guilty verdicts seemed to be the tipping point, later analysis pointed to high unemployment in minority communities, poor housing, conflicts between the black population and the Hispanic population of Los Angeles, and other sociological problems as contributing factors.

There were also riots in: San Francisco; Las Vegas; Atlanta and even as far away as Toronto, Canada.

A t-shirt was sold throughout the Los Angeles area: on the front it read LAPD with a large LAPD logo. On the back it read:

THEY TREAT YOU LIKE A KING

Weeks after the rioting, 11,000 people continued to be arrested.

After the riots, extensive and prolonged civic debate began, at the local, state and national level.

The Justice Department did, as promised, re-open the case and filed federal civil rights charges against LAPD officers Stacey Koon, Laurence Powell, Timothy Wind and Theodor Briseno. Rodney King testified in the case. Koon and Powell were found guilty and sentenced to 32 months in prison; Wind and Briseno were acquitted of all charges. None returned to the LAPD.

In his article "Rodney King and M.L.K.," in the book *Inside the L.A. Riots: What Really Happened and Why It Will Happen Again,* Harvey Wasserman wrote:

Nearly a quarter century—within a year and a few days—passed between the murder of Martin Luther King and the acquittal of the cops who beat Rodney King.

What progress has been made in the interim?

The inner-cities ravaged in the uprising following the King murder were never rebuilt by the time of the King verdict.

We have traded Thurgood Marshall for Clarence Thomas, Lyndon Johnson for George Bush.

* * *

In a quarter-century what lessons have been learned from the death of Martin Luther King? His leadership has never been replaced. The lethal uprisings that followed his murder helped no one, translated into no positive action, raised no conscience or lasting consciousness among the nation's decisions-makers. What came instead was a deep-seated neighborhood hopelessness, fought off with great difficulty by community organizers, but exploited ever since by the likes of Nixon, Reagan and Bush.

* * *

And it is easy to forget that, for nonviolence to ultimately work, it requires a civilized response from those in power.

Twenty-four years after the loss of our greatest preacher of non-violent direct action, do we see any evidence of that moral or mental capacity in our government?

And, if not, what right do we have to be surprised when the torches and bullets once again fly, deadlier than ever?

A statistic accompanying the article revealed:

Average home price, Los Angeles, 1990:
$224,000.
Average home price, South Central L.A., 1990:
$127,000.

Rodney King had drug problems before and after the infamous police beating video. On June 17, 2012, King's girlfriend Cynthia Kelly found him at the bottom of his swimming pool. He was pronounced dead at a Colton, California hospital. An autopsy found alcohol, marijuana, cocaine and the drug PCP in his system. The cause of death was classified as accidental drowning, and probable cardiac arrest, with the autopsy findings listed as contributing factors in his death.

Rodney King was 47.

(Fensch: *At the Dangerous Edge of Social Justice: Race, Violence and Death in America*, pp.167-176)

two

February 26, 2012, Sanford, Florida:

The Death of Trayvon Martin

APPROXIMATELY 7 PM.

(George) Zimmerman: Hey, we've had some break-ins in my neighborhood, and there's a real suspicious guy, uh (near) Retreat View Circle, um, the best address I can give you is 111 Retreat View Circle. The guy looks like he's up to no good, or he's on drugs or something. It's raining and he's just walking around, looking about ...

(Police dispatcher, Sanford Police Department): OK, and this guy, is he white, black, or Hispanic?

Zimmerman: He looks black.

Dispatcher: Did you see what he is wearing?

Zimmerman: Yeah, a dark hoodie, like a grey hoodie, and either jeans or sweatpants and white tennis shoes. He's (unintelligible), he was just staring ...

Dispatcher: OK, he's just walking around the area ...

Zimmerman: ... looking at all the houses.

Dispatcher: OK.

Zimmerman: Now he's just staring at me.

Dispatcher: OK—you said it's 1111 Retreat View? Or 111?

Zimmerman: That's the clubhouse ...

Dispatcher: That's the clubhouse, do you know what the—he's near the clubhouse right now?

Zimmerman: Yeah, now he's coming toward me.

Dispatcher: OK.

Zimmerman: He's got his hand in his waistband. And he's a black male.

Dispatcher: How old would you say he looks?

Zimmerman: He's got a button on his shirt. Late teens.

Dispatcher: Late teens OK.

Zimmerman: Something's wrong with him. Yup, He's coming to check me out. He's got something in his hands. Don't' know what his deal is.

Dispatcher: Just let me know if he does anything, OK?

Zimmerman: How long until you get an officer over here?

Dispatcher: Yeah, we've got someone on the way, just let me know if this guy does anything else.

Zimmerman: OK. These assholes—they always get away. When you come to the clubhouse you come straight in and make a left. Actually you go past the clubhouse.

Dispatcher: So it's on the left side from the clubhouse?

Zimmerman: No you go in straight through the entrance and then you make a left—uh, you go straight in, don't turn, and make a left. Shit, he's running.

Dispatcher: He's running? What way is he running?

Zimmerman: Down toward the other entrance to the neighborhood.

Dispatcher: Which entrance is that—that he's heading towards?

Zimmerman: The back entrance—fucking (unintelligible).

Dispatcher: Are you following him?

Zimmerman: Yeah.

Dispatcher: We don't need you to do that.

Zimmerman: OK.

Dispatcher: Alright sir, what is your name?

Zimmerman: George. He ran.

Dispatcher: Alright George. What is your last name?

Zimmerman: Zimmerman.

Dispatcher: And George, what's the phone number you're calling from?

Zimmerman: (redacted).

Dispatcher: Alright George, we do have them on the way. Do you want to meet with the officer when they get there?

Zimmerman: Alright, where are you going to meet with them at?

Zimmerman: If they come straight through the gate, tell them to go straight past the clubhouse, and uh, straight past the clubhouse and make a left, and then they go past the mailboxes, that's my truck (unintelligible).

Dispatcher: What address are you parked in front of?

Zimmerman: I don't know. It's a cut through so I don't know the address.

Dispatcher: OK. Do you live in the area?

Zimmerman: Yeah, I ... (unintelligible).

Dispatcher: what's your apartment number?

Zimmerman: It's a home. It's 1950, oh crap. I don't want to give it all out. I don't know where this kid is.

Dispatcher: OK. Do you want to just meet with them right near the mailboxes then?

Zimmerman: Yeah, that's fine.

Dispatcher: Alright, George. I'll let them know to meet you there, OK?

Zimmerman: Actually could you have them call me and I'll tell them where I'm at?

Dispatcher: Ok, yeah, that's no problem.

Zimmerman: Should I give out my number or you got it?

Dispatcher: Yeah. I got it. (redacted).

Zimmerman: Yeah, you got it.

Dispatcher: OK, no problem. I'll let them know to call you when you're in the area.

Zimmerman: Thanks.

Dispatcher: You're welcome.

And so it began.

George Zimmerman was 28, his father white, his mother Hispanic, from Peru. Trayvon Martin, 17, was black.

Zimmerman wanted to be a police officer or a judge and was majoring in Criminal Justice at a local community college, but he had been in trouble with the police before. He had been accused of domestic violence by a former girlfriend and had been previously arrested for assaulting a police officer. A cousin of Zimmerman's accused him of years of sexual molestation and she also accused members of Zimmerman's family of being proudly racist against African Americans and she recalled examples of perceived bigotry.

At the time of confrontation with Trayon Martin, Zimmerman was neighborhood watch coordinator for the gated community where Martin was temporarily staying.

From a police report later, Trayvon Martin was doing nothing suspicious or illegal, at the time. *He was just walking home.* He was returning home from a store with a bag of Skittles and an ice tea. From Zimmerman's perspective, the hoodie and Martin's "behavior" made him a suspect; many believe that is racial profiling.

Zimmerman left his truck and confronted Martin. There was an argument—a struggle—a violent encounter. Zimmerman sustained cuts on the back of his head, so inconsequential they need no stitches; he also suffered a bleeding, or perhaps broken nose.

Later, during his trial, tapes were played of the encounter; screams could be heard on the tapes. Martin's mother claimed the screams were Trayvon's; Zimmerman's mother claimed the screams were Zimmerman. A shot was heard on the tape, then the screaming stopped. Most would believe the screams were Trayvon Martin, who stopped screaming when he was shot. Shot by Zimmerman. Trayvon Martin was shot at extremely close range and died almost immediately.

When police arrived, they found that Zimmerman has used a 9 mm handgun. (His "firearm," he said, in police jargon.) He claimed he shot Martin in self-defense.

He was taken to the Sanford Police headquarters, questioned for approximately five hours and released. At the time, police found nothing that would contradict his claim of self-defense.

The initial decision not to charge Zimmerman caused national outrage, a consequence of "Stand Your Ground" laws passed in Florida and elsewhere. (The Sanford Police Chief later resigned, or was forced to resign, for the lack of an immediate arrest.)

From earliest Anglo-Saxon laws, "a man's home is his castle," and homeowners are quite within their rights to shoot intruders. "Stand Your Ground" laws made it acceptable to allow deadly force *anywhere*.

They allow people who believe they are imminently threatened to use deadly force *before* retreating from the threat. Cynics have called them "Make My Day" laws from the "Dirty Harry"/Clint Eastwood character: "Go ahead and do something and I'll shoot you—go ahead—*make my day.*"

"Stand Your ground" laws were first promulgated by the American Legislature Exchange Council (ALEC), a largely right-wing organization, in concert with the National Rifle Association. Their plan was to introduce "Stand Your Ground" legislation to "red" (Republican-controlled) states, then eventually rollout that concept throughout the country.

The history of adoptions of "Stand Your Ground" laws is:

Before 2000: Connecticut, Hawaii, Iowa, Utah;
2004; Illinois;
2005: Florida, Nevada;
2006: Alabama, Alaska, Arizona, Georgia, Idaho, Indiana, Kansas, Kentucky, Louisiana, Michigan, Mississippi,, Oklahoma, South Carolina, South Dakota;
2007: Missouri, North Dakota, Tennessee, Texas, Wisconsin;
2008: Ohio, West Virginia, Wyoming;
2011: New Hampshire, North Carolina, Pennsylvania.

However, during the Zimmerman trial, "Stand Your Ground" became part of the national dialogue; and, perhaps as a surprise to ALEC, nearly 30 major U.S. corporations dropped their membership in ALEC. They included: Kraft Foods; Pepsico; Coca-Cola;; Hewitt-Packard; CVS Caremark; Deer and Co.; MillerCoors; BestBuy; Dell Computer; Amazon; Intuit; Medtronic and others. Their corporate resignations were obviously based on two logical points: "Stand Your Ground" laws had no bearing on the corporate objectives of those companies and, secondly, none wanted the negative publicity associated with ALEC. The National Rifle Association, however, stood—and still stands—resolutely with ALEC.

After the death of Trayvon Martin, President Obama said, 'If I had a son, he would be Trayvon."

In March 22, 2012, a Special Prosecutor was appointed to take over the case: on April 11, 2012 a charge of Murder in the Second Degree was filed against George Zimmerman.

Zimmerman's trial was begun in Sanford, Florida, June 10, 2013, He had requested a "Stand Your Ground" hearing, but his defense attorneys elected to bypass that hearing so his case would be tried before a jury.

The Zimmerman jury was all female; they had three choices: Murder in the Second Degree; Manslaughter and Acquittal. When the jury was dismissed to deliberate Zimmerman's fate, Judge Debra Nelson instructed the jury in the "Stand Your Ground" rationale:

If George Zimmerman was not engaged in an unlawful activity and was attacked in any place where he had a right to be, he had no duty to retreat and had the right to stand his ground and meet force with force.

Presumably, the jury also remembered that Zimmerman had followed Trayvon Martin even after the Sanford Police Dispatcher told him "we don't need you to do that," and they presumably remembered on the Dispatcher's tape, "those assholes—they always get away."

After deliberating 16 hours, the jury found Zimmerman **Not Guilty** in the death of Trayvon Martin.

The verdict had again taken over the national dialogue on race and justice. There have been demonstrations in major cities against the verdict, but they have been, fortunately, for the most part, peaceful. Print publications, television, radio, cable and commentators on all sides of the political spectrum have contributed to the dialogue.

Trayvon Martin has become the Emmett Till of this century.

Artist Nikkolas Smith has contributed a remarkable image, a picture of a dark hoodie, Like Trayvon Martin wore, *with the face of Martin Luther King Jr.* That mage has rocketed back and forth throughout the internet.

What can we say about Florida Governor Rick Scott, who took the "Stand Your Ground" proposed laws and marched them though the Republican-controlled Florida state legislature ... then presented them as a *fait accompli* ...? Doing the bidding of ALEC and the National Rifle Association ...? We can think of Bob Dylan's song about Byron De La Beckwith, who killed Medgar Evers: *he's only pawn in their game* ...

On Friday, July 12, 2013, President Barack Obama entered the press room of the White House, unexpectedly, and in a remarkably personal and candid statement said:

"When Trayvon Martin was first shot, I said that this could have been my son. Another way of saying that is, Trayvon Martin could have been me, 35 years ago."

(Fensch: pp. 184-193.)

three

*In recent history, the U.S Department of
Justice has investigated at least
22 local police departments.
The Albuquerque, New Mexico
Police Department is one of them ...*

Albuquerque, New Mexico:

The Worst Police Department in the Nation?

IN TERMS OF BRUTALITY, corruption and oppression—
and outright and clearly unnecessary killings of civilians—it can easily be argued that the Albuquerque, New
Mexico Police Department has, in recent years, the worst
record in the country, without question.

In an article "New Mexico Law Enforcement Plagued
by Corruption and Abuse of Human Rights," on the website The Cutting Edge News (October 6, 2011), Kent
Paterson wrote:

"The flagrant use of lethal force by APD officers
ranks among the highest in the nation" and "in a recent
18-month period, fatal shootings by members of the APD
claim 14 dead."

19

In an article "Police Department That Kills Highest Rate of Unarmed Citizens" on the website www.popularresistance.org (December 3, 2014) Max Blumentahl wrote:

When an Albuquerque police officer shot his 22-year-old son to death, Mike Gomez was determined to crusade for justice. Three years later, he is simply despondent.

"It's so frustrating," Gomez told me, "There's no accountability here. There's no justice. There's no respect. There's no humanity here. There's nothing. It's so disgusting that they get away with it."

A single father, Mike Gomez struggled for years to help his son, Alan, cope with a substance abuse problem, When Mike Gomez left town on May 10, 2011, Alan Gomez fell back into his addiction and was overcome with paranoid delusions. He began pacing back and forth on the front lawn of his father's house, holding a conversation with an imaginary person about gang members assembling to kill him. Alarmed family members eventually phoned a dispatcher from the Albuquerque police, who summoned police to what she mistakenly believed was a hostage situation.

From across town, an off-duty cop named Sean Wallace heard the alert blare through his scanner, then barreled over to the scene before a crisis intervention officer could arrive. Without provocation, Wallace opened fire, killing Alan Gomez with a high-powered rifle as he entered the house through a screen door. The troubled young man was holding nothing in his hand but a plastic spoon.

With his death, Alan Gomez joined the list of at least 27 people killed by Albuquerque police officers since 2010, and the more than 40 wounded by gunfire.

In a city of just over 540,000, the body count is staggering, Indeed, the rate of officer-involved shootings by Albuquerque police is eight times that of the NYPD and two times higher than in Chicago, a megalopolis with one of the highest levels of crime in the country. (italics added)

And, as of January, 2015, the count is 28 killed, and not one of the Albuquerque officers involved in those shootings has ever been charged with any crime.

What of Albuquerque policeman Wallace, who shot and killed the troubled young man? Blumenthal also wrote:

Wallace joined the Albuquerque police in 2007 during an ill-fated push to expand the force to 1,000 officers. He was among four officers who had just been fired from the New Mexico State Police for taking payments from Wackenhut, a private security contractor, while on duty as state cops. The four barely averted prison terms for the double-dipping scandal.

When the rejects were hired by the Albuquerque PD, then Deputy Police Chief Mike Castro pledged "They do not carry guns, they are not going to be badged." Almost as soon as Wallace reported for duty, however, he was sporting a badge and bearing a high-powered rifle.

Besides killing Alan Gomez, Wallace has shot two other unarmed people in his short career—one died—and terrorized an untold number of others. He was named in a federal lawsuit for ramming the car of a wanted man driving his family to school, then handcuffing the man's children as their schoolmates watched in horror. Though his killing of Gomez cost Albuquerque $900,000, part of a whopping $26 million tab in settlements paid out to families of citizens killed by cops since 2010, Wallace received nothing but rewards from his superiors. (The first time he killed an unarmed person Wallace cost the city $335,000.) For shooting Gomez, the Albuquerque Police Officers Association paid Wallace $500 and gave him three days off. Other cops who shot local residents have received checks ranging from

$300 to $1,000, along with several days of leave—payments the police union calls "decompression money."

In a lengthy article, "When Cops Break Bad: Inside a Police Force Gone Wild," in *Rolling Stone* magazine January 28, 2015, Nick Pinto wrote:

In many respects, the systemic meltdown of the APD (department motto "In step with our community") offers an excellent lens through which to understand how police in America can run amok. Militarization of gear and tactics, an overreliance on specialized tactical units, a blue wall of silence that protects bad cops from the consequences of their actions, and a heavy hand in interactions with mentally ill citizens—all these factors, present in other departments around the country, are painfully evident in the story of how Albuquerque's police came to kill so many of its citizens.

... and, Pinto wrote ...

After more than a year of unsuccessful pleading with local officials to rein in the APD, in November 2012 the relatives of the victims, with the support of groups like the Dr. Martin Luther King Jr. Memorial Center, finally persuaded the U.S. Justice Department to open a civil rights investigation into the Albuquerque Police department. When the DOJ released its findings last April ... they amounted to a scorching indictment of the APD and everyone who had enabled its slide into brutality. Reviewing 20 fatal police shootings from 2009 to 2012, the report found a majority of them to be unconstitutional. "Albuquerque police officers shot and killed civilians who did not pose an imminent threat," the report found, noting that "Albuquerque police officers' own recklessness sometimes led to their use of deadly force."

And, Pinto wrote:

> The Justice report places much of the blame for these problems on a macho, dick-swinging culture of violence among street-level officers, beginning with training "that leads officers to believe that violent outcomes are normal and desirable." But it concludes that the culture has been enabled by the department's leadership and allowed to flourish by ineffective civilian oversight. "Officers have faced little scrutiny from their superiors," the report found. "External oversight is broken and has allowed the department to remain unaccountable."

The Department of Justice Civil Rights Division investigated the Albuquerque Police Department and issued a lengthy report to the Mayor and public April 10, 2014. In three words it is exhaustive, comprehensive—and damning.

(The entire 46-page Department of Justice Report is reprinted in this book.)

The Report, said, in part:

1). Albuquerque police officers too often use deadly force in an unconstitutional manner in their use of firearms. To illustrate, of the 20 officer-involved shootings resulting in fatalities from 2009 to 2012, we concluded that a majority of these shootings were unconstitutional. Albuquerque police officers often use deadly force in circumstances where there is no imminent

threat of death or serious bodily harm to officers or others. Instead, officers used deadly force
against people -who posed a minimal threat, including individuals who posed a threat only to
themselves or who w re unarmed. Officers also
used deadly force in situations where the conduct
of the officers heightened the danger and contributed to the need to use force.
(Department of Justice Report pp. 2-3)

2). Albuquerque police officers also often use less
lethal force in an unconventional manner. We
reviewed a random sample of the department's
use of force reports completed by officers and supervisors between 2009 and 2013. Our sample
consisted of over 200 force reports. We find that
officers frequently misused electronic control
weapons (commonly referred to by the brand
name "Tasers"), resorting to use of the weapon
on people who are passively resisting, observably
non-threatening but unable to comply with orders
due to their mental state, or posed only a minimal threat to the officers. Officers also often used
Tasers in dangerous situations. For example, officers fired Tasers numerous times at a man who
had poured gasoline on himself. The Taser discharges set the man on fire, requiring another
office to extinguish the flames. This endangered
all present. Additionally, Albuquerque police officers often use unreasonable physical force
without regard to the subject's safety or the level
of threat encountered. Officers frequently used
takedown procedures in ways that unnecessarily
increase the harm to the person. Finally, officers
escalate situations in which force could have
been avoided had they instead used de-escalation
measures.
(Report, pp. 3)

3). A significant amount of the force we reviewed was used against persons with mental illness and in crisis. APD's policies, training, and supervision are insufficient to ensure that officers encountering people with mental illness or in distress do so in a manner that respects their rights and is safe for all involved.
(Report, pp. 3)

4). The use of excessive force by APD officers is not isolated or sporadic. The pattern or practice of excessive force stems from systemic deficiencies in oversight, training, and policy, Chief among these deficiencies is the department's failure to implement an objective and rigorous internal accountability system. Force incidents are not properly investigated, documented or addressed with corrective measures.

We found only a few instances in the incidences we reviewed where supervisors scrutinized officers' use of force and sought additional investigation. In nearly all cases, supervisors endorsed officers' version of events, even when the officers' accounts were incomplete, were inconsistent with other evidence, or were based on canned or repetitive language. The department has also failed to implement its force policies consistently, including requirement that officers properly document their use of force, whether by lapel cameras, audio tapes, or in reports. The department does not use other internal review systems, such as internal affairs and the early intervention system, effectively. These internal accountability and policy failures combine with the department's inadequate training to contribute to the uses of excessive force. Additionally, serious limitation in the city's external oversight processes have allowed many of these deficiencies to continue unabated.

As a result of the department's inadequate accountability systems, the department often endorses questionable and sometimes unlawful conduct by officers. The prior criminal history and background of individuals who are the subject of police force also typically receive greater scrutiny than the actions of officers. These practices breed resentment in the community and promote an institutional disregard for constitutional policing. For example, in a 20211 civil trial involving the shooting death of Andrew Lopez in which a state court found that an officer used unreasonable force, the City's expert, a training officer, testified that the officer's actions were "exemplary and that he (the expert) would use this incident to train officers on the proper use of deadly force." The court concluded that the deadly force training provided to APD officers "is designed to result in the unreasonable use of deadly force." We found other examples of similar praise or approval by police supervisors in force investigations we reviewed.
(Report, pp. 3-4)

These topics—and other interrelated topics such as: "supervisory reviews do not address excessive uses of force"; "force incident are not properly documents"; "shooting investigations are inadequate"; "internal review mechanisms are not implemented", and other topics are analyzed in extensive detail in an additional 31 pages, with examples such as the death of Alan Gomez, described above.

Finally the Department of Justice report offers:

- 12 "Remedial Measures" to address the deficiencies in Use of Force policies;
- 5 measures to address interacting with individuals with mental illness of other disabilities:
- 4 measures regarding Tactical Units;
- 4 measures to improve officer training;
- 5 measures to improve Internal Investigations and Citizen Complaints;
- 7 measures to improve Management and Supervision;
- 5 measures to improve recruitment and Selection (of officers); ... and ...
- 4 measures to improve Community Policing and Oversight.

(Report, pp. 41-45)

The Department of Justice reports ends, in part, with:

"We share your sense of urgency in ensuring that the City of Albuquerque has an effective, accountable police department that controls crime, ensures respect for the Constitution, and earns the respect of the public it is charged with protecting."

(Report, pp. 45)

The U.S. Department of Justice Report
on the Albuquerque Police Department

April 10, 2014
The Honorable Richard J. Berry
Mayor, City of Albuquerque
One Civic Plaza NW, 11th Floor
Albuquerque, NM 87102
Re: Albuquerque Police Department

Dear Mayor Berry:

We write to report the findings of the Department of Justice's civil investigation of the Albuquerque Police Department ("APD" or "the department"). Our investigation focused on allegations of use of excessive force by APD officers under the Violent Crime Control and Law Enforcement Act of 1994, 42 U.S.C. § 14141 ("Section 14141"). Section 14141 makes it unlawful for government entities, such as the City of Albuquerque and APD, to engage in a pattern or practice of conduct by law enforcement officers that deprives individuals of rights, privileges, or immunities secured by the Constitution or laws of the United States. The investigation was conducted jointly by the Civil Rights Division and the United States Attorney's Office for the District of New Mexico. This letter is separate from, and does not address, any federal criminal investigation that may be conducted by the Department of Justice.

Based on our investigation, we have reasonable cause to believe that APD engages in a pattern or practice of use of excessive force, including deadly force, in violation of the Fourth Amendment and Section 14141. Our investigation included a comprehensive review of APD's operations and the City's oversight systems. We have determined that structural and systemic deficiencies—including insufficient oversight, inadequate training, and ineffective policies—contribute to the use of unreasonable force. At the conclusion of this letter, we outline the remedial measures that we believe are necessary to ensure that force is used in accordance with the Constitution. In some instances, these recommendations build on measures and initiatives that are already underway within the department.

We recognize the challenges faced by officers in Albuquerque and in communities across the nation every day. Policing can be dangerous; at times, officers must use force, including deadly force, to protect themselves and others in the course of their work. The use of force by police is guided by the need to protect public safety and the duty to protect individuals from unreasonable searches and seizures under the Fourth Amendment. While most force used by APD officers is within these strictures, a significant amount falls short of these requirements. Although APD has taken steps to allay the public's concerns about the department's use of force, these initiatives have been insufficient to ensure consistent accountability. They also have not addressed longstanding deficiencies that have allowed a culture of indifference to constitutional policing and insularity to develop within the department.

We are aware that the release of our findings occurs at a time of transition for the department's leadership and amid continued tension around recent officer-involved shootings. In particular, fatal confrontations with individuals experiencing mental health crises continue to cause significant public concern over the department's ability and willingness to consider the safety and well-being of the individuals in distress. Throughout our investigation, APD leadership has been receptive to our preliminary feedback and technical assistance. However, as outlined in this letter, more work is necessary to ensure that officers have the proper tools, guidance, training, and supervision to carry out their law enforcement responsibilities safely and in accordance with individuals' federal constitutional rights. We appreciate your expressed willingness to embrace many of the changes we have highlighted in our conversations with APD. We will continue to work collaboratively with you, the department's leadership, and other stakeholders to develop sustainable reforms that will resolve our findings. However, if we cannot reach an appropriate resolution, Section 14141 authorizes the Department of Justice to file a civil lawsuit to "eliminate the pattern or practice" of police misconduct. 42 U.S.C. § 14141.

We thank you, APD, and other city officials for your cooperation and professionalism during our investigation. We received invaluable assistance from the department's leadership, counsel, and rank-and-file officers. We also thank community members for bringing relevant information to our attention and for sharing their experiences with us. We are encouraged by the many individuals who took an active interest in our investigation and who offered thoughtful recommendations. We appreciate those individuals who came forward to provide information about specific encounters with APD, even when recounting such events was painful. We know that many residents care deeply about preventing the types of incidents described in this letter and have a genuine interest in supporting the many men and women of APD who uphold their oaths and keep Albuquerque safe. Based on this extensive cooperation and participation, we stand ready, and are encouraged that we will be able, to work together with the City, APD, and other stakeholders to address our findings methodically and expeditiously. By promoting constitutional policing, we will make APD more effective and will help restore the community's trust in the department.

I. SUMMARY OF FINDINGS

While officers may be required to use force during the course of their duties, they must do so respecting constitutional guarantees against unreasonable searches and seizures. For too long, Albuquerque officers have faced little scrutiny from their superiors in carrying out this fundamental responsibility. Despite the efforts of many committed individuals, external oversight is broken and has allowed the department to remain unaccountable to the communities it serves. Based on our investigation, we find that the department engages in a pattern or practice of using excessive force during the course of arrests and other detentions in violation of the Fourth Amendment and Section 14141. We find this pattern or practice in the following areas:

(1) Albuquerque police officers too often use deadly force in an unconstitutional manner in their use of firearms. To illustrate, of the 20 officer-involved shootings resulting in fatalities from 2009 to 2012, we concluded that a majority of these shootings were unconstitutional. Albuquerque police officers often use deadly force in circumstances where there is no imminent threat of death or serious bodily harm to officers or others. Instead, officers used deadly force against people who posed a minimal threat, including individuals who posed a threat only to themselves or who were unarmed. Officers also used deadly force in situations where the conduct of the officers heightened the danger and contributed to the need to use force.

(2) Albuquerque police officers also often use less lethal force[1] in an unconstitutional manner. We

---

1 For purposes of this letter, "less lethal force" means a force application not intended or expected to cause death or serious injury and which is commonly understood to have less potential for causing death or serious injury than conventional, more lethal police tactics. Nonetheless, use of less lethal force can result in death or serious injury.

reviewed a random sample of the department's use of force reports completed by officers and supervisors between 2009 and early 2013. Our sample consisted of over 200 force reports. We find that officers frequently misused electronic control weapons (commonly referred to by the brand name "Tasers"),[2] resorting to use of the weapon on people who are passively resisting, observably non-threatening but unable to comply with orders due to their mental state, or posed only a minimal threat to the officers. Officers also often used Tasers in dangerous situations. For example, officers fired Tasers numerous times at a man who had poured gasoline on himself. The Taser discharges set the man on fire, requiring another officer to extinguish the flames. This endangered all present. Additionally, Albuquerque police officers often use unreasonable physical force without regard for the subject's safety or the level of threat encountered. Officers frequently use takedown procedures in ways that unnecessarily increase the harm to the person. Finally, officers escalate situations in which force could have been avoided had they instead used de-escalation measures.

(3) A significant amount of the force we reviewed was used against persons with mental illness and in crisis. APD's policies, training, and supervision are insufficient to ensure that officers encountering people with mental illness or in distress do so in a manner that respects their rights and is safe for all involved.

---

2 The Department uses the Taser brand electronic control weapons. Throughout this report, we will refer to these weapons as Tasers.

(4) The use of excessive force by APD officers is not isolated or sporadic. The pattern or practice of excessive force stems from systemic deficiencies in oversight, training, and policy. Chief among these deficiencies is the department's failure to implement an objective and rigorous internal accountability system. Force incidents are not properly investigated, documented, or addressed with corrective measures.

We found only a few instances in the incidents we reviewed where supervisors scrutinized officers' use of force and sought additional investigation. In nearly all cases, supervisors endorsed officers' version of events, even when officers' accounts were incomplete, were inconsistent with other evidence, or were based on canned or repetitive language. The department has also failed to implement its force policies consistently, including requirements that officers properly document their use of force, whether by lapel cameras, audio tapes, or in reports. The department does not use other internal review systems, such as internal affairs and the early intervention system, effectively. These internal accountability and policy failures combine with the department's inadequate training to contribute to uses of excessive force. Additionally, serious limitations in the City's external oversight processes have allowed many of these deficiencies to continue unabated.

As a result of the department's inadequate accountability systems, the department often endorses questionable and sometimes unlawful conduct by officers. The prior criminal history and background of individuals who are the subject of police force also typically receive greater scrutiny than the actions of officers. These practices breed resentment in the community and promote an institutional disregard for constitutional policing. For example, in a 2011 civil trial involving the shooting death of Andrew Lopez in which a state court found that an officer used unreasonable force, the City's expert, a training officer, testified that the officer's actions were "exemplary and that he (the expert) would use this incident to train officers on the proper use of deadly force."[3] The court concluded that the deadly force training provided to APD officers "is designed to result in the unreasonable use of deadly force."[4] We found other examples of similar praise or approval by police supervisors in force investigations we reviewed.

We recognize that the department started to institute some preliminary reforms to address our concerns before the conclusion of our investigation. However, the recent remarks by the police chief in response to the James Boyd shooting on March 16, 2014, demonstrate that more work is needed to change the culture of APD.[5] It is imperative that the department continue to build on these reforms and improve its training, recruitment, and internal review mechanisms. The failure to take meaningful remedial action places residents at risk of excessive force and promotes a culture of unjustifiable aggression that further alienates the department from the communities it serves. Making constitutional policing a core agency value and building systems of accountability to carry out that value will support the many APD

---

3 Findings of Fact and Conclusions of Law, *Higgins v. City of Albuquerque*, No. CV-2009-0915 (N.M. 2d Judicial Dist. filed on Aug. 19, 2009), ¶67.

4 *Id.* at ¶66.

5 On March 21, 2014, APD Chief Gorden Eden told reporters at a news conference that the force used against James Boyd was justified after officers responded to reports that an individual was camping illegally in the Sandia foothills. The Boyd shooting is under criminal investigation and is not addressed in this letter. Dan McKay, *Camper Turning from Officers When Shot*, Albuquerque Journal, Mar. 22, 2014, *available at* http://www.abqjournal.com/372844/ news/video-camper-turning-away.html.

officers who strive to and do uphold their oaths. This, in turn, will engender greater trust and confidence in APD from the community.

II. BACKGROUND

A well-functioning police department has the trust of the residents it protects, functions as a part of the community rather than insulated from it, and cultivates legitimacy when the public views it as engaging with them fairly and respecting the rule of law.[6] We started this investigation in November 2012 amid serious public concerns about APD's ability and willingness to fulfill these precepts.

In particular, the department faced community apprehension about its respect for constitutional guarantees against unreasonable force and its ability to protect the safety of all residents. These concerns stemmed from a number of high-profile incidents suggesting unreasonable conduct by some officers, including: (1) a high rate

---

6 *See* generally Tom Tyler & Jeffrey Fagan, *Legitimacy and Cooperation: Why Do People Help the Police Fight Crime in their Communities?*, 6 Ohio St. J. Crim. L. 231 (2008) (finding that cooperation with the police increases when the public views the police as respecting procedural justice and therefore as legitimate authorities); Tom Tyler, Why People Obey the Law 138 (2006) (finding, in a study of over 1,500 Chicago residents, that "[i]nferences about efforts to be fair were the most important criterion of procedural fairness; concerns about politeness and rights (jointly labeled ethicality) were the second-most important"); Jason Sunshine & Tom Tyler, *The Role of Procedural Justice and Legitimacy in Shaping Public Support for Policing*, 37 Law & Soc'y Rev. 513, 519-21 (2003) (study concluding that police treatment of the public and adherence to procedural fairness, such as accurately applying the law, has a stronger effect on police legitimacy than effectiveness in addressing crime).

of shootings,[7] including more than 25 shootings in the two-year period before our investigation started; (2) high profile uses of less lethal force, including Taser deployments and physical force captured on video; (3) a large number of judgments and settlements[8] against the City signifying that many uses of force were unjustified; and (4) concerns raised by local leaders and advocates culminating in a City Council measure seeking an outside investigation by DOJ.[9]

In September 2010, the Police Executive Research Forum ("PERF") started a nine-month study of the department's use-of-force policies and training, as well as the department's management systems. PERF did not evaluate whether officers used force appropriately.[10] Indeed,

---

7 Dan Frosch, *Justice Dept. to Investigate the Police in Albuquerque*, N.Y. Times, Nov. 27, 2012, *available at* http://www. nytimes.com/2012/11/28/us/justice-dept-to-investigate-the-police-in-albuquerque.html?_r=0; Michael Haederle, *In Albuquerque, An Uproar Over Shootings by Police*, Los Angeles Times, Apr. 14, 2012, *available at* http://articles.latimes.com/2012/apr/14/ nation/la-na-albuquerque-police-20120415.

8 Jeff Proctor, *Ellis Case Would Boost APD Payouts*, Albuquerque Journal, Apr. 7, 2013, *available at* http://www.abqjournal. com/186038/news/ellis-case-would-boost-apd-payouts.html; Jeff Proctor, *Police Misconduct Costly*, Albuquerque Journal, Feb. 6, 2012, *available at* http://www.abqjournal.com/85625/news/police-misconduct-costly.html.

9 Council Bill No. R-11-247 (August 2011) (requesting a DOJ investigation into "whether there have been incidents or patterns of civil rights violations by the Albuquerque Police Department"). You vetoed the measure, citing the City's request for a review of the department by the Police Executive Research Forum. Mayor Berry's Veto Message on R-11-247 (Aug. 18, 2011), *available at* http://www.cabq.gov/mayor/news/ read-mayor-berrys-veto-message-on-r-11-247/.

10 PERF, *Review of Use of Force in the Albuquerque Police Department*, 41, 48 (June 23, 2011), *available at* http://alibi.com/

the report noted that "[r]einvestigating officer-involved shooting cases was outside the scope of this study as specified by the city."[11] Instead, PERF focused on "common factors" in the shootings and trends and patterns in the uses of less lethal force, such as frequency of weapons use, officer and subject demographics, and the types of force used.[12] The PERF report noted that shootings increased, even though "both violent crime and assaults on officers have been on a downward trend."[13] The PERF report found that multiple officers were present at 81% of the shooting incidents they reviewed.[14] Given the level of misconduct we uncovered, the presence of multiple officers is significant because officers have a duty to intervene to prevent other officers from using excessive force. *Vondrak v. City of Las Cruces*, 535 F.3d 1198, 1210 (10th Cir. 2008), *cert. denied, 555* U.S. 1137 (2009) (internal citations omitted). The report also noted that in only a small percentage of shooting incidents (11%) did the officer employ less-lethal options before resorting to deadly weapons.[15] The PERF report also noted the significant use of Tasers and pointed out serious limitations in APD's ability to track accurate force data.[16] Our investigation, which included incidents occurring after PERF's review, revealed similar problems.

The Albuquerque Police Department is the largest law enforcement agency in New Mexico, with approximately 1,000 sworn officers and over 600 civilian employees.[17]

---

media/docs/Police%20Executive%20Research%20Forum's%20 review%20of%20APD%20shootings.pdf.

11 *Id.* at 10.

12 *Id.*

13 *Id.* at 2.

14 *Id.* at 14.

15 *Id.*

16 *Id.* at 48.

17 The Albuquerque Police Department's Strategic Plan Fiscal Year 2013 through Fiscal Year 2017, available at http://www.cabq.gov/police/internal-reports.

We recognize that it is a modern policing agency that has made efforts to implement innovative programs, such as the Crisis Intervention Team ("CIT") and the Crisis Outreach and Support Team ("COAST"), which work to diffuse potentially harmful situations and assist people in crisis by providing them with access to mental health care. The department has also partnered with other agencies to maintain the Family Advocacy Center, a safe space that focuses on the needs of victims of domestic violence, sexual abuse, and other trauma. The department has received national accreditation by law enforcement executive associations[18] and has invested in technologies, such as lapel cameras, to address community concerns about officer accountability.

While these measures are noteworthy, the public's confidence in the department remains shaken over concerns that the department is unable to control its officers' use of excessive force. The use of technology and other initiatives have had limited impact in increasing accountability or promoting safer encounters with individuals suffering from mental illness. For instance, although the department is among a few of its size to mandate the use of lapel video cameras, the implementation has been highly inconsistent. The availability of trained CIT officers has not kept up with the needs in the community, and de-escalation techniques employed by these officers are too easily dismissed by heavily-armed tactical units in situations where individuals under police scrutiny are not posing an immediate threat of harm. The mental health professionals and staff on COAST teams operate in a larger mental health system with limited resources and options. It is critical that the

---

18 For example, the department is accredited by the Commission on Accreditation for Law Enforcement Agencies, Inc., which is the credentialing authority through organizations such as the International Association of Chiefs of Police and the National Sheriff's Association, among others. We do not endorse such accreditation. We simply note that such accreditation exists.

City and the department take additional measures to identify, address, and prevent excessive force to protect the public and rebuild the community's trust. Recent shootings have heightened and confirmed the need for further reform.

III. METHODOLOGY AND LEGAL STANDARDS

We conducted our evaluation of the department's use of force in three major phases: fact-gathering, incident analysis based on applicable legal standards, and a comprehensive review of policies and practices to identify significant factors that cause or contribute to misconduct. Our review was informed by many sources, including: (1) individuals participating in community town hall meetings and separate witness interviews; (2) agency stakeholders, such as the department's officers, supervisors, and command staff; (3) other stakeholders in the City, including the officers' union representatives, police oversight commissioners and investigative staff, City officials, and community group leaders; (4) department documents, including use-of-force and shooting files; and (5) information and insights provided by our expert police consultants.

During the first phase of our investigation, we sought relevant information on the department's use of force and worked to gain a comprehensive understanding of the department, including its leadership, systems of accountability, operations, and community engagement. We conducted onsite tours in Albuquerque in December 2012, February and March 2013, and January 2014. Collectively during these tours, we met with command staff and officers of various ranks; representatives from the officers' union; leadership and officers within the internal affairs department; the police academy; and each area command, among others. We spoke to current and former officers in Albuquerque by video conference and telephonically. We also met with stakeholders outside of the department, including the Independent Review Officer, members of the Police Oversight Commission, and community group leaders.[19]

In this fact-gathering phase, we also sought to learn more from those who had direct interactions with the department. We held four community town hall meetings in different regions of the City and conducted initial and follow-up interviews of hundreds of people. We also interviewed dozens of people through additional community outreach efforts. We verified these accounts by reviewing available documentary, photographic, and video support, as well as department records.

In the second phase of our investigation, we carefully analyzed the information we obtained and applied the relevant legal standards to determine whether the department's use of force was justified under federal law. We reviewed an extensive volume of documents provided to us by the department, including a random sample of more than 200 force reports from 2009 through early 2013.[20] We also reviewed the files of officer-involved shootings between 2009 and 2012 that resulted in fatalities. Our review of individual use-of-force complaints and reports informed our investigation into whether a pattern or practice of excessive force exists.

A pattern or practice may be found where incidents of violations are repeated and not isolated instances. *Int'l Bd. of Teamsters v. United States,* 431 U.S. 324, 336 n.16 (1977) (noting that the phrase "pattern or practice" "was not intended as a term of art," but should be interpreted

---

19 *See* a more in depth description of the Police Oversight Commission and the Independent Review Officer at B. 7 *infra.*

20 We reviewed incidents reported by APD as uses of force. APD policy requires that officers report "police actions" that result in death, great bodily harm, or injury. "Police action" is defined as "any offensive or non passive defensive action by an officer, or some intentional action under his/her immediate control." APD Use of Force Policy, 02-52.

according to its usual meaning "consistent with the understanding of the identical words" used in other federal civil rights statutes). Courts interpreting the terms in similar statutes have established that statistical evidence is not required. *Catlett v. Mo. Highway & Transp. Comm'n*, 828 F.2d 1260, 1265 (8th Cir. 1987) (interpreting "pattern or practice" in the Title VII context).

A court does not need a specific number of incidents to find a pattern or practice, and it does not need to find a set number of incidents or acts. *See United States v. W. Peachtree Tenth Corp.*, 437 F.2d 221, 227 (5th Cir. 1971) ("The number of [violations] ... is not determinative.... In any event, no mathematical formula is workable, nor was any intended. Each case must turn on its own facts.").

We assessed officers' conduct under the Fourth Amendment's "right of people to be secure in their persons ... against unreasonable searches and seizures." U.S. Const. amend. IV. Courts apply the Fourth Amendment objective reasonableness standard to all claims of excessive force, including deadly force. *Graham v. Connor*, 490 U.S. 386 (1989); *Tennessee v. Garner*, 471 U.S. 1 (1985). Under this standard, "the nature and quality of the intrusion on the individual's Fourth Amendment interests" is balanced against the "countervailing government interests at stake." *Graham*, 471 U.S. at 396 (internal quotation marks and citations omitted). Ultimately, in evaluating whether there are violations of the Fourth Amendment, the courts are tasked with determining whether the "officers' actions are objectively reasonable in light of the facts and circumstances confronting them, without regard to their underlying intent or motivation." *Id.* at 397 (internal quotation marks and citations omitted); *see also Casey v. City of Federal Heights*, 509 F.3d 1278, 1281 (10th Cir. 2007).

Guiding this balancing of interests are several nonexclusive factors: if a crime was suspected, the severity of that offense; whether the person posed an immediate threat to the safety of the officer or others; and whether the person was actively resisting arrest or attempting to evade arrest. *Graham*, 490 U.S. at 396; *Garner*, 471 U.S. at 8-9. The Tenth Circuit has also considered other factors, including: whether the officer's own conduct contributed to the need to use force; whether the officer issued a warning and the person had the opportunity to comply; whether the person was mentally ill; and whether, during the course of the interaction, new facts developed requiring a change in the amount of force required. *Fancher v. Barrientos*, 723 F.3d 1191, 1201 (10th Cir. 2013) (holding that repeated shooting at person is unreasonable where no threat remained); *Cavanaugh v. Woods Cross City*, 625 F.3d 661, 666 (10th Cir. 2010) ("It is not objectively reasonable to ignore specific facts as they develop (which contradict the need for this amount of force [Taser]), in favor of prior general information."); *Fogarty v. Gallegos*, 523 F.3d 1147, 1159-60 (10th Cir. 2008) (considering whether officers' conduct contributed to the need to use tear gas); *Casey*, 509 F.3d at 1285 (considering whether a person was provided an opportunity to comply before an officer used a Taser); *Allen v. Muskogee, Okla.*, 119 F.3d 837, 840 (10th Cir. 1997) (in shooting, considering person's suicidal state and officer's conduct prior to the person's threat of force); *Cardall v. Thompson*, 845 F. Supp. 2d 1182, 1192 (D. Utah 2012) (noting that person's "mental health also weighed against the use of a [T]aser"). Courts weigh these considerations to determine the reasonableness of the officer's conduct in light of the totality of the circumstances.

In essence, the courts evaluate the full context surrounding the force action. While refraining from engaging in a 20/20 hindsight judgment of the force used, courts review the situation and threat faced by the officer. This also includes the type of force used by the officer—whether that force was physical, the use of weapons such as a Taser or chemical agents, or the use of a firearm. More severe forms of force require more justification. *Cordova v. Aragon*, 569 F.3d 1183, 1190 (10th Cir. 2009) (reasoning that the "general dangers posed" by a reckless driver fleeing the police "does not justify a shooting that is nearly certain to cause the suspect's death"); *Cavanaugh*, 625 F.3d at 665 (holding that an officer's use of the "quiet severe" intrusion of a [T]aser against an unarmed misdemeanant who posed no threat was unreasonable); *Casey*, 509 F.3d at 1286 ("[I]t is excessive to use a Taser to control a target without having any reason to believe that a lesser amount of force—or a verbal command—could not exact compliance."). Courts recognize that while some force may be required to apprehend a person, such force must be limited to what is "reasonably necessary to effect a lawful seizure." *Fisher v. City of Las Cruces*, 584 F.3d 888, 895 (10th Cir. 2009) (holding that a rough handcuffing of a person was unreasonable where no threat remained). We applied these legal standards in our review of APD's force incidents.

In the final phase of our review, we sought to evaluate the causes of, and the factors contributing to, the use of unreasonable force. We reviewed internal and external APD documents addressing a variety of operational issues, including policies and procedures, recruitment, training, internal accountability measures, assessment reports, task force evaluations, and investigations. We were aided in this determination by our expert police consultants who have significant experience in providing constitutional policing services, including reducing improper uses of force, ensuring officer safety and accountability, and promoting respectful police interactions with the community. These consultants joined us during our onsite tours of the department, participated in our town hall meetings, conducted in-person and telephonic interviews with civilians and officers, reviewed APD policies and procedures, and reviewed force and shooting reports. The experience and knowledge of these nationally-recognized law enforcement experts helped to inform our findings. In sum, we relied on a variety of sources to reach the conclusions reported here.

IV. FINDINGS

We have reasonable cause to believe that officers of the Albuquerque Police Department engage in a pattern or practice of use of excessive force, including unreasonable deadly force, in violation of the Fourth Amendment and Section 14141. A significant amount of the force we reviewed was used against persons with mental illness and in crisis. APD's policies, training, and supervision are insufficient to ensure that officers encountering people with mental illness or in distress do so in a manner that is safe and respects their rights. The use of excessive force by APD officers is not isolated or sporadic. The pattern or practice of excessive force stems from systemic deficiencies in oversight, training, and policy. Chief among these deficiencies is the department's failure to implement an objective and rigorous internal accountability system. Force incidents are not properly investigated, documented, or addressed with corrective measures. Other deficiencies relate to the department's inadequate tactical deployments and incoherent implementation of community policing principles.

A. APD Engages in a Pattern or Practice of Unconstitutional Use of Deadly Force.

We find that the Albuquerque Police Department engages in a pattern or practice of unreasonable use of deadly force in officers' use of firearms. We reviewed all fatal shootings by officers between 2009 and 2012[21] and found that officers were not justified under federal law

---

21 Because we wanted to examine both the reasonableness of uses of force and the department's responses to them, we focused on cases closed by APD.

in using deadly force in the majority of those incidents. This level of unjustified, deadly force by the police poses unacceptable risks to the Albuquerque community.

As noted above, the Fourth Amendment permits police officers to use deadly force under certain circumstances, and the courts have identified specific factors they consider in determining the reasonableness of a use of force based on the totality of the circumstances.

Those factors guided our analysis of each fatal police shooting in the 2009 to 2012 time frame. For each officer-involved shooting, we reviewed all police reports from the incident; interviews with witnesses and the officers involved; memoranda from the internal affairs division; reports by the Independent Review Officer and the Police Oversight Commission; reports from the District Attorney's Office; lapel camera footage and audio tape, if they were available; in some cases, accounts that witnesses and family members of those killed gave directly to us; and other relevant information.

Below is a discussion of the most prevalent factors that lead us to find police shootings to be unjustified under federal law, with examples drawn from some of those incidents. We have identified other force incidents that further illustrate the pattern or practice of use of excessive force.

1. Albuquerque police officers shot and killed civilians who did not pose an imminent threat of serious bodily harm or death to the officers or others.

Like other uses of force, the reasonableness of deadly force is evaluated through an objective standard: whether a reasonable officer in the same circumstances—facing the same tensions and uncertainties, and forced to make split-second decisions—would have used deadly force. *See Graham*, 490 U.S. at 396-97. Police officers are permitted to use deadly force to prevent escape when they have "probable cause to believe that the suspect poses a significant threat of death or serious physical injury to the officer or others." *Garner,* 471 U.S. at 3; *Weigel v. Broad,* 544 F.3d 1143, 1151-52 (10th Cir. 2008). The Tenth Circuit has cautioned that this statement must not be read too broadly: "It does not mean that any risk of physical harm to others, no matter how slight, would justify any application of force, no matter how certain to cause death." *Cordova,* 569 F.3d at 1190 (discussing *Scott v. Harris,* 550 U.S. 372 (2007)). In *Cordova,* the Tenth Circuit determined that the general risks created by a motorist's fleeing from the police are, without more, insufficient to justify a shooting that is nearly certain to cause the suspect's death.

We identified several cases in which officers shot and killed civilians who did not pose an immediate threat of death or serious bodily injury to officers or others. For instance, in February 2009, an officer used unreasonable force when he shot and killed Andrew Lopez after officers attempted to pull Lopez over for driving with dim headlights and no tail lights. According to officers, they suspected the vehicle had been involved in a prior incident in which a gun was reported. However, the vehicle Lopez was driving did not match the make, color or type of vehicle that was reported earlier. After leading the officers on a low-speed vehicle chase for more than ten minutes, Lopez stopped the vehicle, exited, and ran toward a driveway of a residence where a truck was parked. One officer gave chase on foot, followed by approximately four other officers. The primary officer stated that he believed Lopez was armed with the biggest handgun he had ever seen and ordered him to drop it. When Lopez reached a fence and began to turn, the officer shot at Lopez three times. One of the shots struck Lopez, causing a non-lethal bullet wound. Lopez fell to the ground and lay motionless on his back. The officer walked around the truck and fired a fourth shot into Lopez's chest, piercing his lung and heart and causing his death. Lopez was unarmed. The officer fired the fourth and final shot when Lopez was not pointing anything at officers and while he lay on his back already wounded.

In a bench trial in state court, a judge found that the officers' testimony about the threat they perceived from Lopez was not credible. The judge concluded that the shooting was unreasonable. The judge further found that the training provided to APD officers on use of deadly force "is not reasonable and is designed to result in the unreasonable use of deadly force."[22] The judge found the City principally responsible for Lopez's death and awarded his estate approximately $4.25 million.

In another incident, in October 2009, an officer shot and killed Dominic Smith, who was unarmed and fleeing the scene of a robbery on foot. Smith did not pose a threat of death or serious bodily injury to officers or others. Smith used a threatening note to rob a pharmacy for drugs before fleeing on foot. No one at the pharmacy saw Smith with any kind of a weapon and he did not commit acts of violence during the alleged robbery. An officer apprehended Smith just minutes later across the street from the pharmacy and stated that Smith appeared heavily intoxicated. The officer stated that he saw no weapons. The officer, with his gun drawn, ordered Smith to stop, but Smith continued walking away from the officer. The officer returned to his car, retrieved an assault rifle, and again confronted Smith, who continued to disregard the officer's orders. With Smith just a few feet away, the officer claimed that Smith motioned near his waist, which the officer believed to indicate that Smith was reaching for a gun. The officer shot and killed Smith. Smith did not have a gun. A reasonable officer confronting Smith as he fled from the pharmacy thus would not have believed that Smith posed an immediate threat of death or serious

---

22 Findings of Fact and Conclusions of Law, *Higgins v. City of Albuquerque*, No. CV-2009-0915 (N.M. 2d Judicial Dist. filed on Aug. 19, 2009), ¶66.

bodily harm. As the Supreme Court stated in *Garner,* "A police officer may not seize an unarmed, nondangerous suspect by shooting him dead." *Id.* at 11.

In another use of deadly force, in May 2011, an officer shot and killed Alan Gomez, who would not allow his brother and his girlfriend to leave their house. Gomez was unarmed and did not pose an immediate risk of death or serious bodily harm to the individuals in the house or officers when he was shot. The incident began in the middle of the night when the girlfriend called APD because Gomez was refusing to let her and her boyfriend leave their house. Officers arrived and surrounded the house. As officers attempted to negotiate with Gomez, police dispatchers spoke on the telephone to the girlfriend who originally called the police. She initially told a dispatcher that Gomez was in possession of a gun. Before the shooting, she told the dispatcher that Gomez no longer had a gun. Officers observed Gomez as he walked in and out of the front door several times without incident. APD officers had not observed Gomez exhibiting any threatening behavior toward the police or the individuals in the house. After officers had been present for nearly an hour, Gomez again came out of the front door briefly and began to turn to go back inside. As he did so, an officer shot Gomez once and killed him. When officers approached Gomez to render aid, they saw that he was not holding a gun and no other object was found anywhere near him

When the officer shot Gomez, the circumstances would not have suggested to a reasonable officer that there was an immediate threat. The officers had not confirmed that Gomez was armed. With the exception of the shooting officer, who gave inconsistent statements, officers did not observe Gomez hold, raise, or aim a gun. No one's life was in immediate danger and an APD negotiator was on his way to the scene. There were insufficient facts to lead officers to believe that Gomez "pose[d] a significant risk of death or serious physical injury to

the officer or others." *Garner*, 471 U.S. at 3. Even if officers were concerned that Gomez might have been going
back to harm the individuals inside the house, that risk
of future harm was not enough to justify the near certainty of Gomez's death from the firearm discharge. *See
Cordova*, 569 F.3d at 1190. Gomez's family sued APD
and in December 2013, the parties reached an out-of-
court settlement in the amount of $900,000. This was
the shooting officer's third shooting in the line of duty.
He shot and killed a man in 2004 while serving with the
New Mexico State Police and wounded another man in
2010. None of the three shooting subjects was armed.
The officer joined APD in 2007 as a lateral hire.

2. Albuquerque police officers used deadly force on individuals in crisis who posed no threat to anyone but themselves.

Just as officers are not reasonable in using deadly
force when a person poses little or no threat to officers
or others, officers are also unreasonable in using deadly
force on individuals in crisis who pose a threat only to
themselves. *Walker v. City of Orem*, 451 F.3d 1139, 1160
(10th Cir. 2006) (concluding that there were sufficient
facts to support a Fourth Amendment violation where
the officer acted precipitously in shooting the subject
who posed a danger only to himself when he held a box
cutter to his wrists); *see Sevier v. City of Lawrence, Kan.*,
60 F.3d 695, 699-701 (10th Cir. 1995) ("The reasonableness of [officers'] actions depends both on whether the
officers were in danger at the precise moment that they
used force and on whether [officers'] own reckless or
deliberate conduct during the seizure unreasonably created the need to use such force.") Although reasonable
officers need not await the "glint of steel" before taking
self-protective action, courts have looked at several factors to assess the threat to officers when an individual is
armed and threatening harm to himself *Estate of Larsen*

v. Murr, 511 F.3d 1255, 1260-61 (10th Cir. 2008) (internal citations omitted). These non-exclusive factors include: (1) whether the officers ordered the suspect to drop his weapon, and the suspect's compliance with police commands; (2) whether any hostile motions were made with the weapon towards the officers; (3) the distance separating the officers and the suspect; and (4) the manifest intentions of the suspect. *Id.* at 1260.

In January 2010, an officer shot and killed Kenneth Ellis, III, a 25-year-old veteran who was suffering from post-traumatic stress disorder. Officers suspected Ellis of vehicle theft and pulled him over in a parking lot. Ellis exited the vehicle holding a gun pointed to his head. Ellis continued to hold the gun to his head as he made several phone calls and the officers attempted to negotiate with him. After several minutes, an officer shot Ellis one time in the neck and killed him.

While it is true that Ellis was holding a gun and thus presented a clear threat of harm, there was never any indication from Ellis' words or actions that he intended to use the gun on anyone but himself. During his encounter with police, he held the gun to his own head and did not point at police or threaten them with harm. It was thus unreasonable for the officer to have used deadly force on Ellis. In addition, when officers are dealing with suicidal subjects, their failure to try to de-escalate the situation is a relevant factor in evaluating the reasonableness of any force they might use. *Allen,* 119 F.3d at 841-44. In February 2013, a judge in a state civil suit granted summary judgment in favor of the plaintiffs, finding that the shooting violated the Fourth Amendment.[23] A jury later returned a verdict finding the City and the officer who shot him liable for Ellis' death and awarding more than $10 million in damages.

---

23 Order on Motion for Summary Judgment, *Wharton v. City of Albuquerque,* No. CV-2010-06590 (N.M. 2d Judicial Dist. filed on May 28, 2010).

3. Albuquerque police officers' own recklessness sometimes led to their use of deadly force.

In evaluating the totality of the circumstances surrounding an officer's use of deadly force, courts have considered "whether the officers' own reckless or deliberate conduct during the seizure unreasonably created the need to use such force." *Medina v. Cram*, 252 F.3d 1124, 1132 (10th Cir. 2001) (citations and internal quotation marks omitted). We reviewed several incidents that provide reasonable cause to believe that the officers were reckless and that their recklessness contributed significantly to their decision to use deadly force.

For example, in March 2012, an officer shot Daniel Tillison after approaching him without waiting for backup. The officer was responding to an anonymous call about an individual selling stereo equipment in a parking lot. When the officer arrived, Tillison was sitting in his car, which the officer believed might be stolen (he had received conflicting information prior to making contact with Tillison). The officer approached the driver's side of the car with his gun drawn. This is an important fact. If the officer believed Tillison posed such a threat to the officer or public safety that it was necessary to draw his weapon, it is not at all clear why the officer did not take cover and wait for other officers to assist him. There was no exigency that required the officer to act immediately; it was the officer who decided when to approach Tillison. The officer spoke to Tillison, recounting that Tillison was evasive and appeared to be reaching for something in the car. Tillison tried to get out of the car, but the officer pushed the door closed. Tillison then backed into the officer's vehicle and an adjacent truck. The officer shot at one of the vehicle's tires. As Tillison attempted to drive forward, the officer stated that he saw something that resembled a gun in Tillison's hand and that Tillison gave him a "warrior stare." The officer then shot directly at Tillison, killing him. The item in Tillison's hand was a cell phone; police found no guns in the car. Based on our review of the facts, Tillison did not pose an immediate threat of death or serious bodily harm and the shooting could have been avoided if the officer had waited for other officers to assist him. The officer was not in control of the situation because he approached Tillison alone and resorted to deadly force.

This incident bears striking similarities to the situation encountered by police in *Zia Trust v. Montoya*, 597 F.3d 1150, 1153 (10th Cir. 2010). In *Zia Trust*, an officer rushed up to a van that he believed was being driven by a domestic violence suspect. The officer had drawn his weapon and approached the van alone. *Id.* The suspect tried to drive his van at the officer, but it was stuck on a pile of rocks and could only move about a foot. *Id.* The officer shot the driver of the van, and he later died. *Id.* The Tenth Circuit found that the officer's recklessness in how he approached the driver could support a finding that the officer's use of deadly force was unreasonable. *Id.* at 1154-55.

In March 2010, a plainclothes detective shot and killed Mickey Owings after Owings' car was boxed in by an unmarked APD vehicle in a commercial parking lot. The encounter began because officers had received information that a stolen car was located in the parking lot. Several officers positioned unmarked cars in the parking lot around the suspected stolen car. Owings then drove a different car into the parking lot and parked directly next to the stolen car. A passenger got out of Owings' car and started to get in the stolen car, and officers drove one unmarked car directly behind Owings while the plainclothes detective approached Owings' car on foot. Owings backed his car into the unmarked police car and another civilian's car, and as he did so, the detective drew his gun, pointed it at Owings, and ran closer to Owings' car. Owings then drove straight forward into two parked cars. As he did so, the detective shot Owings. Owings continued driving forward and actually pushed the two empty, parked cars in front of him out of the way. Owings then drove out of the parking lot but soon seems to have lost consciousness on a nearby road. His car slowed to a stop, and when officers got to him, he had died. Owings was not armed.

The department's use of force policy permits officers to fire at the driver of a moving vehicle only when the car itself poses a threat of death or serious physical injury to the officer or others. (As noted below, the better policy, followed by many departments, is to prohibit officers from firing their weapons at cars altogether.) The use of force policy limits the circumstances in which officers may shoot at drivers because of the substantial risks that are involved: the officer may miss and hit an innocent civilian or fellow officer, or the driver may become incapacitated, leaving the moving car completely out of control. Owings did not pose a threat of death or serious physical injury to the officer or anyone else; he was driving straight into unoccupied, parked cars when he was shot. This damage to property, as serious as it was, did not justify taking Owings' life. The detective who shot Owings could very easily have missed and hit one of the innocent civilians walking through the parking lot; moreover, after Owings was shot, the probability that he would injure someone with his car increased dramatically. *Brosseau v. Haugen,* 543 U.S. 194, 199-201 (2004) (collecting federal appellate cases on police shootings at moving cars and acknowledging that such shootings can be unreasonable); *Vaughan v. Cox,* 343 F.3d 1323, 1333 (11th Cir. 2003) ("[A] reasonable officer would have known that firing into the cabin of a pickup truck, traveling at approximately 80 miles per hour on Interstate 85 in the morning, would transform the risk of an accident on the highway into a virtual certainty."). *But see Scott,* 550 U.S. at 382-84 (2007) (noting that a car can itself be a deadly weapon that can justify the use of deadly force).

Other instances of officer recklessness that led to unreasonable uses of deadly force involved officers from the department's SWAT unit who acted without proper discipline or control. SWAT stands for Special Weapons and Tactics, and officers assigned to SWAT units are generally among the most highly trained in a police department. Officers in the SWAT unit are entrusted with complex weaponry and are called upon to handle the most dangerous situations that police encounter. SWAT units typically operate under strict protocols and carry out operations in a highly planned and organized fashion.

In force incidents we reviewed, we found instances in which the SWAT unit did not operate with the discipline and control that would be expected of them, and this lack of discipline contributed to unreasonable uses of deadly force. The officer who shot and killed Alan Gomez, for example, was assigned to the SWAT unit. When he arrived on the scene, the officer took a position near the house where Gomez was keeping his brother and his girlfriend from leaving without consulting the commanding officer and without following any kind of a plan for handling the crisis. He also did not seek or obtain the approval of the commanding officer before using deadly force. He acted on his own authority from the moment he arrived on the scene until he fired his weapon. The recklessness of his behavior at the scene supports our finding that his use of deadly force was unreasonable. *Zia Trust*, 597 F.3d at 1154-55.

The officer who shot and killed Kenneth Ellis was not a member of the SWAT unit, but commanding officers within and over SWAT were present when Ellis was shot. The department's reports on the shooting make it clear that the SWAT commanding officers failed to exert control over the scene, such as by making a plan for handling the crisis, determining where officers should be positioned, or deciding what roles each officer would fulfill, though our consultants would have expected them to take on these roles and establish control and lines of authority. The lack of scene control contributed to a chaotic environment and allowed the shooting officer to act on his own accord when he shot and killed Ellis. *See Allen,* 119 F.3d at 841-44 (noting that the failure to follow protocols can be a ground for liability for the use of deadly force).

B. APD Engages in a Pattern or Practice of Unconstitutional Use of Less Lethal Force.

We find that the department engages in a pattern or practice of unreasonable use of less lethal force. There is a pattern of APD officers using force that is unnecessary and unreasonable against individuals who pose little, if any, threat, or who offer minimal resistance. Officers too precipitously resort to the use of Tasers, prone restraints (referred to as "face-down stabilization techniques" by APD), leg sweeps, front kicks, face-down arm-bar takedowns, and strikes to legs and thighs. We reviewed incidents where officers applied force against individuals who were unable to understand or yield to commands but posed a minimal threat to the officers. Many subjects of excessive force had indications of mental illness, physical disabilities, intoxication, and other incapacity. In most instances, these individuals were engaging in lawful activities or committing minor infractions.

We formed our conclusions about APD's practices based on a review of APD's own documentation. This information enabled us to review the identical documents that APD supervisors and internal affairs investigators used in making force determinations. This information also allowed us to assess the reasonableness of each incident and the supervisory or investigatory process that followed. In particular, we reviewed 200 incidents through a sampling of use of force reports and internal affairs investigations for a period spanning January 2009 through April 2013. Of the force incidents that we reviewed, APD identified less than 1% of these reports as unreasonable uses of force. In contrast, we concluded that approximately a third of the same incidents involved officer conduct that was unreasonable. The disparity between our conclusions is striking and strongly suggests a pervasive and deliberate leniency in supervisory oversight and accountability.

Although we found unreasonable uses of physical force, such as punches and kicks, the overwhelming majority of our use of force reviews involved inappropriate deployment of Tasers.[24] Residents have complained, and we were able to confirm, that APD officers used Tasers in a manner that was disproportionate to the threat encountered and in situations where lesser force options were more appropriate. Officers engaged in a pattern of using Tasers unreasonably, including in situations that placed individuals at risk of death or serious bodily harm; against individuals experiencing mental health crises, or who, due to inebriation or inability, could not comply; against subjects requiring medical treatment; against unarmed subjects; and against individuals in a punitive manner. We also identified instances where officers fired Tasers numerous times, even when multiple officers were present to help resolve the situation without the need for continued uses of force. The over-reliance on Tasers in situations where more effective and less extreme options, including verbal de-escalation techniques, were far more appropriate, contributes to the pattern or practice of excessive force. *Walter v. Gomez*, No. 12-1496, 2014 U.S. App. LEXIS 4493, at *48 (10th Cir. Mar. 11,

---

24 APD's policies requiring officers to report uses of force with injury and an emphasis on weapons in its data collection process may account for the lower number of reports involving uses of physical force, such as punches, kicks, and takedowns. *See infra* Section IV.C.3. These deficiencies also suggest strongly that APD officers may be underreporting their use of force. PERF also identified missing data and other problems with APD's force tracking process, including incomplete data on the use of weapons. PERF Report, *supra* note 11, at 46-49.

2014) ("Under prevailing Tenth Circuit authority, 'it is excessive to use a Taser to control a target without having any reason to believe that a lesser amount of force—or a verbal command—could not exact compliance.'") (quoting *Casey*, 509 F.3d at 1286).

A Taser is "a weapon that sends up to 50,000 volts of electricity through a person's body, causing temporary paralysis and excruciating pain." *Cavanaugh*, 625 F.3d at 664. Any use of Tasers constitutes a severe intrusion of the interests protected under the Fourth Amendment. *Id.* at 665. The total amount of electricity and severity of the pain inflicted by a Taser depends on the type of application and how frequently electricity is fired into a subject. *See Casey*, 509 F.3d at 1285. Although a Taser may not constitute deadly force, its use unquestionably "seizes" a subject in an abrupt and violent manner. *Cavanaugh*, 625 F.3d, at 664. Inappropriate use of these weapons can result in death.[25] A Taser therefore should be considered, at a minimum, an intermediate level of force.

Most deaths and adverse reactions typically occur with multiple or prolonged deployments of Tasers. Law enforcement research organizations have cautioned that continuous Taser activations of greater than 15 seconds, or three activation cycles, may increase the risk of death or serious injury.[26] In cases we reviewed, officers used more than three cycles in encounters with individuals, without heightened scrutiny from supervisors. Taser deployments can also potentially produce other secondary or indirect effects that may result in death (e.g., using a Taser against a person on a steep slope or tall structure, resulting in a significant fall; deploying a Taser near

---

25 National Institute of Justice, *NIJ Special Report: Study of Deaths Following Electro Muscular Disruption*, (May 2011), *available at* https://www.ncjrs.gov/pdffiles1/nij/233432.pdf.

26 *Id.* at 27; PERF, *2011 Electronic Control Weapon Guidelines*, 18, 20-21 (March 2011)

flammable materials such as gasoline, explosives, volatile inhalants, or flammable propellants used in pepper spray; and using a Taser on a person who is in water). *Id.* at 6. Effective Taser training and oversight are essential to ensure that officers and supervisors understand the circumstances when Taser use is appropriate and when it needlessly exposes an individual to grievous harm.

1. Albuquerque police officers used force against individuals who were passively resisting and posed a minimal threat.

Albuquerque police officers used force that was disproportionate to the threat or resistance posed by civilians. Even where some force is justified, the particular level of force used may still be excessive if it is disproportionate to the resistance or threat encountered. *Casey,* 509 F.3d at 1282 (holding that where a person is suspected of committing a minor misdemeanor, this fact reduces the level of force that was reasonable for an officer to use); *Walker,* 451 F.3d at 1159-60 (no immediate threat where suspect had a knife if he "had not affirmatively led anyone to believe that he had a firearm and had not made any violent threats toward the officers or others"); *Diaz v. Salazar,* 924 F. Supp. 1088, 1094-95 (D.N.M. 1996) (a suspect's refusal to drop his knife is insufficient to establish an immediate threat where suspect does not lunge at the officers or otherwise threaten them).

Albuquerque police used unreasonable force when they deployed a barrage of less lethal weapons at "Albert,"[27] a 60-year-old man who was intoxicated and began arguing with his friend in March 2009.[28] The friend

---

27 We use pseudonyms for individuals who were the subject of force in non-fatal encounters with APD officers to protect against disclosing personally-identifying information.

28 The tactics used by APD against Albert in 2009 resemble the response by officers in the March 16, 2014, shooting death

called police twice, the second time reporting that Albert had threatened him with a knife and a pellet gun. Forty-seven officers responded to the scene, including snipers and officers from specialized tactical units. After some delay, Albert complied with officers' orders to drop a knife that he was holding while standing at the doorway and walked outside unarmed. After additional delay, he stopped and began to turn. At that point, an officer was ordered to "bag him." An officer fired five successive rounds of beanbags at Albert with a shotgun. Another officer deployed a flash-bang grenade. Another officer shot him with a canister of four wooden batons, two of which penetrated his skin. Another officer deployed a police canine that bit Albert in the arm, tearing his flesh as the canine tried to pull him down. Albert grabbed onto a nearby fence. Two officers fired Tasers at Albert; one of them fired six five-second cycles of electricity into him. Albert finally collapsed, and officers carried him away unconscious, leaving behind a trail of blood and urine. In an April 2012 order entering judgment as a matter of law in Albert's favor, District Judge Bruce Black found that "no reasonable person could believe that an inhibited, slow-moving, 60-year-old individual, who made no physical or verbal threats, and wielded no weapons, could constitute a threat to the safety of any of the forty-seven armed and shielded police officers who stood over twenty feet away."[29]

Our investigation uncovered other incidents in which APD officers used force disproportionate to the threat or

---

of James Boyd. Video released to the public of the Boyd incident shows officers using a flash-bang grenade, a Taser rifle, a police canine, multiple beanbag rounds, and firearms. As noted above, the Boyd shooting is currently under investigation and is not addressed in this letter.

29 Am. Mem. Opinion in Support of Judgment as a Matter of Law, *Nelson v. City of Albuquerque*, No. 10-0553 (D.N.M. filed on June 8, 2010), at 7.

resistance encountered. An officer's Taser use on "Ben," a 75-year old man who used a cane to walk, illustrates this problem. The incident happened in September 2012 after officers responded to a bus station because Ben refused to leave. When officers arrived, they offered to take Ben to a homeless shelter and also called a Crisis Intervention Team officer to assist. Ben sat on a bench and told officers that he was not going to leave peacefully and that he was angry with the bus company for refusing to let him board. After officers tried to convince him to leave for about an hour, Ben threatened bus company employees and reached for his cane. Officers ordered him to put his cane down, but he refused. As Ben was trying to stand up using his cane (presumably for support), the CIT-trained officer shot Ben in the abdomen with his Taser. He did so even though the threat from Ben was minimal: Ben had trouble walking on his own, a sergeant and three officers were standing around him, and there were no indications that bystanders were near Ben. The sergeant on the scene found the Taser use reasonable, as did other supervisors. One supervisor praised the officers' conduct as "exceptional." A higher-level commander called for an investigation of the incident, however there is no indication that one was completed.

An incident in which three officers and a sergeant used force against "Charles"—two using physical force and two officers firing Tasers multiple times—also illustrates this problem.

In June 2011, Charles, who was 22 years old and weighed approximately 165 pounds, was riding his bicycle and failed to stop at several stop signs. Officers decided to pursue Charles for the misdemeanor violation. An officer activated his emergency lights and ordered Charles to stop, but Charles continued riding away. Charles then turned into a parking lot and told the officer, "I am just riding my bike." According to officers' reports, one officer got out of his patrol car and again ordered Charles to stop. Another officer then grabbed Charles. As Charles pulled away, Charles and the officer fell to the ground, where Charles continued to move his arms to avoid being handcuffed. The sergeant then fired his Taser at Charles and discharged three cycles. Another officer also fired his Taser. He reported that he discharged three or four Taser cycles. A fourth officer arrived and grabbed Charles's arm and assisted in handcuffing him. A witness stated that Charles was argumentative and trying to get away from the officers and that one of the officers knocked him down off of his bicycle. No charges were ever filed against Charles, and none of the officers, including the sergeant, activated their belt or lapel recorders.

In April 2010, two officers went to an apartment complex after receiving a report about a domestic violence complaint. The officers questioned the property manager and learned that an unauthorized occupant, "David," was inside one of the apartments. The property manager then asked the officers to remove David from the apartment. The officers entered the apartment and found David hiding in the kitchen. As the officers went in the kitchen, they observed David sitting on the floor behind the kitchen cabinets. One officer told David to put his hands where they could see them as the other drew his weapon and grabbed David's arm because he reportedly failed to comply with commands. While one officer was holding David's arm, the other drew his Taser and yelled at David three times before firing his Taser into David's chest and abdomen. David immediately fell against the oven door, causing it to shatter. David cut his face and head on the oven door and lay in a pool of blood before the paramedics arrived. David was taken to the hospital and was later booked for misdemeanor charges. David was unarmed and posed only a minimal threat to officers, who had drawn their weapons because David reportedly failed to comply with commands.

In other incidents, officers increased the risk of death or serious injury by deploying Tasers in dangerous situations that outweighed the threat posed by the subject. *Asten v. Boulder,* 652 F. Supp. 2d 1188, 1203-04 (D. Colo. 2009) (observing that an officer's use of a Taser near broken glass became less reasonable because it would increase the risk of injury to an unresisting, non-threatening subject).

For example, officers used Tasers multiple times on "Edward" even though he had doused gasoline on himself and his home. In December 2009, officers responded to a domestic violence call. Once the officers arrived on the scene, they heard a man and a woman screaming inside an apartment. The officers kicked down the door and immediately smelled a strong odor of gasoline. Sheets, carpet, and even Edward, were saturated in gasoline. One officer reported that he was struck in the face with an object that was later identified as a lighter that came from Edward's direction. The officers tried to speak to Edward, but he refused to follow their commands. An officer fired his Taser at Edward, striking him in the chest. Edward fell to the ground, where he struggled to avoid being handcuffed. Several officers then used their Tasers multiple times in "drive-stun mode"—meaning that they applied the Taser directly to his body instead of firing prongs from across the room—as other officers tried to handcuff Edward. After the officers finally handcuffed him, they tried to remove him from the apartment. As they were doing so, Edward began banging his head against the wall and attempted to kick at the officers. At this point, an officer used his Taser again in drive-stun mode and ignited Edward's shirt in flames. The fire had to be extinguished by another officer. The officer set Edward on fire with his Taser despite clear indications that the apartment and Edward himself were saturated with gasoline. Even if officers believed Edward posed a significant threat before he was handcuffed, once restrained, officers had other options available, such as leg restraints to prevent him from kicking. Instead, officers exposed him and others to the extreme danger of catching fire from the Taser's electrical discharge.

In another example, officers fired Tasers at "Frank," causing him to fall on broken glass; he was shocked with Tasers repeatedly until one officer's Taser ran out of power. In August 2009, two officers responded to a call after someone called 911 and hung-up. Arriving at the address from which the call was made, officers learned that 16-year-old Frank was in the bathroom and had shattered the glass shower door and cut himself. Frank was bleeding and standing on the glass in the bathroom when the officers approached him. Officers commanded him to lay face down on the floor, but he refused. He pounded on the walls with closed fists. An officer reported that Frank "lunged" at the officers. The officer then shot his Taser at Frank, and the Taser's prongs hooked into Frank's chest. Frank fell to the ground, and the officer repeatedly fired his Taser at Frank until the battery died. The officer did not report how many times he fired his Taser, reporting only that Frank "continued to fight." While Frank was lying on broken glass, another officer shocked Frank with his Taser in drive-stun mode while his partner kneed Frank in the back several times. There were at least four officers on the scene. Finally the officers handcuffed and arrested Frank. It turns out that Frank had taken drugs and was experiencing the side effects of the narcotics. The officer who initially deployed his Taser did not use the weapon's auditing function to determine the number of five-second cycles he deployed and the supervisor's report was also missing the information. One of the officers reported that the officer who responded initially fired his Taser five times. Both of these incidents show officers' unreasonable use of their Tasers by exposing subjects to a risk of serious injury that far outweighed the danger posed by the subjects themselves.

2. Albuquerque police officers used excessive force against individuals with mental illness, against individuals with impaired faculties, and against individuals who require medical treatment.

Officers also used excessive force against individuals who suffered from mental illness or who were unable to comply with officers' commands for reasons beyond their control. The Tenth Circuit has recognized that a "detainee's mental health must be taken into account when considering the officers' use of force ... under *Graham*." *Cardall*, 845 F. Supp. 2d at 1190-91 (quoting *Giannetti v. City of Stillwater*, 216 Fed. Appx. 756, 764 (10th Cir. 2007) (unpublished)); *see also Estate of Mathis v. Kingston*, No. 07-2237, 2009 U.S. Dist. LEXIS 32040, at *13-14 (D. Colo. Apr. 16, 2009) (observing that when a subject's diminished capacity is immediately apparent there may be occasions when failure to follow commands may not constitute a refusal to comply). We reviewed many incidents in which we concluded that officers failed to consider an individual's physical, mental, or emotional state in making force determinations. Consequently, we found instances where individuals did not pose an immediate threat to the safety of the officer or the public, and officers deployed a level of force that was unreasonable under the circumstances.

In one example, officers fired Tasers, kicked, and beat "Greg," a 25-year-old man with a developmental disability who could not talk and was unable to follow officers' commands. In this March 2012 incident, two officers responded to a gas station after receiving information that Greg was taking off his clothes and opening packages of food in the gas station. The officers also knew that Greg had injuries to his face, and he was bleeding from his hands. When the officers arrived, they found Greg lying on the floor of the store, shoveling chips into his mouth. The officers ordered

Greg to stand up and place his hands behind his back. Greg stood up, but he refused to put his hands behind his back. One of the officers gave Greg a front kick to the chest—an action the officer described as a "distraction technique"—that sent Greg to the ground. Greg rolled on the ground and moaned. The officer then fired his Taser in drive-stun mode into Greg's upper torso and neck. Greg struggled to his feet when a sergeant arrived and fired his Taser at Greg, causing him to fall back on the ground. Greg got up and walked away as an officer fired his Taser two more times at Greg's back. Greg continued moaning but moved outside. The officer then gave Greg another front kick in the upper torso, sending him once again to the ground. Greg stood up and continued walking in the parking lot. A fourth officer arrived on the scene and swept Greg's legs with a kick. The officers then attempted to forcibly hold Greg down to handcuff him as Greg made incoherent noises and bit. It was evident from Greg's bizarre behavior that he had a diminished capacity, yet officers needlessly fired Tasers, kicked, and beat him. The officers later learned that Greg had wandered away from a group home and had the mental capacity of a five-year old. He was not charged with any crime.

In another example, an officer fired his Taser at "Harry," who could not follow the officer's commands because he was suffering from a severe drug reaction. The incident occurred in November 2011 when an officer responded to a complaint that Harry was threatening suicide and had reportedly overdosed on drugs. As the officer was interviewing Harry's mother, Harry climbed out of a window and tried to leave the house. The officer then ordered Harry to get on the ground, but he refused and replied, "I haven't done anything." The officer again ordered Harry to get on the ground. Harry reportedly took a step toward the officer, and the officer fired his Taser into Harry's stomach, which caused Harry to fall.

While on the ground, Harry attempted to remove the probes as the officer continued to fire electricity into Harry's body.

An officer's decision to use his Taser on "Ivan" when he was obviously inebriated and prone on a couch is another example of this problem. In April 2010, officers responded to a disturbing-the-peace call. Officers arrived on the scene of a party and decided to break it up.

One of the officers approached Ivan, who was lying on a couch, apparently passed out. The officer tried several times to awaken Ivan, including using a "sternum rub," which is a strike to the chest that causes a person to awaken and reflexively jerk their limbs. Ivan woke up, struck the officer on the leg, and lay back down. The officer then attempted to handcuff Ivan, despite the fact that Ivan was clearly intoxicated and unable to respond to the officer's commands. As Ivan pulled away from the officer while still prone on the coach, the officer fired his Taser at Ivan and then used it in drive-stun mode three times before he finally arrested the man.

The officers' use of Tasers and other force in these incidents was not reasonable. None of the subjects posed a significant threat to the officers' safety or that of anyone else. *Graham*, 490 U.S. at 396. Any offense they may have committed was minor. Most importantly, the mental state of the individuals indicated an inability to comply with officers' commands, which did not justify using multiple Taser discharges or severe physical force, like kicking or beating. *Cardall*, 845 F. Supp. 2d at 1192 (observing that courts have stressed that an officer should hesitate to deploy a Taser when the subject is incoherent and he does not appear to understand the officers' commands) (internal citations omitted).

Officers further used force, including Tasers, against individuals in medical crisis or who were otherwise physically vulnerable. In the incidents we reviewed, officers used Tasers, physical blows, and other physical force when individuals with diminished capacity failed to comply with their commands. It is important to note here that when officers use force after they have been called merely to check on a vulnerable person's welfare and not to investigate a crime, the reason for the call is a relevant consideration in determining whether the force used was reasonable. *Mathis*, 2009 U.S. Dist. LEXIS 32040, at * 12-14. We found that officers used unreasonable force against individuals in medical crisis in a number of cases.

In one such example, officers fired Tasers, grabbed, and choked "Jeremy" after they were called to his house to check on his welfare in September 2012. When the officers arrived, Jeremy was locked in the bathroom. His mother told the officers that her son was unarmed and suffered from schizophrenia. The officers asked Jeremy to open the bathroom door, but he refused. The officers then kicked down the door, grabbed Jeremy, and tried to forcefully take him out of the bathroom. Jeremy pulled away from the officers and tried to run into another room. One of the officers tripped him, and Jeremy fell to the floor. Jeremy then jumped back up to his feet and tried to run back into the bathroom. One of the officers shot her Taser at Jeremy, but missed. The officers then returned to the bathroom and grabbed Jeremy by the head and kneed him several times in the leg. One of the officers then began choking Jeremy until he stopped struggling, and he was arrested. Again, Jeremy had committed no crimes when officers arrived. They were called to check on the welfare of a man with mental illness and instead they used severe physical force against him.

In another example, officers beat and fired Tasers at "Ken" who was suffering from a bad drug reaction and posed no threat to the officers. In May 2010, officers responded to a disturbance call. Ken reportedly was having an adverse reaction to his medications and drugs. Once the officers entered his home, Ken was unarmed and naked. He also seemed disoriented, and he said, "Bang bang!" to the officers as they approached him.

Ken then picked up a mop and said, "Boom boom!" as he approached the officers. As Ken was turning away from the officers, one of them fired a Taser at Ken's back. Ken fell to the ground, and officers beat him in an effort to restrain him. Another officer fired his Taser into Ken's body in drive-stun mode, and Ken was then restrained and taken to the hospital.

Neither Jeremy nor Ken posed a significant threat to the officers. Moreover, officers were called to assist the men, who were in obvious distress. The unreasonableness of the force is exacerbated by the officers' neglect of Jeremy's and Ken's conditions, as well as the fact that no crime was involved. *Graham,* 490 U.S. at 396; *Sevier,* 60 F.3d at 701 (observing that officers may precipitate the use of deadly force through their own reckless conduct by confronting a disturbed or suicidal subject with weapons drawn and without gathering more information).

An incident in which an officer fired a Taser at "Larry" repeatedly after he had a car accident, was convulsing in the car, and was non-compliant, provides another example of officers using disproportionate force. In June 2010, officers responded to the scene where Larry had crashed his car. Larry was convulsing inside the car when the officers approached. An officer commanded Larry to open his door, and Larry indicated he would not get out of the car. Larry was in the vehicle with his young child, and, fearing for the child's safety, the officers decided to shatter the passenger-side widow of the vehicle to get the child out of the car. Once they opened the car door, officers again commanded Larry to get out. After he refused, an officer fired his Taser into Larry's back and buttocks. The officer cycled his Taser one time, and then Larry attempted to crawl out of the vehicle. Larry then turned around and got back in the vehicle, and the officer fired his Taser again. Once Larry was finally out of the vehicle, the officer fired his Taser yet again before placing Larry on the ground. Larry drifted in and out of consciousness before an ambulance was able to get to the scene.

The incidents discussed in this letter are not exhaustive. They illustrate the types of encounters that have resulted in a use of force that was not objectively reasonable. We recognize that most encounters with police are resolved without the need to use force and that many APD officers carry out their duties in accordance with the Constitution. However, in a significant number of force cases, force used by APD officers was excessive and placed the community at risk of future harm.

C. Systemic Deficiencies Cause or Contribute to the Use of Excessive Force.

A number of systemic deficiencies contribute to the department's pattern or practice of use of excessive force. The most prevalent deficiency is the department's endorsement of problematic police behavior by failing to conduct thorough and objective reviews of officers' use of force. Despite the use of technology and efforts to implement innovative intervention programs, problematic behavior continues to be viewed as reasonable, even exemplary, by supervisors. These deficiencies demonstrate a failure to embrace policing fundamentals, namely, recognizing and enabling officers' duty to protect both the public's safety and civil rights.

Officers have an obligation to value the life and safety of the individuals they encounter as part of their core mission. As written, APD's policy on use of force is consistent with this principle: "It is the policy of this Department that officers shall use only that force which is reasonably necessary to protect the sanctity of human life, preserve and protect individual liberties, and to effect lawful objectives." APD Procedural Order 2-52. Police leaders must instill these values through accountability measures, training, policy, and the culture they inspire or tolerate.

However, based on our review, APD has failed to abide by these fundamental policing values. We find this failure evident in the following systemic deficiencies: (1) a broken system of internal accountability; (2) inadequate training on use of force, community policing, and constitutional policing; (3) policy deficiencies; (4) an aggressive culture that undervalues civilian safety and discounts the importance of crisis intervention; and (5) insufficient leadership on tactical operations, community policing, and the importance of accountability to external oversight.

The contributing factors we discuss below evidence a breakdown in leadership that is responsible for ensuring that the agency functions in accordance with its mission and core values. The department has invested significant resources to obtain thoughtful recommendations from independent reviews and has participated in discussions on policing issues of national importance over the years, yet it has failed to take basic steps to clarify policies, set expectations through consistent discipline, or ensure the effectiveness and integrity of its training programs. Over the years, the department has reacted hastily in crafting certain measures, such as lapel cameras, which were deployed without making sufficient efforts to ensure the support of the rank-and-file, were not implemented with the necessary supervision and oversight to ensure proper implementation, and appeared directed only at placating public criticism. As a result, there has been an inconsistent approach to reform, and critical systems intended to ensure constitutional policing remain deficient.

1. The Department's Inadequate Internal Accountability Measures Contribute to the Pattern or Practice of Excessive Force.

We identified several deficiencies in APD's internal accountability mechanisms that contribute to the use of excessive force: ineffective supervisory reviews, inadequate documentation of force, inadequate force investigations, and incomplete implementation of APD's internal review mechanisms, including internal affairs, the early intervention process, and the critical incident review process. We did not assess hiring practices; however, we did receive information that causes us concern with regard to those practices. We look forward to working with the City to strengthen background checks and suitability assessments of new and lateral hires.

a. Supervisory reviews do not address excessive uses of force.

We found numerous instances where improper force was used, but the problems were neither identified nor addressed by the chain of command. In nearly all of the incidents that we found problematic, we did not observe *any* findings by *any* supervisor—from the sergeant, who is a patrol officer's immediate supervisor, up through the entire chain of command—that the officer's use of force required corrective action. Data produced by APD corroborates our finding. APD reported 1,863 uses of force from 2010 to 2013. Of these, supervisors found that only 14 uses of force, or less than one per cent, did not comply with agency policy. Supervisors requested a further investigation of 39 uses of force, or two per cent. The overwhelming majority of uses of force during this four-year period were endorsed by supervisors as reasonable. Significantly, in 2010 and 2011, prior to the opening of our investigation, APD supervisors found only two uses of force that failed to comply with policy. As set forth below, however, our investigation revealed numerous instances of policy violations.

APD policy does not require that supervisors conduct a thorough, rigorous and objective review of officers' use of force, including ensuring that officers provide a complete and accurate account of the facts surrounding their use of force. Instead, supervisors are required to review and sign a two-page form (titled "Use of Force

Report Form") that is designed to capture descriptive data about an incident rather than providing for a qualitative review of an officer's use of force. The Use of Force Report Form provides a space for a supervisor to fill in, without more, whether the force was "reasonable" or whether "investigation [is] required." The policy does not provide any guidance on the circumstances that would warrant further investigation; nor does it require that supervisors identify potential policy violations, corrective action, or other training or policy concerns. A separate "Evaluation Form" requires more narrative information and is completed by the commander and the deputy chief after a review of the initial report. However, a commander's responsibility for reviewing force is limited in APD policy to a generalized statement—without additional guidance—requiring that the commander ensure that subordinates conform to the use of force policy.[30] *See* APD Procedural Order 2-52-6(D)-(E).

Not surprisingly, the force reports that we reviewed—and we reviewed hundreds of them—were almost entirely devoid of any analysis of whether force was reasonable. Supervisors marked as "reasonable" almost every use of force report form we saw. Some reports were unmarked altogether. Additionally, we saw few instances where the Evaluation Form was completed or even included, suggesting that these incidents were not subject to review up the chain of command. The PERF report noted similar problems based on PERF's review of use of force data and reports from 2007 through the first quarter of 2011. For example, PERF found that the officer provided no reason

---

30 As background, the force reports APD produced include the Use of Force Report Form, a Use of Force Evaluation Form ("Evaluation Form"), Incident/Offense Reports, Supplemental Incident Reports, witness statements, and supplemental memoranda. The Evaluation Form requires more narrative information and is completed by the commander and the deputy chief after a review of the initial report.

for the force incident in 42% of the incidents reviewed.[31]

These superficial reviews evince the chain of command's disregard for detecting individual and aggregate patterns of unreasonable force by subordinates. They also demonstrate the department's failure to identify and address officers who need correction and inadequate responses to serious policy infractions. Indeed, we reviewed a number of instances that *required* corrective action under the department's policies, but none was taken. For example, in the shooting involving Alan Gomez, the officer shot Gomez without verification of a threat and after receiving information that Gomez could not have been a threat because he was no longer armed. This clearly violated the department's policy, which permits deadly force only where there is an "immediate threat of death or serious physical injury,"[32] but this policy violation was not addressed in the shooting review. Similarly, in the force involving "Edward," it was evident that the officer's decision to fire his Taser at Edward violated the department's policy, which prohibits officers from using the weapon in "any environment where an officer knows that potentially flammable, volatile, or explosive material is present (including ... gasoline ...)."[33] Edward was also handcuffed at the time he was shocked with the Taser. The department's policy prohibits use of the Taser "on a handcuffed prisoner unless they continue to use physical force or violence against the officer, another person or themselves which cannot be controlled by other means."[34] Despite evidence of both policy violations, the supervisor marked this incident as "reasonable" and conducted no additional investigation.

We identified other policy violations that went uninvestigated and uncorrected. For instance, the policy

---

31 PERF Report, *supra* note 11, at 52.

32 Use of Force Policy, 2-52-3(B)(1).

33 Use of Force Policy, 2-52-8(G)(3)(a)(5).

34 Use of Force Policy, 2-52-8(G)(3)(a)(2).

allowing officers to use deadly force to disable a vehicle's tires was violated when officers shot directly at, and killed, Daniel Tillison and Mickey Owings.[35] Other policy infractions that went uncorrected included the policy that fleeing should not be the sole justification for firing a Taser at an individual, the requirement that reports should be completed by all officers witnessing the use of force, and the prohibition of using a Taser against an individual who is passively resisting.[36] We found improper and uncorrected uses of force in violation of all of these policies. Supervisors failed to address these policy violations, either by taking corrective action or referring the incident for further investigation by Internal Affairs, allowing improper conduct to continue unchecked.

b. Force incidents are not properly documented.

Deficient documentation by officers using force and inadequate review of this deficiency up the chain of command contributes to the pattern or practice of excessive force. This documentation deficiency includes failing to document incidents with recording devices, such as lapel cameras and belt tapes,[37] as well as failing to complete use of force reports, failing to accurately describe the force used in incident reports, and failing to report the use of force altogether. The department's internal review mechanisms failed to correct these deficiencies.

For example, the department's use of force policy provides, "Upon firing the [Taser], the officer shall energize the subject the least number of times and no longer than necessary to accomplish the legitimate operational

---

35 Use of Force Policy, 2-52-3(B)(3).

36 Use of Force Policy, 2-52-8(G)(3)(a)(4); 2-52-6(B); and 2-52-8(G)(3)(b), respectively.

37 Before using lapel cameras in 2012, APD officers used belt tapes to capture audio of incidents.

objective."[38] However, officers routinely failed to specify the number of five-second cycles they deployed at an individual, despite the significant risk of serious harm posed by prolonged or repeated Taser deployment. Professional law enforcement and research organizations have warned against continuous deployment of Tasers for more than three cycles, or 15 seconds, and the need for specific justification and investigation in such circumstances.[39]

We also reviewed numerous reports where officers and supervisors on the scene failed to turn on their lapel cameras or belt tapes. Officers failed to record some incidents even when it was the officers themselves who initiated the contact, making their failure to switch on their cameras or recorders before beginning the encounter especially troubling. For example, in an incident where officers fired Tasers at "Mike" after stopping him for speeding, none of the officers present recorded the incident. Many of the reports include repetitive or standardized explanations for failing to record, such as "the immediacy of the situation" and "rapid and unexpected event." These descriptions were provided where it was clear that the officer had a clear opportunity to record the event. We found very few examples of officers being reprimanded for failing to record force incidents. The

---

38 Use of Force Policy, 2-52-8(G)(6)(b).

39 NIJ Special Report, *supra* note 23, at 4 ("A preliminary review of deaths following [Taser] exposure found that many are associated with continuous or repeated shocks. There may be circumstances in which repeated or continuous exposure is required, but law enforcement officers should be aware that the associated risks are unknown. Therefore, caution is urged in using multiple activations."); PERF Guidelines, *supra* note 24, at 19, 21-22; International Association of Chiefs of Police ("IACP") Model Policy, Electronic Control Weapons, April 2010, and IACP National Law Enforcement Policy Center, Electronic Control Weapons, Concepts and Issues Paper, April 2010.

fact that few officers were reprimanded for this failure suggests that supervisors have also failed to insist on this form of accountability. The reports reflect some of the justifications we heard onsite for not recording force incidents. We were informed, during our onsite visits and after, that some officers found the equipment cumbersome and difficult to operate. However, we observed a number of officers successfully using the lapel cameras during our onsite tours. In the time since our onsite tours, the department has procured new lapel cameras that are reportedly easier to operate. We have not assessed officers' use of that new equipment. However, the department's failure to record incidents consistently indicates that officers have not embraced these accountability mechanisms.

We also reviewed numerous reports that did not provide sufficient information to justify the force used, did not explain fully what type of force was used, and did not accurately describe the level of threat, if any, posed by those against whom force was used.[40] Many of the reports included canned language, such as "aggressive posture" and "aggressive manner," but the overall description of the incident did not support such characterizations. For example, obviously disoriented subjects were described as approaching officers in an aggressive manner. In many instances where multiple officers witnessed an incident, officers did not complete supplemental reports as required by APD policy.[41] Other common documentation deficiencies include

- Failing to take a statement from the person who was subjected to force;

---

40 This issue was also noted by PERF. PERF Report, *supra* note 11, at 48 ("[L]imitations to the data make it impossible to distinguish between events where a weapon was not needed and events where a weapon was used but the weapon use was not reported.").
41 Use of Force Policy, 2-52-6(B).

- Failing to provide photographic documentation of the injuries sustained; and
- Failing to investigate discrepancies in the report.

Despite these deficiencies, supervisors noted no problems with the reports, marking questionable force incidents as reasonable. The reports also reveal that officers often failed to canvass for witnesses to the use of force, which led to reports that were usually one-sided.

Finally, the verified information we received from community witnesses indicates that officers underreport force incidents. We note first that the policy effective during our review period required officers to complete reports only where the officer's actions resulted in an injury.[42] This standard is too narrow and allows officers not to report force, even significant force, if they do not believe an individual was injured. For example, we reviewed video of officers putting one man in a chokehold, but there was no force report completed regarding this encounter despite the risk of serious harm. *See Walton v. Gomez*, No. 12-1496, 2014 U.S. App. LEXIS 4493, at *49 (10th Cir. Mar. 14, 2014) (noting that police training materials recommend against applying chokeholds for longer than one minute because brain damage or death could occur and observing that courts from various jurisdictions have held chokeholds on a non-resisting subject to be excessive). In situations where officers do not use weapons, supervisors are only expected to review force from "hand-to-hand action resulting in injury,"[43] which excludes other significant physical force, such as kicks, leg sweeps, prone restraints, and other forceful takedowns. Not surprisingly, we heard from credible witnesses who suffered injuries as a result of their encounters with officers, yet no force reports were completed. The failure

---

42 Use of Force Policy, 2-52-6(A), (B).
43 Use of Force Policy, 2-52-6(D)(2).

to provide clear policy guidance on reportable and reviewable force results in underreporting of force and contributes to the use of unreasonable force.

c. Shooting investigations are inadequate.

Officer-involved shooting investigations are conducted by the department's homicide detectives with the aid of a multijurisdictional team.[44] While these investigations are more thorough than reviews of less lethal force incidents, we noticed several deficiencies in the investigations. First, as a matter of policy, the department does not subject incidents where officers shoot to disable a vehicle to the same scrutiny as shootings of persons, despite the significant risks of death or serious injury to the occupants of the disabled vehicle or to bystanders.[45] Although shooting at a vehicle's tires, as permitted by APD policy, may not pose the same certainty of death or serious injury as shooting at the driver himself, the risk is at least equal to, if not greater than, ramming a moving vehicle to disable it. *See Scott,* 550 U.S. at 384 (observing that the term "deadly force" encompasses a range of applications of force, some more certain to cause death than others and noting that ramming a vehicle poses a "high likelihood" of death or serious injury to the driver); *see also Cordova,* 569 F.3d at 1188-89 (distinguishing the ramming technique in *Harris* to the near certainty of death or serious injury resulting from shooting a driver in the back of the head). Given the significant risks involved when officers discharge their firearms at moving vehicles, APD should respond to such incidents with the

---

44 The team includes homicide detectives, an internal affairs investigator, and representatives from the Sheriff's Office, the Independent Review Office, the District Attorney's Office, and the State Police. A homicide detective leads the team.

45 Investigation of Shootings and the Use of Deadly Force Involving Department Personnel, 2-31.

same level of resources and heightened scrutiny as other firearm discharges.[46]

We also observed deficiencies in how detectives approached shooting incidents that were questionable, i.e., not clearly justified. Based on our review, detectives approached these incidents with less scrutiny than required, such as by failing to canvass for witnesses, to test the officer's account, and to address contradictions. For example, in the shooting of Dominic Smith, the review team failed to reconcile inconsistencies in the physical evidence when compared with the officer's statement. The officer claimed that Smith came towards him and reached in his waistband. However, the physical evidence indicated that Smith had a defensive wound and was shot through the forearm. This discrepancy was not addressed in the shooting review. In the shooting review of Daniel Tillison, detectives failed to canvass the area for witnesses even though the shooting occurred in a parking lot within sight of a number of residences. In addition, in some reviews, the shooting officer's interview was attended by other officers who were involved in the incident. This practice encourages collusion and discourages candor. Finally, the reviews seemed biased in favor of clearing the officer as opposed to gaining a full understanding of the incident. These deficiencies contribute to the pattern or practice of unnecessary uses of deadly force.

d. Internal review mechanisms are not implemented.

We observed additional deficiencies in the department's internal review mechanisms, including internal affairs reviews, the early intervention system, and the critical incident review board. First, under the

---

46 Of course, it would be preferable to prohibit officers from shooting at moving vehicles altogether, as recommended by PERF and consistent with the practice of many other police departments.

department's use of force policy, the internal affairs unit is responsible for reviewing all reported uses of force to determine whether: (a) departmental policies, rules or procedures were violated; (b) the relevant policy was clearly understandable and effective to cover the situation; and (c) department training was adequate.[47] However, we found no evidence that the internal affairs unit consistently carried out this critical task. Nor does the internal affairs policy specify how the unit should conduct these substantive force reviews. The internal affairs policy states explicitly that the unit is responsible for conducting administrative investigations of cases where an individual is killed or seriously injured, or an officer discharges his firearm.[48] However, it is silent on how other uses of force should be reviewed. The policy also fails to list force reviews or investigations as part of the internal affairs unit's major purposes.

Thus, in many cases, we found that the internal affairs unit did not make recommendations to the chain of command where officers clearly violated policy, despite its responsibility to "identify personnel guilty of misconduct so that proper corrective action may be taken."[49] We also found that the internal affairs unit relies too heavily on interviews conducted in the initial shooting review. We reviewed a number of files where internal affairs failed to re-interview civilian witnesses. The unit is thus deficient in carrying out one of its most basic duties.

Second, the department's implementation of the early intervention system is ineffective. An early intervention system should be non-punitive, proactive, and geared toward identifying officers who may require retraining and counseling. These officers may have had a number of force incidents, community complaints, policy violations, or other issues that indicate that they

---

47 Use of Force Policy, 2-52-7(B)(1).

48 Internal Affairs Policy, 3-41-3(A)(6), (7).

49 Internal Affairs Policy, 3-41-2(A)(2).

may need some level of supervisory intervention to prevent them from engaging in future improper conduct. Administrative Order 03-49 outlines APD's early intervention system. However, based on our interviews, the purpose of the early intervention process appears to be a mystery to line officers. During our onsite meetings, many officers expressed concern that the process was used to punish them instead of correcting or disrupting potentially problematic conduct. Their understanding of the system is disconnected from the policy itself and what we heard from commanders. This lack of clarity suggests a lack of buy-in by officers to the process. Part of the confusion may be due to the initial policy statement, which states that the early intervention system is an essential part of the department's overall discipline system, rather than a management tool that is non-disciplinary.[50] To be fully effective, early intervention must be accepted by officers, supervisory personnel, and the community as an important alternative and complement to the agency's discipline system.

Also, we are concerned with the early intervention policy's high threshold for reassigning officers who have been required to attend multiple early intervention meetings in a 12-month period. The threshold of five meetings—which means the officer engaged in more than 15 uses of force, or a combination of 25 other triggering events, including firearm discharges and missing court—is too high. The seven data elements or performance indicators captured by APD's early intervention system may also be too limited for APD's size and risk management needs. APD should consider adding elements related to vehicle pursuits, incidents involving resisting arrest, injuries, sick days and other absences.

The department is also not using the early intervention process in the way it was intended, which is to disrupt patterns of problematic behavior. We reviewed a

---

50 Early Intervention System Policy, 3-49.

sampling of the early intervention files and found lacking documentation, superficial reviews, and a failure of the supervisors to discuss underlying incidents with officers. For example, reports with officers flagged because of multiple force incidents did not include the underlying force reports, and many made no mention of supervisors having discussed the incidents with the officer. Many of the reports were so cursory that it was difficult to discern what was discussed with the officer in the meeting. We question the effectiveness of such meetings.

Finally, the department's critical incident review board is ineffectively implemented. As with the early intervention system, the critical incident review board is a necessary and good idea. The board was established to identify deficiencies or required changes in policies and training through a review of serious incidents. The board consists of a diverse group, including commanders, a training representative, and a patrol supervisor. Despite the laudable purpose of the board, we are concerned with its effectiveness. Specifically, there is no communication to others within the agency about its findings, no documentation of the board's meetings, and no corrective actions stemming from the board's meetings. In sum, the process appears to be superficial. Such anemic internal review mechanisms contribute to the pattern or practice of unreasonable force.

2. The Department's Training Deficiencies Contribute to the Pattern or Practice of Unreasonable Use of Force.

In our review of the department's training programs, it was clear that the department has recently taken a number of steps to improve the training it provides to officers, most prominently by hiring a new training director. As we expressed to then-Chief Schultz during our meetings with him, we believe that the director is taking the training program in the right direction, and we commend

the department for all of the support it has shown for the
new director's efforts. Nonetheless, we found numerous
deficiencies in the department's training program that
have contributed to the pattern of unreasonable uses of
force. While many of these deficiencies seem to be under
review by the director, we will address them here because doing so provides a more complete picture of the
department's approach to the use of force. Our observations about the training programs are based on on-site
reviews of training materials and interviews with training staff; reviews of training curricula, lesson plans, and
classroom materials; and consultation with our police
practices consultants.

The most significant deficiency we observed in the
department's training programs—both at the academy,
where new recruits are trained, and in the ongoing training that officers receive regularly—is the over-emphasis
on using force, especially weapons, to resolve stressful
encounters, and insufficient emphasis on de-escalation
techniques. Much of the training leads officers to believe
that violent outcomes are normal and desirable. Even
scenario-based trainings, where officers role-play in
simulated interactions with civilians, tended to escalate
to the use of force, even though scenario-based training can be very effectively used to teach officers how to
diffuse tensions and end stressful civilian encounters
peacefully. As in many police departments, Albuquerque
officers are trained on a computer-assisted Firearms
Training Simulator, and we note particularly that this
simulator could be used more effectively to teach verbal
de-escalation strategies.

Also concerning is that it is impossible to ensure that
the training that officers receive accurately reflects
the department's policies, the state of the law, and best
practices in policing. Most of the individuals who deliver
lectures during police academy sessions do not provide
the department with lesson plans or classroom materials, which prevents the department from validating

those materials to ensure that they are consistent with the department's policies and values. It is also impossible to tell whether the content of the training is the same from one academy session to the next, and thus whether officers come into the field with the same base of knowledge.

We understand that much of the department's training program is mandated by New Mexico's Peace Officer Standards and Training Program, and the department does not have complete flexibility in determining what training officers receive. However, the department can and does supplement the training required by the state, and has the ability to tailor the training program to its needs. We also know that APD's training director shares all of these concerns, and we commend the steps he is taking to remedy the problems, such as by hiring a curriculum writer who can create training programs that are fully documented and validated by the department. The department should also require any individuals who train its officers to provide their complete lesson plans, classroom materials, and any other information the department may require to ensure that the training provided meets the department's standards.

As mentioned above, the department offers training to new recruits at its police academy and to officers already working in the department through regular in-service, or annual training updates called "maintenance of effort," training. It appeared to us that the maintenance-of-effort training was largely a lost opportunity. Officers we spoke to perceived it as a waste of their time, and much of it seemed to focus on the use of weaponry. We believe that the maintenance-of-effort trainings are another area where the department also can focus on subjects that are not included in the training required by the state and can take a more active role in designing its own original curriculum.

We found a number of areas in which training seemed to be entirely lacking or at least dangerously deficient. It appeared that officers are not given refresher trainings on critical policies, such as the use-of-force policy, when those policies have been implicated in major incidents. Similarly, major incidents themselves do not give rise to new training scenarios, though many officers expressed a desire to see the department as a whole learn from such incidents.

In addition, when new or different policies are put into effect, or when officers are provided with new equipment, the department fails to provide new training to prepare officers for the changes, which predictably leads to policy violations and the misuse of equipment. For example, when the department issued lapel cameras and then added a new policy that required officers to record civilian encounters, our understanding is that officers were not provided sufficient training on the lapel camera policy or on how to use the lapel cameras, especially in situations in which the use of force is likely. As noted elsewhere in this letter, officers have consistently failed to follow the department's lapel camera policy and have failed to record critical encounters. The lack of training on the lapel cameras is partially to blame.

We also found that the department should provide substantially more training on constitutional law. It appears that officers receive only a few hours of training on constitutional standards at the police academy, and very little (if any) time is put into these topics during maintenance-of-effort trainings. We also note with concern that the legal training materials provided to officers contain a number of cartoons that are likely intended to break up the monotony of the material, but that nevertheless are unprofessional and, in some cases, offensive. These cartoons send the wrong message to officers about the importance of civilians' legal rights.

Officers should also receive more training on community policing—which is widely embraced by the field as effective at building community trust in police departments and in ensuring public safety. As noted below, officers at all levels of the chain of command seemed to have a poor understanding of what community policing is or how it can improve their encounters with civilians and better protect the public. Any efforts the department takes to adopt a true community policing model should include robust training on what community policing is and how it should impact officers' work.

Because so much of the department's training program is not documented, it was difficult for us—as it is for the department itself—to fully evaluate most of the training that officers receive. From our review of other aspects of the department, however, it is apparent that training is deficient in several other areas. The department clearly has not provided sufficient training on the use of Tasers, including when their deployment may pose substantial risks to the safety of officers and the individuals on whom they are being used. We also believe that the way officers have communicated with (or failed to communicate with) individuals in mental health crisis show a clear lack of appropriate training on mental illness. In addition, the department should fully re-assess the training it provides to officers on how to write police reports, as well as its training for supervisors on how to review the police reports filed by their subordinates. Several of the first- and second-line supervisors we spoke to (those at the ranks of sergeant and lieutenant) also expressed an interest in seeing the department offer training specifically for new supervisors.

3. The Department's Deficient Policies Contribute to the Pattern or Practice of Unreasonable Use of Force.

The department's use-of-force policies and procedures fail to provide its officers with the operational guidance they need to ensure constitutional policing. These policy deficiencies begin with the failure to clearly define "force" in terms that allow officers to distinguish between reportable uses of force and non-reportable uses of force. The department's definition of "force" should be articulated clearly to allow for consistent, practical applications. In addition, the current definition of "police action" is too vague. For instance, it is unclear if the definition includes escorting an individual, pointing a firearm, or placing an individual in a prone restraint. The absence of clear guidance on what force officers are required to report leaves significant gaps. These gaps affect the quantity and quality of force reports that should be generated after force is used in incidents that do not result in fatalities.

APD's use of force policy is also too restrictive in requiring officers to report only force that results in injury. The policy states that "in all instances where police actions are used which result in an injury, officers shall document the injury or alleged injury in the report of the incident." The term "injury" is not sufficiently defined in the policy. Not surprisingly, we found that officers have varied interpretations of the policy, and many seemed uncertain when a use of force should be reported. We interviewed one sergeant who told us that no report was required where an officer used pepper spray. He also stated that even officers' use of physical force did not require documentation where there was no obvious injury. The varying interpretations of the current policy further limit the quantity of reports generated after incidents. The broadly drafted and unclear policy is ineffective, encourages abuse, and allows officers to conceal uses of force that should ordinarily be reported and reviewed.

The department's policy regarding shooting at moving vehicles is outdated and inconsistent with best police practices. As noted above, shooting at vehicles is generally a poor tactical choice and exacerbates the chances of vehicles becoming more dangerous instruments. The department's policy does not prohibit firing at moving vehicles. It specifically permits officers to fire at tires in certain situations. Under policy 2-52-3(B), officers are permitted to disable the tires of a moving vehicle by shotgun or rifle in circumstances where the officers are protecting themselves or others from what is reasonably believed to be an immediate threat of death or serious physical injury or preventing the escape of one reasonably believed to have committed a felony. This policy is inconsistent with modern and acceptable police practices; moreover, we found little evidence that officers have been following this policy.

Indeed, our review of incident reports revealed a practice of officers firing and injuring subjects in the cabin of their vehicle. In the fatal shooting of Mickey Owings, an officer shot him through the passenger window as he attempted to leave a busy department store parking lot. Owings' vehicle eventually slowed down as he lost consciousness and then died. The officer's action clearly violated the department's policy and placed citizens in the parking lot area in danger. Although the department concluded that the officer's conduct was justified, it appears that the only immediate threat that Owings posed was property damage, and the officer could have employed other tactics to avoid having to use deadly force under these circumstances. Furthermore, it appears that the officer did not try to place himself in a tactically advantageous position, but instead reacted in a manner that was inconsistent with the department's own policies.

The department has been aware of the problems with this policy and the risks associated with allowing officers to fire at vehicles since at least June 2011, when PERF recommended that the department prohibit officers from firing from or at moving vehicles under all circumstances.[51] Despite PERF's guidance, APD has not revised its policy to address the likely dangers associated with allowing its officers to fire at moving vehicles. This delay in implementing needed reform signals that

---

51 PERF Report, *supra* note 11, at 22-23.

APD does not acknowledge the dangers associated with firing at moving vehicles. The department's failure to update its policy to conform to modern police practices places its officers and citizens at a higher risk of harm.

The use of force policy also includes terms that imply the justified use of force. For example, officers are required to describe the force they use in an "offense" report, which suggests that the subject of force was committing or suspected of committing a crime.[52] Based on our review, some individuals are the subject of force during welfare checks or when they are not engaged in criminal activity. Subjects of force are also referred to as "combatants" in APD policy.[53]

As discussed earlier, the use of force policy is wholly inadequate in requiring thorough and objective supervisory reviews of force. The policy does not describe the collection and preservation of evidence regarding an officer's use of force, canvassing the scene for witnesses, obtaining information from subjects of force, reviewing photographs and other demonstrative evidence, or referring a use of force for administrative or criminal investigation. The policy also does not prohibit having those supervisors who used, authorized, or directed force subsequently review the reasonableness of the force. We reviewed incidents in which supervisors who were on the scene and participated in the use of force also determined that the force they used or authorized was reasonable and did not warrant further investigation. Other policy deficiencies include permitting canines to be deployed for crowd control, which is inconsistent with contemporary policing practices.

Underreporting appears to be correlated with poor interpretations of the force policy and officers' resistance to reporting incidents. Underreporting inhibits the department from learning from use-of-force incidents.

---

52 Use of Force Policy, 2-52-6(B)(1).
53 Use of Force Policy, 2-52-6(B)(1)(d).

It also limits the quantity of incidents that supervisors could review, and it leads to officers not being held accountable for their actions. The high number of force incidents involving Tasers in our review sample suggests either that Tasers are used with considerable frequency or, more likely, that other forms of force are being under-reported. APD's policy of requiring use of force reports when there is an injury allows officers to avoid reporting incidents where there is no visible or apparent injury. We also obtained recordings of force provided by individuals without corresponding APD reports. It appears that the department has failed to account for the full range of force that its officers use against its citizens. This failure has a contributed to the pattern or practice of excessive force.

4. Under-Use of the Crisis Intervention Team Contributes to the Pattern or Practice of Unconstitutional Force.

As noted above, the Crisis Intervention Team ("the Team") is a specialized unit in APD that is trained and equipped to create safer encounters with individuals who are in mental health crisis and may harm themselves or others. After interviewing and observing the Team and some of the patrol officers they have trained and certified, we are encouraged by the innovations and passions that many on the Team have brought to the department. In many ways, the Team provides a template for the department as it considers how to remedy its pattern of unreasonable uses of force. Members of the Team demonstrate an understanding of the illnesses that individuals suffer, they are informed about the challenges those individuals face, and they approach encounters with an eye toward preserving the health and safety of everyone involved.

Given the Team's skills, the department could gain substantially—and could greatly impact its overemphasis on the use of force—by involving the Team in far more of its encounters than it currently does and by permitting the Team greater latitude in the course of an encounter to broker a peaceful outcome. Reaching this goal may require adding personnel to the Team and training and certification of additional patrol officers across the city. Our understanding is that currently, if officers encounter someone in mental health crisis, they can call for a Team member or a specially trained patrol officer assigned to their part of the city, but there is no guarantee that either will be available. We recommend that the department conduct a staffing study to determine how many officers would need to be added to the Team, as well as how many patrol officers would need to be trained and certified, to ensure that someone with the appropriate skills is always available in all parts of the city when an encounter with someone in mental health crisis occurs.

The department could also make a significant impact on officers' tendency to use force during stressful encounters by providing officers more training on the use of de-escalation techniques. The Team currently provides this kind of training to new recruits at the police academy, but our observations of, and interviews with, officers indicate that the Team's training has so far failed to make an impact on the overall culture of the department and the general approach of most officers. We also found it troubling that many officers did not seem conversant with the Team's function or its relevance to their encounters with those in mental health crisis. A clear example of this lack of familiarity was evident in the use-of-force reports that we reviewed. In far too many of those reports, officers encountered a person who was clearly in mental health crisis, but they made no attempt to contact the Team or patrol officers in their area who had been trained and certified by the Team. Partially as a result of the officers' failure to use the resources available to them, far too many of these encounters had a violent outcome.

One area where we believe the department can immediately begin leveraging the skills and training of the Team is in what officers call "welfare checks"—where someone has called 911 to ask officers to check on a person who may be at risk of harming himself or who seems to be in crisis. In the use-of-force reports we reviewed, far too many encounters that began as welfare checks ended in violence, and far too often the officers' use of force was unreasonable. The inclusion of the Team or patrol officers trained and certified by the Team on welfare checks could make a substantial impact on the department's use of force and could lead to better overall outcomes for residents in mental health crisis.

5. The Department's Ineffective Use of Its Tactical Deployments Contributes to the Use of Excessive Force.

Through our review of use-of-force reports, officer-involved shooting investigations, and interviews with citizens, we conclude that the department inadequately conducts tactical deployments. Tactical deployments are a significant component of a police department's strategic response to high-intensity incidents. These incidents include encounters with suicidal subjects, barricaded subjects, hostage situations, and high-risk traffic stops.

In our review of the Department's SWAT, we found deficiencies in the leadership of this specialized unit. At the time of our review, the SWAT commander had not received adequate training and appeared to lack the experience to direct a disciplined and effective SWAT unit. It is critical that supervisors be taught the skills necessary to oversee a specialized unit. Beyond the commander's lack of SWAT experience, we note that the unit does not have clear command structure or deployment guidance. As a consequence, we found that SWAT members do not have sufficient understanding of incident

deployment, scene control, or proper reporting protocols. We further noted a near absence of organizational
accountability. Officers are simply afforded too much
autonomy, which has contributed to even greater insularity from the department's accountability systems,
ineffective deployments and tragic shootings that could
have been avoided.

SWAT's deficient on-scene supervisory oversight contributes to the pattern of unreasonable use of force. Based
on our review, SWAT officers failed to conduct any pre-
deployment planning and rarely coordinated with patrol
officers once they arrived on the scene of incidents. We
further found that SWAT officers were unable to provide
operational or strategic guidance once they arrived on
scene. In many instances, despite being tactical experts,
SWAT command failed to provide any meaningful assistance during dangerous situations.

In the fatal shooting of Alan Gomez, 26 officers responded to a possible hostage situation. Even though
SWAT responded to the scene, it appeared that SWAT
command failed to establish scene control. A SWAT officer acted independently in setting up on the scene, and
it appears that little, if any, coordination was conducted
to ensure that patrol officers could effectively address
the situation. The SWAT officer also failed to participate
in negotiations, even though the discussions with Gomez
lasted nearly one hour. While the patrol officers were
negotiating with Gomez, the SWAT officer unilaterally
took a shooting position near the house. As the officers
continued to negotiate with Gomez, the SWAT team
member shot Gomez before he received approval from a
supervisor.

Similarly, we reviewed another incident where
several patrol officers responded to a home after learning that "Steve" had been involved in multiple armed
robberies and was staying at the home. As the patrol officers arrived on the scene, Steve left the home and was

followed by multiple patrol officers. Steve reportedly had suicidal thoughts and was carrying a firearm in a duffle bag. The patrol officers were able to negotiate with Steve in an open field and to convince him to get on his knees, although he maintained control of the duffle bag. As the patrol officers continued to negotiate with Steve for over one hour, a SWAT officer arrived on the scene. The SWAT officer failed to coordinate with the patrol officers, and SWAT command seemed to play no role in handling the situation. The SWAT officer instead positioned himself in a tactical shooting position. The SWAT officer also failed to communicate with his supervisor, even though the supervisor was on his way to the scene. This lack of communication is a pervasive practice that has contributed to tactical shortcomings at APD. As the patrol officers were awaiting a SWAT supervisor, the SWAT officer shot Steve multiple times. Several officers reported that they were surprised that the SWAT officer shot Steve. This is another example of how a SWAT command failure and deployment failure led to a fatal shooting.

In addition to its lacking deployment oversight, we also identified a troubling trend where SWAT officers failed to document and videotape deployments. This stands in stark contrast to the canine unit, which is actually a component of the SWAT unit and which more consistently documents and evaluates deployments. SWAT has the ability to document and record deployments just as thoroughly as the canine unit, but it has not done so. Supervisors—and again, the same supervisors who oversee SWAT also oversee the canine unit—have therefore been unable to determine whether SWAT's actions were reasonable, appropriate, and complied with the department's standards. They also could not assess the tactical effectiveness of deployments. This deficient control and understanding of SWAT officers' conduct contributes to the pattern of unreasonable use of force.

6. The Department's Aggressive Organizational Culture Contributes to Excessive Force Incidents.

The department's lack of internal oversight has allowed a culture of aggression to develop. This culture is manifested in the routine nature of excessive force and lack of corrective actions taken by the leadership to address force incidents. This culture is evident in the department's training, permissive policy on weapons, under-utilization of its crisis intervention team, overuse of SWAT, and the harsh approaches to ordinary encounters with residents. The failure of the department's leadership to address unnecessary uses of force reinforces the aggressive culture.

A lack of accountability in the use of excessive force promotes an acceptance of disproportionate and aggressive behavior towards residents. We reviewed numerous incidents demonstrating this approach. For example, in the incident involving "Charles," where he was stopped by officers for failing to stop at a sign while riding his bicycle, the officers escalated the situation and shocked him with Tasers multiple times. According to the incident report, the officer essentially fired his Taser at Charles for failing to completely submit and obey commands. The initial officer called for backup when Charles failed to stop his bicycle immediately upon the officer's command; ultimately three officers approached him. Their use of force against a perplexed cyclist is just one of many episodes in which officers expressed hostility toward people not engaged in the commission of any crimes. An officer's decision to use his Taser on Ivan is another example. Ivan was unconscious on a couch during a party. When he was roused by the officer and obviously confused, he started to struggle while still prone on the couch. The officer escalated the situation instead of altering his approach given Ivan's condition. Both of these incidents were approved by supervisors in subsequent reports that found the force reasonable.

As mentioned above, APD's training is focused so heavily on weaponry and force scenarios that officers do not get essential tools to engage in effective de-escalation methods. The training is an element of the culture of aggression. Once officers complete their training, they are allowed to carry non-standard issued weapons that are approved by the range master.[54] We were informed that many officers purchase expensive, high-powered guns as soon as they are allowed, using their own money. Officers see the guns as status symbols. APD personnel we interviewed indicated that this fondness for powerful weaponry illustrates the aggressive culture.

This aggressive culture is also evident in many of the force reports that we reviewed, in incidents recounted to us by community witnesses, and in widely available videos of officers using force against non-combative individuals. We interviewed numerous people who relayed accounts of harsh treatment by officers. The incident involving "Nick" illustrates this point. He provided video footage showing an officer choking him after he stepped out of his car during a stop for driving while intoxicated. In another incident, an officer grabbed, yelled at, and attempted to handcuff "Omar" when he was helping an accident victim and did not get out of the officers' way quickly enough for the officer. Omar tried to explain that he was compressing the victim's wound and using his training as an emergency medical technician, but the officer seemed concerned only with his immediate compliance. Additionally, we have reviewed reports and publicly available videos of officers slamming a man's head against a tree plantar on a sidewalk, using a Taser on an obviously subdued man, and punching a man who had done nothing to the officer or anyone else. Few supervisors tried to address these problems. When supervisors did attempt to correct these officers, many complained about the dearth of support from department leadership

---

54 Firearms and Ammunition Authorization Policy 2-22.

when they attempted to address problematic conduct. These incidents and the failure to require corrective action demonstrate a culture that emphasizes force and complete submission over safety. The department's leadership does not address these issues and, as such, sends a message that such conduct is acceptable. This culture contributes to the use of excessive force.

7. The Department's Limited External Oversight Contributes to the Pattern or Practice of Unconstitutional Uses of Force.

Independent, external oversight of a police agency—oversight that is exercised by individuals or institutions that are not part of or beholden to the agency or its leadership—helps strengthen community trust. Independent oversight can identify deficiencies in a police agency's own internal reviews, provide a transparent process for resolving complaints against an agency, and build confidence in an agency by bringing the public into the process of assessing and improving it.

Albuquerque has adopted an external oversight structure that has two primary components: the Police Oversight Commission ("the Commission") and the Independent Review Officer ("the Review Officer"). Briefly, the Review Officer is appointed by the Mayor and paid by the City to investigate all officer-involved shootings and all complaints filed against the Department by civilians. The Review Officer is assisted by a staff of paid investigators, and she reports her findings at public meetings of the Police Oversight Commission. The Commission is made up of volunteer Commissioners from across the city appointed by the Mayor. The Commission holds regular public meetings to consider the reports of the Review Officer and make recommendations to the Chief of Police on whether officers have violated the Department's policies. The Chief retains complete discretion over whether policy violations in fact occurred and whether officers should be disciplined.

To assess the effectiveness of Albuquerque's external oversight structure, we interviewed the current Review Officer and members of the Commission. We also reviewed the reports of the Review Officer and recommendations of the Commission for all fatal police shootings between 2009 and 2012 for which such reviews have occurred. In addition, we analyzed the city ordinance that established and governs the Commission and the Review Officer, as well as other information we received.

Albuquerque's external oversight structure could do much more to address unreasonable uses of deadly force, and it is apparent from our review of documents and interviews that the failure to do so in the past has contributed to the pattern of unreasonable force that we have found. Members of the Albuquerque community have expressed concern that the Commission does not provide meaningful oversight of the department and that the Commission and the Review Officer have not weighed the evidence from their investigations appropriately.

We note that the Commission's work is limited in some ways by the collective bargaining agreement reached between the City and the officers' union, the Albuquerque Police Officers Association. That agreement limits the amount of information that the Commission can consider in reviewing specific cases, such as the identity of the officer whose alleged conduct is at issue and the officer's disciplinary history. Knowing an officer's identity and disciplinary history could provide important context for individual allegations of misconduct and help the Commission assess whether there is a pattern of problematic behavior.

Albuquerque's independent oversight structure could also do far more to involve the community and to provide opportunities to be heard to those making allegations of misconduct. Community members have limited opportunities to speak during the Commission's public meetings. Those who have filed complaints against officers are not provided any opportunities to be heard at any of the Commission's meetings before a decision is made on their cases except in the very limited public comment period, and so they cannot meaningfully contribute to the Commission's decision-making process.

Along those same lines, citizen complaints are subject to strict limitations that keep the Commission from being able to address potentially serious allegations of misconduct. The ordinance that created the Police Oversight Commission requires complaints to be filed within 90 days of the incident or they will not be considered. In addition, by an agreement between the City of Albuquerque and the Albuquerque Police Officers Association, complaints must be personally signed by the complainant for the department to consider them "official" complaints that will be taken through the full review process. We believe these limitations unnecessarily restrict the work of the Commission and the ability of the public to bring police misconduct to light.

The ordinance that created the Commission and the position of the Review Officer directs the Review Officer to "play an active public role in the community." The current Review Officer has engaged in some public outreach, and we understand that her office would reach out to the public more frequently if it were able to hire a full-time staff member dedicated to community outreach. We believe this is an important function of the Review Officer, and we urge the City to support her in these efforts.

Nonetheless, from our review it appears that the Review Officer is more closely aligned with the department than with the community that the Review Officer serves. The Review Officer has failed to find violations of department policy in cases where it is more likely than not that violations clearly occurred, and, in at least one case, she has interpreted the department's policies in ways that are contrary to the policies themselves but favorable to officers. This occurred in the case of Mickey Owings, which was discussed above and involved an officer who shot Owings while he was fleeing in a car. The Review Officer interpreted the department's policy on firing at moving vehicles to apply only when an officer fires at the vehicle itself and not at the driver of a vehicle. The point of the policy, however, is not to protect cars from being damaged by gunshots; it is to keep officers from firing their weapons where doing so poses substantial risks to public safety. When an officer fires his gun at the driver of a moving vehicle, he is both firing at the vehicle and creating risks to public safety, issues that the Review Officer should have recognized.

The current Review Officer and her predecessor found very few violations of the department's policy on the use of deadly force in officer-involved shootings, which is at odds with the evidence as detailed in this letter. If we had reached different conclusions in just a handful of cases, it might have been attributable to a difference of opinion on the very fact-intensive questions that arise when analyzing officers' use of force. But we have reached different conclusions on far more than a handful of cases. Nor can the different conclusions we reached be attributed to any difference in the underlying materials that we reviewed; the current Review Officer and her predecessor had at least as much access to reports, witnesses, and other pertinent information on force encounters as we did. We are left with the conclusion that the current Review Officer and her predecessor have simply been too forgiving of the department's use of deadly force. They thus deprived the department of critical opportunities to correct its course, which contributed to the overwhelming pattern of unconstitutional use of deadly force that we find.

8. Inadequate Community Policing Contributes to the Department's Pattern or Practice of Unconstitutional Force.

Community policing is an effective strategy that enables law enforcement agencies and individuals and organizations they serve to develop solutions to problems and increase trust in police. The department's leadership does not prioritize community policing, has not communicated its importance throughout the agency, and tolerates a culture that is hostile to community partnerships. These deficiencies have led to a mutual distrust between officers and the residents they encounter. It has contributed to the pattern or practice of excessive force.

Despite references to community policing in its policies and officer evaluations, the department does not consistently support the concepts of community policing. Community policing, also known as "smart policing," involves building partnerships between law enforcement and the people and organizations within its jurisdiction, engaging in problem-solving through proactive measures, and managing the police agency to support community partnerships and community problem-solving.[55] The focus on developing partnerships with the community is to engender trust and encourage the public to participate in identifying and addressing public safety concerns.[56] During our onsite tours, we observed

---

55 U.S. Department of Justice, Community Oriented Policing Services (COPS), Community Policing Defined (Undated) at 1; Drew Diamond and Deirdre Meid Weiss, Advancing Community Policing through Community Governance: A Framework Document (2009) at 4.

56 Community Policing Defined at 3; *see also* Tyler and Fagan, *Legitimacy and Cooperation*, 6 Ohio St. J. Crim. L. 231, 267 (cooperation with the police increases when the public views the police as fair and legitimate); Tyler, Why People Obey the Law at 163 (study verified that people believed procedures to be fair and

that there was no consistent understanding of the department's community policing program within the ranks. Even commanders had inconsistent understandings of the agency's program. Moreover, commanders have no systems in place to analyze citizen contacts with officers outside of incident reports. They do not consistently review complaints to measure how officers are engaging the community.

The lack of organizational support for community policing was evident in the numerous, credible complaints we reviewed regarding the aggressive behavior of officers. Residents told us of encounters where officers were disrespectful and aggressive in their approach. For example, "Steven" contacted APD after accidentally shooting his wife in the hip. When officers arrived, they approached Steven in his front yard and immediately placed him in handcuffs. Officers knocked on the front door and pointed their weapons at Steven's sister-in-law as soon as she opened the door. The officers then entered the home and pointed their weapons at Steven's son, even though he was rendering aid to his mother. In another example, an officer threw "Rita's" documents on the street after a traffic stop when she challenged the basis of the stop. The citation was subsequently dismissed. The "Omar" incident where the officer grabbed and yelled at a man providing medical aid to an accident victim also shows a disregard for the community. These are but a few of the instances where residents expressed concerns about their negative interactions with officers.

A disconnect exists between officers and residents about the perception of overly aggressive conduct by officers. We observed that many officers were dismissive of community concerns. For instance, many officers complained that the media generated the complaints about their perceived aggressiveness in citizen encounters.

---

authorities legitimate when they were provided opportunities to participate in the decision-making process).

Some officers also complained that the citizens were the ones who were aggressive towards them. This perception persists even though the data suggests otherwise.[57] These concerns suggest an unwillingness to embrace community policing. This rejection of one of the basic elements of community policing contributes to the department's pattern or practice of unjustified force.

V. REMEDIAL MEASURES

APD should implement the following remedial measures to address the deficiencies discussed in this letter:

A. Use of Force Policies

1. Revise the use of force policy to require that officers report any use of force, including the active pointing of firearms, above un-resisted handcuffing, and, even in cases of un-resisted handcuffing, when the subject complains of injury or excessive force.

2. Revise the use of force policy to clearly define "force" and specify the types of physical force that must also be reported, such as chokeholds, prone restraints, kicks, takedowns, leg sweeps.

3. Revise the use of force policy to prohibit shooting at vehicles.

---

57 PERF Report, *supra* note 11, at 39-40 (noting that while assaults against police officers rose between 2006 and 2007, they declined between 2007 and 2008 and overall during 2005 to 2008). The FBI Law Enforcement Officers Killed and Assaulted reports from 2009 to 2011 show a steady rate of assaults on officers in the region; there was a slight increase in 2012. *See* FBI Law Enforcement Officers Killed and Assaulted *available at* http://www.fbi.gov.

4. Revise the use of force policy to place more emphasis on de-escalation techniques and require officers to consider less-intrusive alternatives before employing force.

5. Revise the use of force policy to prohibit the use of canines for crowd control.

6. Revise the use of force policy to prohibit supervisors and officers who were involved in, ordered, or authorized a use of force from assessing the reasonableness of the force.

7. In addition to a comprehensive use of force policy that incorporates all force options, including deadly and less lethal force, develop specific policies for each of the following areas: (a) deadly force; (b) firearms; (c) canines; (d) less lethal munitions; (e) Tasers; (f) chemical agents; (g) batons and impact weapons; (h) other force technology or weapon authorized by the department.

8. Require that a failure to report a use of force or prisoner injury by an officer shall subject the officer, including supervisors and commanders, to disciplinary action.

9. Ensure that officers request medical services immediately when an individual is injured or complains of injury following a use of force.

10. Establish policies regarding force reviews and investigations. Require that force reviews and investigations determine whether the officer's conduct was justified and within agency policy.

11. Develop a reliable and accurate tracking system for all officers' use of force, all force reviews

conducted by supervisors, all force investigations conducted by the internal affairs unit, and all command-level reviews.

12. Ensure that uses of force are promptly referred to the appropriate investigative unit or agency whenever a supervisor or reviewing officer finds evidence indicating apparent misconduct or criminal conduct by an officer.

B. Interacting with Individuals with Mental Illness and other Disabilities.

1. Develop policies and implement procedures to improve the response to individuals in behavioral or mental health crisis, and to minimize the use of unnecessary force against such individuals.

2. Develop and implement protocols with the Crisis Intervention Team on how to handle interactions with individuals with known or suspected mental health issues, including those observably undergoing a mental health crisis, individuals with developmental disabilities, and individuals who appear to be intoxicated or impaired.

3. Require all officers to participate in crisis intervention training.

4. Expand the number of officers trained on how to handle interactions with individuals with mental health issues and individuals who appear to be intoxicated.

5. Review current policies and protocols concerning interactions with individuals with mental illness, developmental disabilities or other impairments to ensure they are consistent with

applicable legal standards and generally accepted policing practice.

C. Tactical Units

1. Revise policies and procedures governing response to, and investigation of, high-risk incidents including specific guidance covering: encountering suicidal subjects, barricaded subjects, hostage situations, and high-risk traffic stops.

2. Require training for all tactical team members and supervisors in topics including: pre-deployment guidance and planning; incident deployment; scene control; and post-deployment reporting.

3. Establish eligibility criteria for all staff and supervisors assigned to tactical units and conduct regular (at least annual) reviews of tactical team members to ensure that they meet delineated criteria.

4. Provide tailored annual training to all staff and supervisors assigned to tactical units, including training on effective deployment, scene control, and post-deployment reporting.

D. Training

1. Implement scenario-based training and role playing to ensure officers understand de-escalation techniques and when force is justified. This should also include training on changes to policy, new equipment, and tactical methods.

2. Train officers to use appropriate hands-on techniques following the first application of less-lethal

force, when feasible, to complete an arrest, and to use as few cycles of Taser as possible.

3. Train officers to avoid using more intrusive forms of force on individuals who do not pose a threat to the safety of the officers and others.

4. Train officers to give verbal warnings, where feasible, before using force.

E. Internal Investigations and Civilian Complaints

1. Revise the civilian complaint policy to eliminate the 90-day reporting period, allow for the investigation of anonymous and third-party complaints, and eliminate the requirement that complainants sign the complaint.

2. Revise all forms and instructions on the civilian complaint process that can be construed as discouraging civilians from submitting complaints, including warnings regarding potential criminal prosecution for false or untrue complaints.

3. Develop investigative standards and protocols for force investigations conducted by the internal affairs unit.

4. Require that all officers and employees report misconduct, including apparent, alleged, or perceived misconduct, by another officer or employee to a supervisor or directly to the internal affairs unit for review and investigation.

5. Ensure that investigations of officer misconduct are thorough and that findings are consistent with the facts.

F. Management and Supervision

1. Require that supervisors perform the following actions in response to any use-of-force incident: (a) ensure that a medical unit report to the scene of every use of force resulting in injury, actual or complained; (b) conduct a thorough analysis of the incident based on all obtainable physical evidence, adequately descriptive use-of-force reports, witness statements, and independent investigation; (c) resolve any discrepancies in use-of-force reports or witness accounts and explain all injuries; (d) ensure that the recording policy was followed; and (e) complete a summary analysis regarding the reasonableness, proportionality, and legality of the force. If the supervisor cannot resolve any factual discrepancies, determine the source of any injury, or determine the lawfulness of a use of force, the supervisor should refer the matter immediately and directly to his or her supervisor and to internal affairs. Every level of supervision should be held accountable for the quality of the first-line supervisor's force investigation.

2. Require a critical firearm discharge review process led by a command-level review team to evaluate all investigations involving critical firearm discharges. The team should be chaired by the commanding officer. The process should include specific determinations regarding whether the force used was consistent with the department's policy and training, whether lesser force alternatives were available, what non-disciplinary corrective actions should be taken, and what policy or training amendments should be effectuated. An annual review of patterns in critical incidents should be completed and reported to the Chief.

3. Require supervisors to review and take appropriate disciplinary or non-disciplinary corrective action, where warranted, in situations where he or she becomes aware of potential misconduct or criminal behavior by an officer.

4. Expand the Early Intervention System to track supervisor and area command activity. Require supervisors to conduct timely reviews that identify patterns in officer behavior and specific training deficiencies.

5. Change the Early Intervention System thresholds by: (a) adjusting thresholds based on comparison data that takes officer assignment into account; (b) creating single-event thresholds for events so critical that they require immediate department intervention; (c) implementing rolling thresholds, so that an officer who has received an intervention for use of force should not, for example, be permitted to engage in four additional uses of force before again triggering a review; (d) expand the elements or performance indicators tracked by the system; and (e) evaluate whether thresholds are in line with national standards.

6. Monitor uses of force to ensure consistency with the policies, and enforce the policies when force is used inappropriately.

7. Ensure that an adequate number of qualified first-line supervisors are deployed in the field to allow supervisors to provide close and effective supervision to each officer under the supervisor's direct command, provide officers with the direction and guidance necessary to improve and develop as officers, and to identify, correct, and prevent misconduct.

G. Recruitment and Selection

1. Ensure that the department's officer hiring and selection processes meet minimum standards for recruiting and an objective process for selection that employs reliable and valid selection devices that comport with generally accepted policing practices and federal anti-discrimination laws.

2. Require that all candidates for sworn personnel positions, including new recruits and lateral hires, undergo a valid psychological, medical, and polygraph examination to assess their fitness for employment.

3. Ensure that thorough, objective, and timely background investigations of candidates for sworn personnel positions are conducted in accordance with generally- accepted policing practice and federal anti-discrimination laws.

4. Develop objective selection criteria to ensure promotions are based on knowledge, skills, and abilities that are required to perform supervisory and management duties successfully in core substantive areas. Provide clear guidance on promotional criteria, and prioritize effective, ethical, and community-oriented policing as criteria for promotion. These criteria should account for experience, civil rights and discipline record.

5. Establish procedures that govern the removal of officers from consideration from promotion for disciplinary action related to serious misconduct.

H. Community Policing and Oversight

1. Develop a comprehensive program of community outreach that emphasizes the department's role as part of the Albuquerque community and in partnership with and service to all residents of the City.

2. Provide necessary information and sufficient resources to civilian oversight entities, so that they can meaningfully evaluate citizen complaints against officers and engage the community.

3. Create robust community relationships and engage constructively with the community to ensure collaborative problem-solving and consistent feedback from diverse sectors of the community.

4. Revise the civilian oversight process to ensure that an effective system of review and approval is implemented that includes review of serious uses of force and officer- involved shootings. The oversight process should also have the resources and support necessary to assess and make recommendations regarding the department's operations and performance that need improvement.

We share your sense of urgency in ensuring that the City of Albuquerque has an effective, accountable police department that controls crime, ensures respect for the Constitution, and earns the trust of the public it is charged with protecting. Recent events have galvanized many in the Albuquerque community to join the public discourse over the future of the Albuquerque Police Department and its relationship with the community. We look forward to working with you, the department, and the community to address our findings and forge a path forward to restore public trust and promote constitutional policing in Albuquerque. Those affected by our findings and the men and women of APD who serve the City honorably deserve no less. Please note that this letter is a public document and will be posted on the Civil Rights Division's website.

We hope to hear from you soon to begin discussions of the necessary reforms.

Sincerely,

/s/

Jocelyn Samuels
Acting Assistant Attorney General
Civil Rights Division

/s/

Damon P. Martinez
Acting U.S. Attorney
District of New Mexico

cc: Gorden E. Eden, Jr.
    Police Chief
    Albuquerque Police Department
    David Tourek, Esq.
    City Attorney
    City of Albuquerque

four |

November 29, 2012, Cleveland, Ohio:

A Police Force Out of Control— The Deaths of Timothy Russell & Malissa Williams

A CHASE BY CLEVELAND Police units on Nov. 29, 2012, caught on videotape by streetcorner surveillance cameras and by citizens with cellphones, revealed how completely out of control the Cleveland PD has become.

And if the scenes had become a part of a Hollywood film, even by today's mediocre Hollywood standards, they would have been considered so over-the-top as to be unbelievable.

The Cleveland Plain Dealer summarized the story in an article published on its website Feb. 5, 2013:

Cleveland police chase and shooting:
State report on officers involved

CLEVELAND, Ohio—On the evening of Nov. 29, 2012, Cleveland police began pursuing a 1979 Chevy Malibu driven by 43-year-old Timothy Russell with passenger Malissa Williams, 30.

The chase lasted more than 25 minutes and reached speeds in excess of 100 mph. At one point, more than 62 police vehicles from multiple law-enforcement agencies took part in the chase.

It ended in the dead-end parking lot of Heritage Middle School in East Cleveland, where Cleveland police fired close to 140 times at the Malibu, killing Russell and Williams. While police said they believed they were being fired upon, no gun was found in the Malibu.

Police officers also believed that the Malibu rammed a police car during the chase when in fact a police car making tight turn glanced the rear of the Malibu.

And while they said they saw officers down, no police officer was injured in the shootout.

The sum total of this astonishing and tragic event:

More than 62 police vehicles in the chase, covering 19-plus miles ...

Of the 62 police officers involved, 59 did not have permission to join the chase ... officers involved in the pursuit accounted for one-third of Cleveland officers on that duty shift ...

137 shots fired ...

When the fleeing car was stopped, Officer Michael Brelo stood on the hood of the car, fired down through the windshield and killed both. Counting Brelo's shots and others, Williams was hit by 24 bullets; Russell by 23 ...

Brelo was ultimately charged with two counts of manslaughter.

Street surveillance camera footage and citizen cell-phone recordings were spliced together to count the number of police vehicles involved in the chase. And while both occupants of the Malibu had criminal records, there is no excuse for more than 62 police cruisers to be involved in the chase (threatening their safety and the safety of other vehicles or pedestrians in close proximity to the chase) and clearly no excuse for 140 shots being fired and the two occupants killed.

On Feb. 8, 2013, Jeffrey Follmer, head of the Cleveland Police union called the police pursuit "a perfect chase," because no civilians were injured.

Police magazine followed this massive pursuit with multiple articles.

By mid-March, 2013, the U.S. Department of Justice began an investigation of the Cleveland Police Department. On March 14, the magazine summarized the Department of Justice investigation under the headline:

Feds Launch Use-of-Force Probe of Cleveland Police.

The article read, in part:

> The U.S. Department of Justice opened an investigation to determine whether Cleveland police use excessive force and evaluate the department's training, supervision, and accountability mechanisms.
>
> The DOJ investigation came in response to a deadly pursuit that involved one-third of the Cleveland Division of Police's on-duty force and resulted in the deaths of two subjects in a hail of gunfire. Mayor Frank Jackson requested the DOJ review.
>
> As part of the civil-rights probe, federal investigators will seek input from community members

and groups "for help in identifying potential problems within the police department," according to a DOJ release.

Another article in *Police* magazine, April 30, 2013 explained the continuing—and growing—scandal in the Cleveland PD:

Cleveland Police Supervisors
Face Discipline in Deadly Pursuit

Twelve Cleveland police supervisors face disciplinary hearings for failing to control a deadly high-speed chase that resulted in the deaths of two unarmed suspects at an East Cleveland school.

Police Chief Michael McGrath said Tuesday that his office and the agency's Integrity Control section have reviewed the supervisors' actions on Nov. 29 and determined they violated the department's mission statement, standards of conduct and several rules on vehicle pursuits, reports the *Cleveland Plain Dealer.*

The supervisors include a captain, lieutenant and 10 sergeants. All have been with the department since 1998 and one is a 20-year veteran. Other officers could also face disciplinary action, and 13 officers who used deadly force face possible criminal charges. Cuyahoga County Prosecutor Timothy McGinty is now completing that investigation, the agency announced here last week. Those 13 officers will be subject to a departmental review following the criminal investigation.

On August 2, 2013 the magazine published a follow-up article under the headline:

75 Cleveland Officers Disciplined
for Deadly Pursuit

Cleveland Police Chief Michael McGrath said Friday that 75 officers will be disciplined for violating agency protocols while participating in a deadly chase that ended with the deaths of two unarmed subjects.

Of the 75 officers, 19 will be referred to the Department of Public Safety for disciplinary hearings and could receive suspensions. The officers are charged with various violations including engaging in a chase without permission and providing false information on police reports.

The discipline stems from a November chase that resulted in the deaths of Timothy Russell and Malissa Williams in a hail of police gunfire. The 13 officers who played a role in the chase's climax aren't included in this group.

At the end of August, the Cleveland Police Department instituted a new policy that prohibited Cleveland police officers from shooting at, or from, a moving vehicle.

One reader, R. Wierzslow, contributed this, to *Police* magazine: "As a retired sergeant from this department, I can say there has always been a policy prohibiting officers to shoot at moving vehicles. The exception being the occupant used the vehicle as a form of deadly force against the officer. This new policy appears to indicate that officers cannot use deadly force against a vehicle that is trying to run them down (even if the officer did everything possible to stay out of harm's way). This new policy attempts to cover the city government against liable and leaves the officer and the police union to fend for themselves. Of course, liable policy writing has been tried in other issues. It almost never works out in the end."

On October 15, 2013, *Police* magazine reported:

63 Cleveland Officers Suspended for Deadly Pursuit

More than 60 Cleveland police officers received suspensions for improperly joining a deadly November chase that left two unarmed suspects dead in a hair of police gunfire, Chief Michael McGrath announced Tuesday.

The chief announced suspensions of no more than 10 days each for 63 of the more than 100 Cleveland Division of Police officers who participated in the Nov. 29 chase if Timothy Russell and Malissa Williams. These officers are not among the 13 who fired 137 rounds at Russell and Williams near at East Cleveland middle school.

The 178 suspension days will be distributed among ther63 officers. Chief McGrath told the *Cleveland Plain Dealer* that officers under a stressful at must "follow your rules and procedures" to avoid "some type of chaos or problems."

The previous June, 12 supervisors were disciplined, including one sergeant who was fired. On December 4, 2014. *Los Angeles Times* writer Richard Serrano covered the story, as then-Attorney General Eric Holder was concluding the DOJ's investigation.

Cleveland police use 'unnecessary' force, Justice Department finds

Cleveland police routinely engage in "unreasonable and unnecessary" force, exemplified by a half-hour chase involving 100 officers that left two unarmed African Americans dead when police mistook the car backfiring for gunshots and shot each of them more than 20 times, a Justice Department investigation revealed Thursday.

"The investigation concluded that there is reasonable cause to believe that Cleveland police engage in a pattern or practice of unreasonable force in violation of the 4th amendment," Atty. Gen. Eric H. Holder, Jr. said Thursday. "Our investigation revealed that the causes of these patterns or practices were systemic and resulted from organizational deficiencies."

The probe, a part of an ongoing series of "pattern or practice" investigations into the nation's police department, also found that Cleveland police often needlessly shot residents, struck them with head blows and subjected them to Taser weapons and chemical spray.

Attorney General Holder announced the findings one day after he opened an investigation into the July 17, 2014 chokehold death of New York resident Eric Garner, who was doing nothing more than selling cigarettes one-by-one on a sidewalk.

Cleveland Police officer Michael Brelo, who stood on the hood of the Chevrolet Malibu and shot down through the windshield, killing Timothy Russell and Malissa Williams, was charged with two counts of manslaughter. Prosecutors claimed his actions crossed the line to manslaughter when he stood on the hood of the Chevrolet Malibu and fired through the windshield.

The Brelo trial was held in front of a judge; it apparently was not a jury trial. Results were announced Saturday, May 23, because any protestors after the verdict would not impede weekday traffic. 137 shots were fired at Russell and Williams; in total, Brelo fired 49 times. He stood on the hood of the Chevy Malibu and fired 15 rounds through the windshield, killing both. **He was found not guilty of two counts of manslaughter.**

Cuyahoga County Common Pleas Judge John P. O'Donnell said he would not "sacrifice" Brelo if the evidence did not merit a conviction. Police subsequently arrested 71 protestors in the wake of the acquittal of Michael Brelo. The U.S, Department of Justice said it would continue to pursue the matter.

Note: On May 25, 2015, the City of Cleveland and the U.S. Department of Justice reached a settlement which would avoid a long and costly court fight. The settlement would call for independent monitors to oversee changes within the Police Department. The new agreement with the Department of Justice now holds the Cleveland Police Department to the most exacting standards in the nation.

The Department of Justice claimed that the Cleveland Police often used excess force; used excessive force against mentally ill people and inappropriately used stun guns, chemical sprays and punches. The report also said that supervisors endorsed questionable and sometimes unlawful conduct by officers. Cleveland police were not provided with adequate training, policy guidance or supervision, the Justice Department found. The agreement with the Department of Justice would also prohibit police chases, a policy which New York City adopted in 1972.

The City of Cleveland eventually paid out $3 million to the families of Russell and Williams to settle wrongful death lawsuits.

five

July 17, 2014, Staten Island, New York City:

The Death of Eric Garner

I CAN'T BREATHE ... is now as famous as *Hands Up, Don't Shoot* ...

Eric Garner was 43, a 350- pound black man, formerly employed as a horticulturalist at the New York City Department of Parks and Recreation, who subsequently resigned "for health reasons."

He was described by friends as a "neighborhood peacemaker," and as "a generous, congenial person." He was married, the father of six children and three grandchildren. As the time of his death, he had a three-month- old child. (www.Wikipedia.com, "Death of Eric Garner")

On July 17, 2014, Garner was approached by a plainclothes police officer Justin Damico, in front of 202 Bay Street in the Tompkinsville area of Staten Island.

Others at the scene, including Garner friend Ramsey Orta, who videotaped the incident, Garner had just broken up a fight ("a neighborhood peacemaker ...").

That earlier incident may have drawn Damico and his partner, officer Daniel Pantaleo, to Garner.

Garner has been selling cigarettes on the sidewalk one-by-one (called *loosies*), strictly speaking against the law, but surely the most harmless of illegal activities.

Previously—since 1980—Garner had been arrested by the NYPD *30 times* on charges such as assault, resisting arrest, and grand larceny. There were multiple counts of selling unlicensed cigarettes.

In 2007, Garner filed a handwritten complaint in federal court, accusing a police officer of conducting a cavity search on the street, "digging his fingers into my rectum in the middle of the street," while people passed by. Garner told lawyers at Legal Aid that he intended to take all the cases against him to trial.

At the time of the sidewalk confrontation with police officers Pantaleo and Damico, Garner was out on bail for selling untaxed cigarettes, driving without a license, marijuana possession and false impersonation.

(Wikipedia, Garner, pp. 3).

As Damico and Pantaleo approached Garner, Ramsey Orta began videotaping ...

Garner is heard on the videotape:

Get away (garbled) for what? Every time you see me, You want to mess with me. I'm tired of it. It stops today. Why would you ...? Everyone standing here will tell you I didn't do nothing. I did not sell nothing. Because every time you see me, you want to harass me. You want to stop me (garbled) selling cigarettes. I'm minding my business, officer. I'm minding my business. Please just leave me alone. I told you the last time, please just leave me alone.
(Wikipedia, Garner, pp. 3)

Pantaleo then approaches Garner from behind and attempts to handcuff him. Garner swats his arms away, and says "please don't touch me."

Pantaleo then puts Garner in a chokehold from behind and pulls backwards attempting to force Garner to the ground. They fall against a storefront window, but do not break it.

As Garner is falling, he is surrounded by other officers.

Garner falls to his knees and is momentarily silent, surrounded then by three uniformed officers and the two plainclothes officers, Pantelo and Damico.

Pantaleo then removes his arm from around Garner's neck, then uses his hands to push Garner's face into the sidewalk.

Garner is heard to say *I can't breathe* "multiple times," (Wikipedia entry, pp. 3) while lying face down on the sidewalk. Quite possibly 11 times ...

I can't breathe ...

I can't breathe ...

I can't breathe ...

I can't breathe ...

I can't breathe ...

I can't breathe ...

I can't breathe ...

I can't breathe ...

I can't breathe ...

I can't breathe ...

I can't breathe ...

(Wikipedia entry, pp. 1)

The arrest was supervised by a female NYPD African American Sergeant Kizzy Adoni, who did not intercede and who was quoted in the original police report as saying, "The perpetrator's condition did not seem serious and he did not appear to get worse."

Garner then apparently became unconscious and lay motionless, handcuffed, for several minutes.

No NYPD officer moved to help, except one, who told Garner to "breathe in, breathe out," (Wikipedia, pp. 4).

Ultimately the NYPD defended their decision not to aid Garner because they assumed he was still breathing and using CPR on someone who was breathing on their own was improper.

When an EMS unit arrived, two medics and two EMTs inside the ambulance did not administer any first aid, or even properly put him on a stretcher.

The NYPD later claimed he had a heart attack on the way to the Richmond University Medical Center.

He was pronounced dead on arrival at the hospital an hour later.

New York Police Department's Patrolmen's Benevolent Association (police union) leader Patrick Lynch vehemently—*vehemently*—denied that Garner died from a chokehold. Union officials and Pantaleo's lawyer argued that he did not use a chokehold, but a "takedown" maneuver because Garner was resisting arrest, but medical examiners concluded that Garner was killed by "compression of neck (choke hold), compression of chest and prone positioning during physical restraint by police," although no damage to his windpipe or neck was found.

We are shocked—Shocked!—that anyone would think the NYPD uses chokeholds—

In the article "Eric Garner and the NYPD's History of Deadly Chokeholds," in *The Atlantic Monthly* on their website, Dec. 4, 2014, Conor Friedersdorf wrote:

> The NYPD banned chokeholds outright in November, 1993. "The policy in New York grew from concern about the rising number of deaths in police custody over the last eight years, including that of Federico Pereira, a 21-year-old Queens man who in 1991 died of what the medical examiners called traumatic asphyxia," *The New York Times* reported. "Five officers were charged, but the charges against four were dropped and the fifth was acquitted." Same as it ever was.

*   *   *

... On December (1995) Anthony Ramon Baez was throwing a football with his brothers "when two throws within minutes of each other hit two separate parked police cars near the corner of Cameron Place and Jerome Avenue in the University Heights section of the Bronx. Neither the Police Department, nor the family has suggested that the ball was thrown at the cars intentionally." According to the man's family, "two officers grabbed Mr. Baez around the neck and handcuffed him for no good reason." Police said he died of an asthma attack. "His family accused the police of choking him to death and the Medical Examiners' office indicated that the cause of death was probably asphyxiation."

He was killed for the sake of playing street football.

Officer Francis Livoti was charged with criminally negligent homicide and acquitted. "Unbound by double jeopardy, Federal prosecutors stepped in... Livoti was eventually convicted by a Federal court in June 1998 for violating Baez's civil rights. He was a sentenced to seven years in a federal prison."

That same year, the NYPD settled a lawsuit over the case for $3 million.

Nine police brutality cases had been filed against Livoti before the death of Anthony Baez.

From 2006-2010, Friedersdorf writes, 200 chokehold cases per year were filed with the Civilian Complaint Review Board; between July 2013 and June 2014, 219 chokehold complaints were filed.

(Atlantic Monthly, pp. 1-2)

On August 1, 2015, the medical examiner ruled Garner's death a homicide, with qualifications: "a homicide is a death caused by the intentional actions of another person or persons, *which is not necessarily an intentional death or a criminal death."*

(Wikipedia, pp. 1-2) Italics added.

Asthma, heart disease and obesity were also listed as contributing factors.

(Wikipedia entry, pp. 4)

On August 19, Staten Island District Attorney Daniel Donovan announced the case against Daniel Pantaleo would be presented to a Grand Jury; the Grand Jury began hearing the case September 29. It heard the case for two months; on December 3, the Grand Jury **decided not to indict** Pantaleo.

The decision came barely a week after a similar Grand Jury found no criminality in the case against office Darren Wilson, who shot and killed Michael Brown, in Ferguson, Missouri.

And what of officer Pantaleo, who administered the chokehold? His father was a New York City firefighter;

his uncle, an NYPD officer. Pantaleo had a bachelor's degree from the University of Staten Island, but was the subject of two civil rights cases in 2013, when plaintiffs accused Pantaleo of falsely arresting them and abusing them. In one of the cases, Pantaleo and other officers allegedly ordered two black men to strip naked on the street for a search. The charges against the two men were dismissed.

(Wikipedia, pp. 3).

Pantaleo was eventually stripped of his badge and gun and placed on NYPD desk duty. Justin Damico was also placed on desk duty, but allowed to keep his badge and handgun.

Four of the EMTs and paramedics who took Garner to the hospital were suspended; two have returned to duty, two are doing non-medical work at the hospital pending the hospital's own investigation.

(Wikipedia, pp. 4)

To no one's surprise, protest and demonstrations began immediately after the Grand Jury decision: in New York City; San Francisco; on the Boston Common in Boston; in Chicago; Washington, D.C,; Baltimore; Minneapolis and Atlanta. 300 protestors were arrested in New York on December 4 and 5; 300 protestors marched in Berkeley, California the next day. Protestors were even arrested in west London, England.

Protestors often chanted _I can't breathe, I can't breathe, I can't breathe ..._ during demonstrations.

New York City Mayor Bill de Blasio called the death "a terrible tragedy"; President Barack Obama said it was "an American problem"; former president George W. Bush said he found the verdict "hard to understand."

Basketball superstars LeBron James, Kobe Bryant and members of the Los Angeles Lakers—and the Phoenix Suns—wore t-shirts during warm-ups before professional basket games—black with white lettering:

I CAN'T BREATHE

The Georgetown University's men's basketball team and the Notre Dame women's basketball team wore the same t-shirts.

They did, however, spark a backlash of sorts: others wore t-shirts that read:

BREATHE EASY, DON'T BREAK THE LAW

... and ...

I CAN BREATHE—THANKS TO THE NYPD

Ultimately, failure to indict officer Daniel Pantaleo in the Eric Garner death was yet another example of ...

No justice, No peace ...

(Note: Many of the citations in this chapter are from: www.Wikipedia.org: "Death of Eric Garner." Some critics have been skeptical of Wikipedia because entries can be changed. In this case, there are 133 major media sources, with original publication dates, which can be researched, as appendix material in the "Death of Eric Garner" Wikipedia entry.)

six

August 9, 2014, Ferguson, Missouri:

The Death of Michael Brown

FERGUSON.
MICHAEL BROWN.

Now just those names represent injustice today just as profoundly—or more so—than Rodney King did in 1991.

As in any sudden and violent encounter, some facts are still in dispute, but the core of the Michael Brown death is the timeline:

Saturday, August 9, 2014, just before noon.

Michael Brown 18, and a friend Dorian Johnson stop at the Ferguson Market and Liquor (store). Surveillance cameras capture a man pushing a clerk before walking out with a pack of cigarillos. Johnson's attorney later claimed Brown took the package—a case of simple shoplifting.

Subsequently, Brown and Johnson were walking down the middle of Canfield Drive, when they were confronted by officer Darren Wilson in a Chevy Tahoe police vehicle.

Some describe Wilson telling the two "get out of the street" or "get on the sidewalk"; others said that Wilson said "Get the f* * * on the sidewalk" or "get the f* * * out of the street."

Brown or Johnson or both said, "We're almost where we're going."

Whatever the language Wilson or the two used, that was the flashpoint.

Wilson drove away briefly, then backed up, at a slight angle, almost hitting Brown and Johnson.

Wilson tried to open the door, but was so close to the two, that the door bounced off both and closed on Wilson.

Wilson grabbed Brown by the neck—Brown attempted to pull away. Reports said Wilson pulled his weapon and said, "I'll shoot."

Brown was shot in the chest from inside the cruiser. Later blood was found on Wilson's uniform and inside the cruiser.

Johnson said they did not struggle over the weapon because Wilson already had it drawn.

Brown's friend Johnson then hid behind the first car he saw.

Brown began running from the scene away from the front of the cruiser.

Wilson fired a second shot.

Brown apparently got about 35 feet away then stopped and began to return.

Some said it wasn't clear whether Brown wanted to surrender or confront Wilson again.

Johnson's attorney later said Brown had his hands up, over his shoulders and was beginning to say that he was unarmed and to stop shooting.

Wilson fired several more shots. The last shot hit Brown in the forehead. He fell two or three feet in front of Wilson.

Brown was hit by six shots.

Michael Brown died there. He was 18. He was not armed.

At 12:10 a paramedic arrives and determines that Brown had jnjuries "incompatible with life."

At 12:15 St. Louis county officers arrive. A crowd begins to gather. A sheet is put over Brown's body.

At about 1:08 crews from television station KMOV arrive. Reporter Cory Stark reports a heavy police presence and a man lying dead in the street.

At 1:30 additional police and detectives arrive, from other police agencies.

By mid-afternoon officers on the scene broadcast a Code 1000, summoning help to control the crowd,

Brown's body was left on the street until 4 p.m.

By late afternoon, Brown's step-father Louis Head, posed for a photo with a sign that read "Ferguson police just executed my unarmed son" The photo goes viral on social media immediately.

About 7 pm Brown's mother, Lesley McSpadden and crowd members create a makeshift memorial on the spot where he was killed.

About 7:18 a crowd marches to the Police Department headquarters in protest.

The crowd did not disperse until almost 10 pm.

The second day—Sunday, August 10, 2014

Day Two was a day of increasing protests. Residents gathered holding their arms up, chanting "Hands Up, Don't Shoot. Hands Up, Don't Shoot. Hands Up, Don't Shoot." It became a sad and tragic mantra. Chanting also included "No Justice, No Peace" and "Black Lives Matter."

Protestors were met with—to the astonishment of many spectators and national television viewers—a massive police presence, including military-style weapons and equipment.

Watching the protests on television without a caption at the bottom of the screen, viewers would be forgiven if they assumed the protestors and the military-style police were in the middle of a revolution in some Third World country, instead of Middle America.

In the article "War Gear Flows to Police Departments," *in The New York Times* June 8, 2014, reporter Matt Apuzzo writes:

> During the Obama administration, according to Pentagon data, police departments have received tens of thousands of machine guns, nearly 200,000 ammunition magazines, thousands of pieces of camouflage and night-vision equipment and hundreds of silencers, armored cars and aircraft.
>
> The equipment has been added to the armories of police departments that already look and act like military units. Police SWAT teams are now deployed tens of thousands of times each year, increasingly for routine jobs. Masked, heavily armed police officers in Louisiana raided a nightclub in 2006 as part of a liquor inspection. In Florida in 2010, officers in SWAT gear and with guns drawn carried out raids on barbershops that led only to charges of "barbering without a license."

Reporter Apuzzo also writes:

> Congress created the military-transfer in the early 1900s, when violent crime plagued America's cities and the police felt outgunned by drug gangs. Today, crime has fallen to its lowest levels in a generation, wars have wound down and despite current fears, the number of domestic terrorist attacks has declined sharply from the 1960s and 1970s.
>
> Police departments, though, are adding more firepower and military gear than ever. Some,

especially in larger cities, have used federal grant money to buy armored cars and other tactical gear. And the free surplus program remains a favorite of many police chiefs who say they could not otherwise afford such equipment.

What exactly is this gear? Apuzzo's article included a chart:

- 432 MRAPS, Mine-Resistant, Ambush-Protected armored vehicles;
- 435 other armored vehicles;
- 44,900 night-vision pieces;
- 533 aircraft;
- 93,763 machine guns;
- 180,718 magazines, without ammunition.
- Not on the chart: 5,235 Humvees.

In the article "11 chilling facts about America's militarized police force," Alex Kane, writing for the website alternet, July 4, 2014 said:

The 'war on terror" has come home—and it's wreaking havoc on innocent American lives.

The culprit is the militarization of the police.

Among the 11 chilling facts are:

- It harms, and sometimes kills, innocent people;
- The use of SWAT teams is unnecessary;
- The "war on terror" is fueling militarization (of police departments);
- Asset forfeitures are funding police militarization;
- There's little debate and oversight;
- And, perhaps most importantly,
- Communities of color bear the brunt (of being targeted by police practices).

During the second day, police in body-armor and in military style vehicles were heard to refer to Ferguson protestors—perhaps not surprisingly—as "the enemy." Instead of calming the situation, military-looking police and excessive military vehicles, only inflame the situation.

Day Three—August 11, 2014

The F.B.I. opens a Civil Rights investigation. Hours after President Obama denounced both the police and protestors, and Missouri Governor Jay Nixon orders the Missouri State Highway Patrol to take over security plans. Captain Ronald S. Johnson, who is black and a officer of the Highway Patrol, appears in public to calm protestors and orders police to remove tear gas masks. Armored vehicles are taken away—the military-style approach is largely abandoned, but unrest continues and a curfew is established. Governor Nixon is booed during public appearances.

August 15, 2014
Officer Darren Wilson is identified as the policeman who shot Michael Brown.

August 17, 2014
The Brown family releases an autopsy report; Michael Brown was shot six times, including two shots to the head, all from the front.

August 18, 2014
The curfew fails to hold and Governor Nixon calls in the Missouri National Guard to maintain order.

August 20, 2014.
Protests continue. Attorney General Eric Holder arrived in Missouri and promises Ferguson residents that a Justice Department investigation will be opened.

August 24, 2014

Michael Brown's funeral, in the Friendly Temple Missionary Baptist Church in St. Louis. An article in *The Huffington Post* on the internet titled "Michael Brown Funeral Filled With Cries for Justice" said "a massive crowd" attended the service including "600 members of Brown's extended family."

The Rev, Al Sharpton attended, as did Rev. Jesse Jackson, filmmaker Spike Lee and others, including officials from The White House and a variety of politicians. *The Huffington Post* article included a key sentence:

> *The calls for justice for Brown have been folded into a broader movement in the greater St. Louis area—and around the country—for improved relationships between police and the communities they are supposed to protect.* (Italics added)

September 3, 2014

The U.S Department of Justice under Attorney General Eric Holder announced it will open a civil rights investigation to determine if the Ferguson police have a history of discrimination or abused of force beyond the Michael Brown case. The F.B.I. is also investigating the Michael Brown case.

September 8, 2014

The Ferguson City Council agrees to establish a Citizen Review Board and also agreed to revamp its court system, which unfairly targets minority and lower-income residents, often passing young black men from jail to jail when picked up for unpaid fines.

September 25, 2014

The Ferguson Police Chief, Thomas Jackson, apologizes, publically:

"I want to say this to the Brown family. None who has not experienced the loss of a child can understand what you're feeling" and "I am truly sorry for the loss of your son. I'm also sorry it took so long to remove Michael from the street. The time that it took involved very important work on the part of investigators who were trying to collect evidence and gain a true picture of what happened that day. But it was just too long, and I'm truly sorry for that."

October 9, 2014

Critics call for the demilitarization of local police around the county, but in a Senate Hearing, the Department of Homeland Security defended the practices claiming that such militarization was responsible for the capture of suspects in the Boston Marathon bombing.

October 17, 1014

Officer Darren Wilson explains his account of the events leading up to Michael Brown's death. Wilson said he was initially pinned in his vehicle and feared for his life. Witness statements have contradicted part of Wilson's account. Wilson's account does not explain—if he was so fearful for his own life—why he then got out of the police vehicle and then fired at Brown multiple times. If indeed, he feared for his life, he could have locked himself inside the Chevy Tahoe police vehicle.

November 17, 2014

Missouri Governor Jay Nixon activates the state National Guard ahead of the announcement by the Grand Jury regarding the possible indictment of Darren Wilson.

Many legal experts expect the Grand Jury will not indict a police officer for an on-duty shooting, especially since he was on duty in a confrontational situation and, as he had previously stated, he feared for his own life, while he was inside the police vehicle struggling with Michael Brown.

November 24, 2014

As many expected the Grand Jury **does not indict** Darren Wilson in the death of Michael Brown. Protests only intensify, as officials feared.

November 29, 2014

Officer Darren Wilson resigns from the Ferguson Police Department almost four months after the confrontation that lead to the death of Brown.

March 4, 2015

The U.S. Department of Justice, Civil Rights Division issues its report: "Investigation of the Ferguson Police Department."

To say it is a *scathing analysis* is a vast understatement.

Virtually every page is damning.

(The entire 102-page Department of Justice Report is reprinted in this book.)

The Investigation report is divided into four key sections:

- Ferguson's Police Practices;
- Fergusons' Municipal Court practices;
- Ferguson Law Enforcement Practices Disproportionally Harm Ferguson's African-American Residents and Are Driven in Part by Racial Bias;
- Ferguson Law enforcement Practices Erode Community Trust, especially Among Ferguson's African-American Residents, and Make Policing Less Effective, More Difficult and Less Safe.

There are graphic examples of misconduct in each section.

What did the Department of Justice discover about the Ferguson Police Department?

- Officers expect and demand compliance even when they lack legal authority. They are inclined to interpret the exercise of free-speech rights as unlawful disobedience, innocent movements as physical threats, indications of mental or physical illnesses as belligerence.
- Police supervisors and leadership do too little to ensure that officers act in accordance with law and policy, and rarely respond meaningfully to civilian complaints of officer misconduct. (pp. 2)
- Ferguson's approach to law enforcement both reflects and reinforces racial bias, including stereotyping. The harms of Ferguson's police and court practices are borne disproportionally by African Americans, and there is evidence that this is due in part to intentional discrimination on the basis of race. (pp. 4)
- Our investigation has shown that distrust of the Ferguson Police Department is long standing and largely attributable to Ferguson's approach to law enforcement. (pp. 5)
- Of the 54 sworn (police) officers, currently serving in the FPD, four are African American. (pp. 7)
- The Municipal Judge, Court Clerk, Prosecuting Attorney and all assistant court clerks are white. (pp. 8)
- A Municipal Judge presides over local court sessions.

... City officials informed us (the Department of Justice) that they are consider plans to bring the court under the supervision of the city Finance Director. (pp. 8– see section Ferguson; s Municipal Court practices, below.)

The second section, "Ferguson's Municipal Court Practices," includes the following: it has been a standard practice to encourage police to build revenue for the city by the use of court fees and fines, to be added to the city budget. A March 2011 message from Police Chief Thomas Jackson to the City Manager said

> ... court revenue in February was $179,862.50 and the total "beat our next biggest month in the last four years," to which the City manager responded; "wonderful." (pp. 13)

Substantial court fees and fines fall primarily on minority citizens who often could not obtain transportation to go to Ferguson's Municipal Court to pay a minor fine. When that was the case, the court added additional "failure to appear" fines and warrants issued for arrest for failure to pay fines.

The Department of Justice report cited one case in which a woman received two parking tickets for a single violation in 2007 that totaled $151 plus fees. Over seven years later, she still owed Ferguson $541, after already paying $550 in fines and fees, having multiple arrest warrants issued against her (a standard practice if a person missed paying a minor fine) and being arrested and jailed on several occasions. (pp. 42)

This perpetual financial slavery has not been seen since Charles Dickens' father was incarcerated in a debtors' prison in England circa 1820.

Similar practices have been SOP (Standard Operating Procedures) in other municipalities in the area. (pp. 49)

High fines which ultimately went into the City of Ferguson budget have been an exceptional burden on low-income residents: Typically fines were:

Peace Disturbance violation: $427;
High grass and Weeds $531;
Resisting Arrest $777;
Failure to Obey (a police officer) $792;
Failure to Comply (with a police officer) $527.
(pp. 52)

Additionally the Department of Justice Report showed extraordinary bias by the Ferguson Police department:

African Americans experience disparate impact in nearly every aspect of Ferguson's law enforcement system. Despite making up 67 % of the population, African Americans accounted for 85 % of FPD's (Ferguson Police Department's) traffic stops, 90 % of FPD's citations and 93 % of FPD's arrests from 2012 to 2014. (pp. 62)

The Department of Justice additionally found extensive examples of systemic racial prejudice in e-mails sent through the official City of Ferguson e-mail system, involving several police and court supervisors including FPD supervisors and commanders. (pp. 72)

Additionally:

FPD also has not significantly altered its use of-force tactics, even though FPD records make clear that current force decisions disparately impact black suspects, and that officers appear to assess threat differently depending on the race of the suspect. FPD, for example, has not reviewed or revised its canine program even though available records show that *canine officers have exclusively set their dogs against black individuals.* (pp. 78—italics added)

... and ...

... when police and courts treat people unfairly, unlawfully, or disrespectfully, law enforcement loses legitimacy in the eyes of those who have experienced or even observed, the unjust conduct. (pp. 80)

The Department of Justice Report on Ferguson concludes with:

- 13 major topic areas for improvement of Ferguson police practices;
- 13 major topic areas for improvement of the Ferguson courts system. (pp. 90-102)

The Department of Justice Report validated everything that minority and low-income Ferguson residents knew, or suspected, for years, about the Ferguson Police and Courts system.

Yet Ferguson wasn't alone. Under the headline, "This Tiny Town Near St. Louis Is Making Minor-Crime Arrests 100 Times The National Average " (*The Huffington Post*, May 4, 2015) stated that Beverly Hills, Missouri, has a population of 574. Police there, which also covered the nearly Velda Village area, actually made more arrests ... each year than the number of people that actually lived in the areas—100 times the national rate of arrests per population, to supplement the municipal budget, just as Ferguson had done.

Another article, with the headline "Fleece Force: How Police and Courts Around Ferguson Bully Residents and Collect Millions," in *The Huffington Post* March 26, 2015 tells the same story, of other municipalities near St. Louis and Ferguson.

Mid-March, 2015

The fall-out from the Michael Brown shooting and the Department of Justice resulted in:

- Municipal Court Judge Ronald Brockmeyer and City Manager John Shaw resigned;
- Embattled Police Chief Thomas Jackson resigned;
- Reportedly he will receive $100,000 and health insurance for one year;
- Municipal official vow to keep the Ferguson Police Department intact despite critics who claim it should be abolished in favor of some other form of law enforcement for Ferguson;
- When asked about the possibility of dismantling the Ferguson Police Department, Attorney General Eric Holder said "If that's what's necessary, then we are prepared to do that," in the article "2 Ferguson police officers quit, court clerk fired after Justice report", www.cnn.com, March 6, 2015;
- Because of the racial e-mails scandal Police Captain Rick Henke and Sgt. William Mudd resigned and the city's top court clerk, Mary Ann Twitty, was fired.

May 15, 2015

... was the last day of the current session of the Missouri State Legislature. Observers and activists **counted more than 100 proposed bills** relating to improvements for criminal justice and policing in Missouri and bills that would improve Ferguson and other towns and villages like Ferguson.

It was, as some said, a "menu of reforms," which would have: developed standards for eyewitness identification; required body cameras for police; restricted police from racial profiling; required diversity and sensitivity training and would have modified state rules governing the use of lethal force. Governor Jay Nixon supported that proposed law.

More than 100 proposed laws ...
How many do you think were passed?
Think hard.
Then think again.
One.

One law was passed—which did call for limiting municipal reliance on fines for revenue. The bill lowers the cap on how much revenue a municipality can generate from traffic tickets from 30 percent to 20 percent and to 12.5 percent in St. Louis County, which is home to Ferguson. The bill also bans courts from throwing individuals in jail over minor traffic offenses.

Activists might have seen this coming.

On January 7, 2015, Missouri House speaker John Diehl (R) said, "We're not going to have a Ferguson agenda here in the House. I think the Senate has indicated the same thing. I view the situation of Ferguson as really a reflection of decades of bad government policy," in "Dozens of Ferguson-related reforms proposed in Missouri. Just one passed," *The Washington Post*, May 16, 2015.

May 18, 2015

The Obama administration announced it will ban the provision of some types of military-style equipment to local police departments and sharply restrict the availability of others, top administration officials said.

President Obama is intensifying his push to ease tensions between citizens and police departments in reaction to deaths in Ferguson, Baltimore and other cities.

A task force he crested in January, 2014 urged that police departments should be barred from using federal funds to acquire armored vehicles, highest-caliber fire-arms and ammunition and camouflage uniforms.

The effort is being made to restore trust "between law enforcement agencies and the citizens they are charged with protecting."

The Obama administration will also try to retrieve military-style equipment already given to, or sold at a discount to, municipal law enforcement agencies.

Investigation of the Ferguson Police Department

United States Department of Justice
Civil Rights Division
March 4, 2015

TABLE OF CONTENTS

VI. CONCLUSION 102

I. REPORT SUMMARY

The Civil Rights Division of the United States Department of Justice opened its investigation of the Ferguson Police Department ("FPD") on September 4, 2014. This investigation was initiated under the pattern-or-practice provision of the Violent Crime Control and Law Enforcement Act of 1994, 42 U.S.C. § 14141, the Omnibus Crime Control and Safe Streets Act of 1968, 42 U.S.C. § 3789d ("Safe Streets Act"), and Title VI of the Civil Rights Act of 1964, 42 U.S.C. § 2000d ("Title VI"). This investigation has revealed a pattern or practice of unlawful conduct within the Ferguson Police Department that violates the First, Fourth, and Fourteenth Amendments to the United States Constitution, and federal statutory law.

Over the course of the investigation, we interviewed City officials, including City Manager John Shaw, Mayor James Knowles, Chief of Police Thomas Jackson, Municipal Judge Ronald Brockmeyer, the Municipal Court Clerk, Ferguson's Finance Director, half of FPD's sworn officers, and others. We spent, collectively, approximately 100 person-days onsite in Ferguson. We participated in ride-alongs with on-duty officers, reviewed over 35,000 pages of police records as well as thousands of emails and other electronic materials provided by the police department. Enlisting the assistance of statistical experts, we analyzed FPD's data on stops, searches, citations, and arrests, as well as data collected by the municipal court. We observed four separate sessions of Ferguson Municipal Court, interviewing dozens of people charged with local offenses, and we reviewed third-party studies regarding municipal court practices in Ferguson and St. Louis County more broadly. As in all of our investigations, we sought to engage the local

community, conducting hundreds of in-person and telephone interviews of individuals who reside in Ferguson
or who have had interactions with the police department. We contacted ten neighborhood associations and
met with each group that responded to us, as well as
several other community groups and advocacy organizations. Throughout the investigation, we relied on two
police chiefs who accompanied us to Ferguson and who
themselves interviewed City and police officials, spoke
with community members, and reviewed FPD policies
and incident reports.

We thank the City officials and the rank-and-file officers who have cooperated with this investigation
and provided us with insights into the operation of
the police department, including the municipal court.
Notwithstanding our findings about Ferguson's approach
to law enforcement and the policing culture it creates, we
found many Ferguson police officers and other City employees to be dedicated public servants striving each day
to perform their duties lawfully and with respect for all
members of the Ferguson community. The importance of
their often-selfless work cannot be overstated.

We are also grateful to the many members of the
Ferguson community who have met with us to share
their experiences. It became clear during our many conversations with Ferguson residents from throughout the
City that many residents, black and white, genuinely embrace Ferguson's diversity and want to reemerge from
the events of recent months a truly inclusive, united
community. This Report is intended to strengthen those
efforts by recognizing the harms caused by Ferguson's
law enforcement practices so that those harms can be
better understood and overcome.

Ferguson's law enforcement practices are shaped by
the City's focus on revenue rather than by public safety
needs. This emphasis on revenue has compromised the
institutional character of Ferguson's police department,
contributing to a pattern of unconstitutional policing,

and has also shaped its municipal court, leading to procedures that raise due process concerns and inflict unnecessary harm on members of the Ferguson community. Further, Ferguson's police and municipal court practices both reflect and exacerbate existing racial bias, including racial stereotypes. Ferguson's own data establish clear racial disparities that adversely impact African Americans. The evidence shows that discriminatory intent is part of the reason for these disparities. Over time, Ferguson's police and municipal court practices have sown deep mistrust between parts of the community and the police department, undermining law enforcement legitimacy among African Americans in particular.

Focus on Generating Revenue

The City budgets for sizeable increases in municipal fines and fees each year, exhorts police and court staff to deliver those revenue increases, and closely monitors whether those increases are achieved. City officials routinely urge Chief Jackson to generate more revenue through enforcement. In March 2010, for instance, the City Finance Director wrote to Chief Jackson that "unless ticket writing ramps up significantly before the end of the year, it will be hard to significantly raise collections next year.... Given that we are looking at a substantial sales tax shortfall, it's not an insignificant issue." Similarly, in March 2013, the Finance Director wrote to the City Manager: "Court fees are anticipated to rise about 7.5%. I did ask the Chief if he thought the PD could deliver 10% increase. He indicated they could try." The importance of focusing on revenue generation is communicated to FPD officers. Ferguson police officers from all ranks told us that revenue generation is stressed heavily within the police department, and that the message comes from City leadership. The evidence we reviewed supports this perception.

Police Practices

The City's emphasis on revenue generation has a profound effect on FPD's approach to law enforcement. Patrol assignments and schedules are geared toward aggressive enforcement of Ferguson's municipal code, with insufficient thought given to whether enforcement strategies promote public safety or unnecessarily undermine community trust and cooperation. Officer evaluations and promotions depend to an inordinate degree on "productivity," meaning the number of citations issued. Partly as a consequence of City and FPD priorities, many officers appear to see some residents, especially those who live in Ferguson's predominantly African-American neighborhoods, less as constituents to be protected than as potential offenders and sources of revenue.

This culture within FPD influences officer activities in all areas of policing, beyond just ticketing. Officers expect and demand compliance even when they lack legal authority. They are inclined to interpret the exercise of free-speech rights as unlawful disobedience, innocent movements as physical threats, indications of mental or physical illness as belligerence. Police supervisors and leadership do too little to ensure that officers act in accordance with law and policy, and rarely respond meaningfully to civilian complaints of officer misconduct. The result is a pattern of stops without reasonable suspicion and arrests without probable cause in violation of the Fourth Amendment; infringement on free expression, as well as retaliation for protected expression, in violation of the First Amendment; and excessive force in violation of the Fourth Amendment.

Even relatively routine misconduct by Ferguson police officers can have significant consequences for the people whose rights are violated. For example, in the summer of 2012, a 32-year-old African-American man sat in his car cooling off after playing basketball in a Ferguson public park. An officer pulled up behind the man's car, blocking him in, and demanded the man's Social Security number and identification. Without any cause, the officer accused the man of being a pedophile, referring to the presence of children in the park, and ordered the man out of his car for a pat-down, although the officer had no reason to believe the man was armed. The officer also asked to search the man's car. The man objected, citing his constitutional rights. In response, the officer arrested the man, reportedly at gunpoint, charging him with eight violations of Ferguson's municipal code. One charge, Making a False Declaration, was for initially providing the short form of his first name (e.g., "Mike" instead of "Michael"), and an address which, although legitimate, was different from the one on his driver's license. Another charge was for not wearing a seat belt, even though he was seated in a parked car. The officer also charged the man both with having an expired operator's license, and with having no operator's license in his possession. The man told us that, because of these charges, he lost his job as a contractor with the federal government that he had held for years.

Municipal Court Practices

Ferguson has allowed its focus on revenue generation to fundamentally compromise the role of Ferguson's municipal court. The municipal court does not act as a neutral arbiter of the law or a check on unlawful police conduct. Instead, the court primarily uses its judicial authority as the means to compel the payment of fines and fees that advance the City's financial interests. This has led to court practices that violate the Fourteenth Amendment's due process and equal protection requirements. The court's practices also impose unnecessary harm, overwhelmingly on African-American individuals, and run counter to public safety.

Most strikingly, the court issues municipal arrest warrants not on the basis of public safety needs, but rather as a routine response to missed court appearances and required fine payments. In 2013 alone, the court issued over 9,000 warrants on cases stemming in large part from minor violations such as parking infractions, traffic tickets, or housing code violations. Jail time would be considered far too harsh a penalty for the great majority of these code violations, yet Ferguson's municipal court routinely issues warrants for people to be arrested and incarcerated for failing to timely pay related fines and fees. Under state law, a failure to appear in municipal court on a traffic charge involving a moving violation also results in a license suspension. Ferguson has made this penalty even more onerous by only allowing the suspension to be lifted after payment of an owed fine is made in full. Further, until recently, Ferguson also added charges, fines, and fees for each missed appearance and payment. Many pending cases still include such charges that were imposed before the court recently eliminated them, making it as difficult as before for people to resolve these cases.

The court imposes these severe penalties for missed appearances and payments even as several of the court's practices create unnecessary barriers to resolving a municipal violation. The court often fails to provide clear and accurate information regarding a person's charges or court obligations. And the court's fine assessment procedures do not adequately provide for a defendant to seek a fine reduction on account of financial incapacity or to seek alternatives to payment such as community service. City and court officials have adhered to these court practices despite acknowledging their needlessly harmful consequences. In August 2013, for example, one City Councilmember wrote to the City Manager, the Mayor, and other City officials lamenting the lack of a community service option and noted the benefits of such a program, including that it would "keep those people that simply don't have the money to pay their fines from constantly being arrested and going to jail, only to be released and do it all over again."

Together, these court practices exacerbate the harm of Ferguson's unconstitutional police practices. They impose a particular hardship upon Ferguson's most vulnerable residents, especially upon those living in or near poverty. Minor offenses can generate crippling debts, result in jail time because of an inability to pay, and result in the loss of a driver's license, employment, or housing.

We spoke, for example, with an African-American woman who has a still-pending case stemming from 2007, when, on a single occasion, she parked her car illegally. She received two citations and a $151 fine, plus fees. The woman, who experienced financial difficulties and periods of homelessness over several years, was charged with seven Failure to Appear offenses for missing court dates or fine payments on her parking tickets between 2007 and 2010. For each Failure to Appear, the court issued an arrest warrant and imposed new fines and fees. From 2007 to 2014, the woman was arrested twice, spent six days in jail, and paid $550 to the court for the events stemming from this single instance of illegal parking. Court records show that she twice attempted to make partial payments of $25 and $50, but the court returned those payments, refusing to accept anything less than payment in full. One of those payments was later accepted, but only after the court's letter rejecting payment by money order was returned as undeliverable. This woman is now making regular payments on the fine. As of December 2014, over seven years later, despite initially owing a $151 fine and having already paid $550, she still owed $541.

Racial Bias

Ferguson's approach to law enforcement both reflects and reinforces racial bias, including stereotyping. The

153

harms of Ferguson's police and court practices are borne disproportionately by African Americans, and there is evidence that this is due in part to intentional discrimination on the basis of race.

Ferguson's law enforcement practices overwhelmingly impact African Americans. Data collected by the Ferguson Police Department from 2012 to 2014 shows that African Americans account for 85% of vehicle stops, 90% of citations, and 93% of arrests made by FPD officers, despite comprising only 67% of Ferguson's population. African Americans are more than twice as likely as white drivers to be searched during vehicle stops even after controlling for non-race based variables such as the reason the vehicle stop was initiated, but are found in possession of contraband 26% less often than white drivers, suggesting officers are impermissibly considering race as a factor when determining whether to search. African Americans are more likely to be cited and arrested following a stop regardless of why the stop was initiated and are more likely to receive multiple citations during a single incident. From 2012 to 2014, FPD issued four or more citations to African Americans on 73 occasions, but issued four or more citations to non-African Americans only twice. FPD appears to bring certain offenses almost exclusively against African Americans. For example, from 2011 to 2013, African Americans accounted for 95% of Manner of Walking in Roadway charges, and 94% of all Failure to Comply charges. Notably, with respect to speeding charges brought by FPD, the evidence shows not only that African Americans are represented at disproportionately high rates overall, but also that the disparate impact of FPD's enforcement practices on African Americans is 48% larger when citations are issued not on the basis of radar or laser, but by some other method, such as the officer's own visual assessment.

These disparities are also present in FPD's use of force. Nearly 90% of documented force used by FPD officers was used against African Americans. In every canine bite incident for which racial information is available, the person bitten was African American.

Municipal court practices likewise cause disproportionate harm to African Americans. African Americans are 68% less likely than others to have their cases dismissed by the court, and are more likely to have their cases last longer and result in more required court encounters. African Americans are at least 50% more likely to have their cases lead to an arrest warrant, and accounted for 92% of cases in which an arrest warrant was issued by the Ferguson Municipal Court in 2013. Available data show that, of those actually arrested by FPD only because of an outstanding municipal warrant, 96% are African American.

Our investigation indicates that this disproportionate burden on African Americans cannot be explained by any difference in the rate at which people of different races violate the law. Rather, our investigation has revealed that these disparities occur, at least in part, because of unlawful bias against and stereotypes about African Americans. We have found substantial evidence of racial bias among police and court staff in Ferguson. For example, we discovered emails circulated by police supervisors and court staff that stereotype racial minorities as criminals, including one email that joked about an abortion by an African-American woman being a means of crime control.

City officials have frequently asserted that the harsh and disparate results of Ferguson's law enforcement system do not indicate problems with police or court practices, but instead reflect a pervasive lack of "personal responsibility" among "certain segments" of the community. Our investigation has found that the practices about which area residents have complained are in fact unconstitutional and unduly harsh. But the City's personal-responsibility refrain is telling: it reflects many of the same racial stereotypes found in the emails between police and court supervisors. This evidence of bias and stereotyping, together with evidence that Ferguson has long recognized but failed to correct the consistent racial disparities caused by its police and court practices, demonstrates that the discriminatory effects of Ferguson's conduct are driven at least in part by discriminatory intent in violation of the Fourteenth Amendment.

Community Distrust

Since the August 2014 shooting death of Michael Brown, the lack of trust between the Ferguson Police Department and a significant portion of Ferguson's residents, especially African Americans, has become undeniable. The causes of this distrust and division, however, have been the subject of debate. Police and other City officials, as well as some Ferguson residents, have insisted to us that the public outcry is attributable to "outside agitators" who do not reflect the opinions of "real Ferguson residents." That view is at odds with the facts we have gathered during our investigation. Our investigation has shown that distrust of the Ferguson Police Department is longstanding and largely attributable to Ferguson's approach to law enforcement. This approach results in patterns of unnecessarily aggressive and at times unlawful policing; reinforces the harm of discriminatory stereotypes; discourages a culture of accountability; and neglects community engagement. In recent years, FPD has moved away from the modest community policing efforts it previously had implemented, reducing opportunities for positive police-community interactions, and losing the little familiarity it had with some African-American neighborhoods. The confluence of policing to raise revenue and racial bias thus has resulted in practices that not only violate the Constitution and cause direct harm to the individuals whose rights are violated, but also undermine community trust, especially among many African Americans. As a consequence of these practices, law enforcement is seen as illegitimate, and the partnerships necessary for public safety are, in some areas, entirely absent.

Restoring trust in law enforcement will require recognition of the harms caused by Ferguson's law enforcement practices, and diligent, committed collaboration with the entire Ferguson community. At the conclusion of this report, we have broadly identified the changes that are necessary for meaningful and sustainable reform. These measures build upon a number of other recommended changes we communicated verbally to the Mayor, Police Chief, and City Manager in September so that Ferguson could begin immediately to address problems as we identified them. As a result of those recommendations, the City and police department have already begun to make some changes to municipal court and police practices. We commend City officials for beginning to take steps to address some of the concerns we have already raised. Nonetheless, these changes are only a small part of the reform necessary. Addressing the deeply embedded constitutional deficiencies we found demands an entire reorientation of law enforcement in Ferguson. The City must replace revenue-driven policing with a system grounded in the principles of community policing and police legitimacy, in which people are equally protected and treated with compassion, regardless of race.

II. BACKGROUND

The City of Ferguson is one of 89 municipalities in St. Louis County, Missouri.[1] According to United States Census Data from 2010, Ferguson is home to roughly

---

1 *See 2012 Census of Governments,* U.S. Census Bureau (Sept. 2013), *available at* http://factfinder.census.gov/bkmk/table/1.0/en/COG/2012/ORG13.ST05P?slice=GEO~0400000US29 (last visited Feb. 26, 2015).

21,000 residents.[2] While Ferguson's total population has stayed relatively constant in recent decades, Ferguson's racial demographics have changed dramatically during that time. In 1990, 74% of Ferguson's population was white, while 25% was black.[3] By 2000, African Americans became the new majority, making up 52% of the City's population.[4] According to the 2010 Census, the black population in Ferguson has grown to 67%, whereas the white population has decreased to 29%.[5] According to the 2009-2013 American Community Survey, 25% of the City's population lives below the federal poverty level.[6]

Residents of Ferguson elect a Mayor and six individuals to serve on a City Council. The City Council appoints a City Manager to an indefinite term, subject to removal by a Council vote. *See* Ferguson City Charter § 4.1. The City Manager serves as chief executive and administrative officer of the City of Ferguson, and is responsible for all affairs of the City. The City Manager directs and supervises all City departments, including the Ferguson Police Department.

---

2 *See 2010 Census,* U.S. Census Bureau (2010), *available at* http://factfinder.census.gov/bkmk/table/1.0/en/DEC/10_SF1/ QTP3/1600000US2923986 (last visited Feb. 26, 2015).

3 *See 1990 Census of Population General Population Characteristics Missouri,* U.S. Census Bureau (Apr. 1992), *available at* ftp://ftp2.census.gov/library/publications/1992/dec/ cp-1-27.pdf (last visited Feb. 26, 2015).

4 *See Race Alone or in Combination: 2000,* U.S. Census Bureau (2000), *available at* http://factfinder.census.gov/ bkmk/table/1.0/en/DEC/00_SF1/QTP5/1600000US2923986 (last visited Feb. 26, 2015).

5 *2010 Census, supra* note 2.

6 *See Poverty Status in the Past 12 Months 2009-2013 American Community Survey 5-Year Estimates,* U.S. Census Bureau (2014), *available at* http://factfinder.census.gov/bkmk/table/1.0/en/ ACS/13_5YR/S1701/1600000US2923986 (last visited Feb. 26, 2015).

The current Chief of Police, Thomas Jackson, has commanded the police department since he was appointed by the City Manager in 2010. The department has a total of 54 sworn officers divided among several divisions. The patrol division is the largest division; 28 patrol officers are supervised by four sergeants, two lieutenants, and a captain. Each of the four patrol squads has a canine officer. While all patrol officers engage in traffic enforcement, FPD also has a dedicated traffic officer responsible for collecting traffic stop data required by the state of Missouri. FPD has two School Resource Officers ("SROs"), one who is assigned to the McCluer South-Berkeley High School and one who is assigned to the Ferguson Middle School. FPD has a single officer assigned to be the "Community Resource Officer," who attends community meetings, serves as FPD's public relations liaison, and is charged with collecting crime data.

FPD operates its own jail, which has ten individual cells and a large holding cell. The jail is staffed by three non-sworn correctional officers. Of the 54 sworn officers currently serving in FPD, four are African American.

FPD officers are authorized to initiate charges—by issuing citations or summonses, or by making arrests—under both the municipal code and state law. Ferguson's municipal code addresses nearly every aspect of civic life for those who live in Ferguson, and regulates the conduct of all who work, travel through, or otherwise visit the City. In addition to mirroring some non-felony state law violations, such as assault, stealing, and traffic violations, the code establishes housing violations, such as High Grass and Weeds; requirements for permits to rent an apartment or use the City's trash service; animal control ordinances, such as Barking Dog and Dog Running at Large; and a number of other violations, such as Manner of Walking in Roadway. *See, e.g.,* Ferguson Mun. Code §§ 29-16 *et seq.*; 37-1 *et seq.*; 46-27; 6-5, 6-11; 44-344.

FPD files most charges as municipal offenses, not state violations, even when an analogous state offense exists. Between July 1, 2010, and June 30, 2014, the City of Ferguson issued approximately 90,000 citations and summonses for municipal violations. Notably, the City issued nearly 50% more citations in the last year of that time period than it did in the first. This increase in enforcement has not been driven by a rise in serious crime. While the ticketing rate has increased dramatically, the number of charges for many of the most serious offenses covered by the municipal code—e.g., Assault, Driving While Intoxicated, and Stealing—has remained relatively constant.[7]

Because the overwhelming majority of FPD's enforcement actions are brought under the municipal code, most charges are processed and resolved by the Ferguson Municipal Court, which has primary jurisdiction over all code violations. Ferguson Mun. Code § 13-2. Ferguson's municipal court operates as part of the police department. The court is supervised by the Ferguson Chief of Police, is considered part of the police department for City organizational purposes, and is physically located within the police station. Court staff report directly to the Chief of Police. Thus, if the City Manager or other City officials issue a court-related directive, it is typically sent to the Police Chief's attention. In recent weeks, City officials informed us that they are considering plans to bring the court under the supervision of the City Finance Director.

A Municipal Judge presides over court sessions. The Municipal Judge is not hired or supervised by the Chief of Police, but is instead nominated by the City Manager and elected by the City Council. The Judge serves a two-year term, subject to reappointment. The current Municipal

---

7 This is evidenced not only by FPD's own records, but also by Uniform Crime Reports data for Ferguson, which show a downward trend in serious crime over the last ten years. *See Uniform Crime Reports*, Federal Bureau of Investigation, http://www.fbi. gov/about-us/cjis/ucr/crime-in-the-u.s (last visited Feb. 26, 2015).

Judge, Ronald Brockmeyer, has presided in Ferguson for approximately ten years. The City's Prosecuting Attorney and her assistants officially prosecute all actions before the court, although in practice most cases are resolved without trial or a prosecutor's involvement. The current Prosecuting Attorney was appointed in April 2011. At the time of her appointment, the Prosecuting Attorney was already serving as City Attorney, and she continues to serve in that separate capacity, which entails providing general counsel and representation to the City. The Municipal Judge, Court Clerk, Prosecuting Attorney, and all assistant court clerks are white.

While the Municipal Judge presides over court sessions, the Court Clerk, who is employed under the Police Chief's supervision, plays the most significant role in managing the court and exercises broad discretion in conducting the court's daily operations. Ferguson's municipal code confers broad authority on the Court Clerk, including the authority to collect all fines and fees, accept guilty pleas, sign and issue subpoenas, and approve bond determinations. Ferguson Mun. Code § 13-7. Indeed, the Court Clerk and assistant clerks routinely perform duties that are, for all practical purposes, judicial. For example, documents indicate that court clerks have disposed of charges without the Municipal Judge's involvement.

The court officially operates subject to the oversight of the presiding judge of the St. Louis County Circuit Court (21st Judicial Circuit) under the rules promulgated by that Circuit Court and the Missouri Supreme Court. Notwithstanding these rules, the City of Ferguson and the court itself retain considerable power to establish and amend court practices and procedures. The Ferguson municipal code sets forth a limited number of protocols that the court must follow, but the code leaves most aspects of court operations to the discretion of the court itself. *See* Ferguson Mun. Code Ch. 13, Art. III. The code also explicitly authorizes the Municipal Judge to "make and adopt such rules of practice and procedure as are necessary to hear and decide matters pending before the municipal court." Ferguson Mun. Code § 13-29.

The Ferguson Municipal Court has the authority to issue and enforce judgments, issue warrants for search and arrest, hold parties in contempt, and order imprisonment as a penalty for contempt. The court may conduct trials, although it does so rarely, and most charges are resolved without one. Upon resolution of a charge, the court has the authority to impose fines, fees, and imprisonment when violations are found. Specifically, the court can impose imprisonment in the Ferguson City Jail for up to three months, a fine of up to $1,000, or a combination thereof. It is rare for the court to sentence anyone to jail as a *penalty* for a violation of the municipal code; indeed, the Municipal Judge reports that he has done so only once. Rather, the court almost always imposes a monetary penalty payable to the City of Ferguson, plus court fees. Nonetheless, as discussed in detail below, the court issues arrest warrants when a person misses a court appearance or fails to timely pay a fine. As a result, violations that would normally not result in a penalty of imprisonment can, and frequently do, lead to municipal warrants, arrests, and jail time.

As the number of charges initiated by FPD has increased in recent years, the size of the court's docket has also increased. According to data the City reported to the Missouri State Courts Administrator, at the end of fiscal year 2009, the municipal court had roughly 24,000 traffic cases and 28,000 non-traffic cases pending. As of October 31, 2014, both of those figures had roughly doubled to 53,000 and 50,000 cases, respectively. In fiscal year 2009, 16,178 new cases were filed, and 8,727 were resolved. In 2014, by contrast, 24,256 new offenses were filed, and 10,975 offenses were resolved.

The court holds three or four sessions per month, and each session lasts no more than three hours. It is not uncommon for as many as 500 people to appear before the court in a single session, exceeding the court's physical capacity and leading individuals to line up outside of court waiting to be heard. Many people have multiple offenses pending; accordingly, the court typically considers 1,200-1,500 offenses in a single session, and has in the past considered over 2,000 offenses during one sitting. Previously there was a cap on the number of offenses that could be assigned to a particular docket date. Given that cap, and the significant increase in municipal citations in recent years, a problem developed in December 2011 in which more citations were issued than court sessions could timely accommodate. At one point court dates were initially scheduled as far as six months after the date of the citation. To address this problem, court staff first raised the cap to allow 1,000 offenses to be assigned to a single court date and later eliminated the cap altogether. To handle the increasing caseload, the City Manager also requested and secured City Council approval to fund additional court positions, noting in January 2013 that "each month we are setting new all-time records in fines and forfeitures," that this was overburdening court staff, and that the funding for the additional positions "will be more than covered by the increase in revenues."

III. FERGUSON LAW ENFORCEMENT EFFORTS ARE FOCUSED ON GENERATING REVENUE

City officials have consistently set maximizing revenue as the priority for Ferguson's law enforcement activity. Ferguson generates a significant and increasing amount of revenue from the enforcement of code provisions. The City has budgeted for, and achieved, significant increases in revenue from municipal code enforcement over the last several years, and these increases are projected to continue. Of the $11.07 million in general fund revenue the City collected in fiscal year 2010, $1.38 million came from fines and fees collected by the court;

similarly, in fiscal year 2011, the City's general fund revenue of $11.44 million included $1.41 million from fines and fees. In its budget for fiscal year 2012, however, the City predicted that revenue from municipal fines and fees would increase over 30% from the previous year's amount to $1.92 million; the court exceeded that target, collecting $2.11 million. In its budget for fiscal year 2013, the City budgeted for fines and fees to yield $2.11 million; the court exceeded that target as well, collecting $2.46 million. For 2014, the City budgeted for the municipal court to generate $2.63 million in revenue. The City has not yet made public the actual revenue collected that year, although budget documents forecasted lower revenue than was budgeted. Nonetheless, for fiscal year 2015, the City's budget anticipates fine and fee revenues to account for $3.09 million of a projected $13.26 million in general fund revenues.[8]

City, police, and court officials for years have worked in concert to maximize revenue at every stage of the enforcement process, beginning with how fines and fine enforcement processes are established. In a February 2011 report requested by the City Council at a Financial Planning Session and drafted by Ferguson's Finance Director with contributions from Chief Jackson, the Finance Director reported on "efforts to increase efficiencies and maximize collection" by the municipal court. The report included an extensive comparison of

---

8 Each of these yearly totals excludes certain court fees that are designated for particular purposes, but that nonetheless are paid directly to the City. For example, $2 of the court fee that accompanies every citation for a municipal code violation is set aside to be used for police training. That fee is used only by the City of Ferguson and is deposited in the City's general fund; nonetheless, the City's budget does not include that fee in its totals for "municipal court" revenue. In 2012 and 2013, the police training fee brought in, respectively, another $24,724 and $22,938 in revenue.

Ferguson's fines to those of surrounding municipalities and noted with approval that Ferguson's fines are "at or near the top of the list." The chart noted, for example, that while other municipalities' parking fines generally range from $5 to $100, Ferguson's is $102. The chart noted also that the charge for "Weeds/Tall Grass" was as little as $5 in one city but, in Ferguson, it ranged from $77 to $102. The report stated that the acting prosecutor had reviewed the City's "high volume offenses" and "started recommending higher fines on these cases, and recommending probation only infrequently." While the report stated that this recommendation was because of a "large volume of non-compliance," the recommendation was in fact emphasized as one of several ways that the code enforcement system had been honed to produce more revenue.

In combination with a high fine schedule, the City directs FPD to aggressively enforce the municipal code. City and police leadership pressure officers to write citations, independent of any public safety need, and rely on citation productivity to fund the City budget. In an email from March 2010, the Finance Director wrote to Chief Jackson that "unless ticket writing ramps up significantly before the end of the year, it will be hard to significantly raise collections next year. What are your thoughts? Given that we are looking at a substantial sales tax shortfall, it's not an insignificant issue." Chief Jackson responded that the City would see an increase in fines once more officers were hired and that he could target the $1.5 million forecast. Significantly, Chief Jackson stated that he was also "looking at different shift schedules which will place more officers on the street, which in turn will increase traffic enforcement per shift." Shortly thereafter, FPD switched to the 12-hour shift schedule for its patrol officers, which FPD continues to use. Law enforcement experience has shown that this schedule makes community policing more difficult—a concern that we have also heard directly from FPD officers.

Nonetheless, while FPD heavily considered the revenue implications of the 12-hour shift and certain other factors such as its impact on overtime and sick time usage, we have found no evidence that FPD considered the consequences for positive community engagement. The City's 2014 budget itself stated that since December 2010, "the percent of [FPD] resources allocated to traffic enforcement has increased," and "[a]s a result, traffic enforcement related collections increased" in the following two years. The 2015 budget added that even after those initial increases, in fiscal year 2012-2013, FPD was once again "successful in increasing their proportion of resources dedicated to traffic enforcement" and increasing collections.

As directed, FPD supervisors and line officers have undertaken the aggressive code enforcement required to meet the City's revenue generation expectations. As discussed below in Part III. A., FPD officers routinely conduct stops that have little relation to public safety and a questionable basis in law. FPD officers routinely issue multiple citations during a single stop, often for the same violation. Issuing three or four charges in one stop is not uncommon in Ferguson. Officers sometimes write six, eight, or, in at least one instance, fourteen citations for a single encounter. Indeed, officers told us that some compete to see who can issue the largest number of citations during a single stop.

The February 2011 report to the City Council notes that the acting prosecutor—with the apparent approval of the Police Chief—"talked with police officers about ensuring all necessary summonses are written for each incident, i.e. when DWI charges are issued, are the correct companion charges being issued, such as speeding, failure to maintain a single lane, no insurance, and no seat belt, etc." The prosecutor noted that "[t]his is done to ensure that a proper resolution to all cases is being achieved and that the court is maintaining the correct volume for offenses occurring within the city." Notably, the "correct volume" of law enforcement is uniformly presented in City documents as related to revenue generation, rather than in terms of what is necessary to promote public safety.[9] Each month, the municipal court provides FPD supervisors with a list of the number of tickets issued by each officer and each squad. Supervisors have posted the list inside the police station, a tactic officers say is meant to push them to write more citations.

The Captain of FPD's Patrol Division regularly communicates with his Division commanders regarding the need to increase traffic "productivity," and productivity is a common topic at squad meetings. Patrol Division supervisors monitor productivity through monthly "self-initiated activity reports" and instruct officers to increase production when those reports show they have not issued enough citations. In April 2010, for example, a patrol supervisor criticized a sergeant for his squad only issuing 25 tickets in a month, including one officer who issued "a grand total" of 11 tickets to six people on three days "devoted to traffic stops." In November 2011, the same patrol supervisor wrote to his patrol lieutenants and sergeants that "[t]he monthly self-initiated activity totals just came out," and they "may want to advise [their] officers who may be interested in the open detective position that one of the categories to be considered when deciding on the eligibility list will be self-initiated activity." The supervisor continued: "Have any of you

---

9 FPD's financial focus has also led FPD to elevate municipal enforcement over state-law enforcement. Even where individuals commit violations of state law, if there is an analogous municipal code provision, the police department will nearly always charge the offense under municipal law. A senior member of FPD's command told us that all Ferguson police officers understand that, when a fine is the likely punishment, municipal rather than state charges should be pursued so that Ferguson will reap the financial benefit.

heard comments such as, why should I produce when I know I'm not getting a raise? Well, some people are about to find out why." The email concludes with the instruction to "[k]eep in mind, productivity (self-initiated activity) cannot decline for next year."

FPD has communicated to officers not only that they must focus on bringing in revenue, but that the department has little concern with how officers do this. FPD's weak systems of supervision, review, and accountability, discussed below in Part III.A., have sent a potent message to officers that their violations of law and policy will be tolerated, provided that officers continue to be "productive" in making arrests and writing citations. Where officers fail to meet productivity goals, supervisors have been instructed to alter officer assignments or impose discipline. In August 2012, the Captain of the Patrol Division instructed other patrol supervisors that, "[f]or those officers who are not keeping up an acceptable level of productivity and they have already been addressed at least once if not multiple times, take it to the next level." He continued: "As we have discussed already, regardless of the seniority and experience take the officer out of the cover car position and assign them to prisoner pick up and bank runs.... Failure to perform *can* result in disciplinary action not just a bad evaluation." Performance evaluations also heavily emphasize productivity. A June 2013 evaluation indicates one of the "Performance-Related Areas of Improvements" as "Increase/consistent in productivity, the ability to maintain an average ticket [sic] of 28 per month."

Not all officers within FPD agree with this approach. Several officers commented on the futility of imposing mounting penalties on people who will never be able to afford them. One member of FPD's command staff quoted an old adage, asking: "How can you get blood from a turnip?" Another questioned why FPD did not allow residents to use their limited resources to fix equipment violations, such as broken headlights, rather than paying that money to the City, as fixing the equipment violation would more directly benefit public safety.[10]

However, enough officers—at all ranks—have internalized this message that a culture of reflexive enforcement action, unconcerned with whether the police action actually promotes public safety, and unconcerned with the impact the decision has on individual lives or community trust as a whole, has taken hold within FPD. One commander told us, for example, that when he admonished an officer for writing too many tickets, the officer challenged the commander, asking if the commander was telling him not to do his job. When another commander tried to discipline an officer for over-ticketing, he got the same response from the Chief of Police: "No discipline for doing your job."

The City closely monitors whether FPD's enforcement efforts are bringing in revenue at the desired rate. Consistently over the last several years, the Police Chief has directly reported to City officials FPD's successful efforts at raising revenue through policing, and City officials have continued to encourage those efforts and request regular updates. For example, in June 2010, at the request of the City, the Chief prepared a report comparing court revenues in Ferguson to court revenues for cities of similar sizes. The Chief's email sending the report to the City Manager notes that, "of the 80 St. Louis County Municipal Courts reporting revenue, only 8, including Ferguson, have collections greater than one million dollars." In the February 2011 report referenced above, Chief Jackson discussed various obstacles to officers writing tickets in previous months, such as training, injury leave, and officer deployment to Iraq, but noted

---

10 After a recommendation we made during this investigation, Ferguson has recently begun a very limited "correctable violation" or "fix-it" ticket program, under which charges for certain violations can be dismissed if corrected within a certain period of time.

that those factors had subsided and that, as a result, revenues were increasing. The acting prosecutor echoed these statements, stating "we now have several new officers writing tickets, and as a result our overall ticket volume is increasing by 400-700 tickets per month. This increased volume will lead to larger dockets this year and should have a direct effect in increasing overall revenue to the municipal court."

Similarly, in March 2011, the Chief reported to the City Manager that court revenue in February was $179,862.50, and that the total "beat our next biggest month in the last four years by over $17,000," to which the City Manager responded: "Wonderful!" In a June 2011 email from Chief Jackson to the Finance Director and City Manager, the Chief reported that "May is the 6th straight month in which court revenue (gross) has exceeded the previous year." The City Manager again applauded the Chief's efforts, and the Finance Director added praise, noting that the Chief is "substantially in control of the outcome." The Finance Director further recommended in this email greater police and judicial enforcement to "have a profound effect on collections." Similarly, in a January 2013 email from Chief Jackson to the City Manager, the Chief reported: "Municipal Court gross revenue for calendar year 2012 passed the $2,000,000 mark for the first time in history, reaching $2,066,050 (not including red light photo enforcement)." The City Manager responded: "Awesome! Thanks!" In one March 2012 email, the Captain of the Patrol Division reported directly to the City Manager that court collections in February 2012 reached $235,000, and that this was the first month collections ever exceeded $200,000. The Captain noted that "[t]he [court clerk] girls have been swamped all day with a line of people paying off fines today. Since 9:30 this morning there hasn't been less than 5 people waiting in line and for the last three hours 10 to 15 people at all times." The City Manager enthusiastically reported the Captain's email to the City

Council and congratulated both police department and court staff on their "great work."

Even as officers have answered the call for greater revenue through code enforcement, the City continues to urge the police department to bring in more money. In a March 2013 email, the Finance Director wrote: "Court fees are anticipated to rise about 7.5%. I did ask the Chief if he thought the PD could deliver 10% increase. He indicated they could try." Even more recently, the City's Finance Director stated publicly that Ferguson intends to make up a 2014 revenue shortfall in 2015 through municipal code enforcement, stating to Bloomberg News that "[t]here's about a million-dollar increase in public-safety fines to make up the difference."[11] The City issued a statement to "refute[]" the Bloomberg article in part because it "insinuates" an "over reliance on municipal court fines as a primary source of revenues when in fact they represented less than 12% of city revenues for the last fiscal year." But there is no dispute that the City budget does, in fact, forecast an increase of nearly a million dollars in municipal code enforcement fines and fees in 2015 as reported in the Bloomberg News report.

The City goes so far as to direct FPD to develop enforcement strategies and initiatives, not to better protect the public, but to raise more revenue. In an April 2014 communication from the Finance Director to Chief Jackson and the City Manager, the Finance Director recommended immediate implementation of an "1-270 traffic enforcement initiative" in order to "begin to fill the revenue pipeline." The Finance Director's email attached a computation of the net revenues that would be generated by the initiative, which required paying five officers overtime for highway traffic enforcement for a

---

11 Katherine Smith, *Ferguson to Increase Police Ticketing to Close City's Budget Gap*, Bloomberg News (Dec. 12, 2014), http://www.bloomberg.com/news/articles/2014-12-12/ ferguson-to-increase-police-ticketing-to-close-city-s-budget-gap.

four-hour shift. The Finance Director stated that "there is nothing to keep us from running this initiative 1, 2, 3, 4, 5, 6, or even 7 days a week. Admittedly at 7 days per week[] we would see diminishing returns." Indeed, in a separate email to FPD supervisors, the Patrol Captain explained that "[t]he plan behind this [initiative] is to PRODUCE traffic tickets, not provide easy OT." There is no indication that anyone considered whether community policing and public safety would be better served by devoting five overtime officers to neighborhood policing instead of a "revenue pipeline" of highway traffic enforcement. Rather, the only downsides to the program that City officials appear to have considered are that "this initiative requires 60 to 90 [days] of lead time to turn citations into cash," and that Missouri law caps the proportion of revenue that can come from municipal fines at 30%, which limits the extent to which the program can be used. *See* Mo. Rev. Stat. § 302.341.2. With regard to the statewide-cap issue, the Finance Director advised: "As the RLCs [Red Light Cameras] net revenues ramp up to whatever we believe its annualized rate will be, then we can figure out how to balance the two programs to get their total revenues as close as possible to the statutory limit of 30%."[12]

---

12 Ferguson officials have asserted that in the last fiscal year revenue from the municipal court comprised only 12% of City revenue, but they have not made clear how they calculated this figure. It appears that 12% is the proportion of Ferguson's *total* revenue (forecasted to amount to $18.62 million in 2014) derived from fines and fees (forecasted to be $2.09 million in 2014). Guidelines issued by the Missouri State Auditor in December 2014 provide, however, that the 30% cap outlined in Mo. Rev. Stat. § 302.341.2 imposes a limit on the makeup of fines and fees in *general* use revenue, excluding any revenue designated for a particular purpose. Notably, the current 30% state cap only applies to fines and fees derived from "traffic violations." It thus appears that, for purposes of the state cap, Ferguson must ensure that its

The City has made clear to the Police Chief and the Municipal Judge that revenue generation must also be a priority in court operations. The Finance Director's February 2011 report to the City Council notes that "Judge Brockmeyer was first appointed in 2003, and during this time has been successful in significantly increasing court collections over the years." The report includes a list of "what he has done to help in the areas of court efficiency and revenue." The list, drafted by Judge Brockmeyer, approvingly highlights the creation of additional fees, many of which are widely considered abusive and may be unlawful, including several that the City has repealed during the pendency of our investigation. These include a $50 fee charged each time a person has a pending municipal arrest warrant cleared, and a "failure to appear fine," which the Judge noted is "increased each time the Defendant fails to appear in court or pay a fine." The Judge also noted increasing fines for repeat offenders, "especially in regard to housing violations, [which] have increased substantially and will continue to be increased upon subsequent violations." The February 2011 report notes Judge Brockmeyer's statement that "none of these changes could have taken place without the cooperation of the Court Clerk, the Chief of Police, and the Prosecutor's Office." Indeed, the acting prosecutor noted in the report that "I have denied defendants' needless requests for continuance from the payment docket in an effort to aid in the court's efficient collection of its fines."

Court staff are keenly aware that the City considers revenue generation to be the municipal court's primary purpose. Revenue targets for court fines and fees are created in consultation not only with Chief Jackson, but also the Court Clerk. In one April 2010 exchange with Chief Jackson entitled "2011 Budget," for example, the

---

traffic-related fines and fees do not exceed 30% of its "General Fund" revenue. In 2014, Ferguson's General Fund revenue was forecasted to be $12.33 million.

Finance Director sought and received confirmation that the Police Chief and the Court Clerk would prepare targets for the court's fine and fee collections for subsequent years. Court staff take steps to ensure those targets are met in operating court. For example, in April 2011, the Court Clerk wrote to Judge Brockmeyer (copying Chief Jackson) that the fines the new Prosecuting Attorney was recommending were not high enough. The Clerk highlighted one case involving three Derelict Vehicle charges and a Failure to Comply charge that resulted in $76 in fines, and noted this "normally would have brought a fine of all three charges around $400." After describing another case that she believed warranted higher fines, the Clerk concluded: "We need to keep up our revenue." There is no indication that ability to pay or public safety goals were considered.

The City has been aware for years of concerns about the impact its focus on revenue has had on lawful police action and the fair administration of justice in Ferguson. It has disregarded those concerns—even concerns raised from within the City government—to avoid disturbing the court's ability to optimize revenue generation. In 2012, a Ferguson City Councilmember wrote to other City officials in opposition to Judge Brockmeyer's reappointment, stating that "[the Judge] does not listen to the testimony, does not review the reports or the criminal history of defendants, and doesn't let all the pertinent witnesses testify before rendering a verdict." The Councilmember then addressed the concern that "switching judges would/could lead to loss of revenue," arguing that even if such a switch did "lead to a slight loss, I think it's more important that cases are being handled properly and fairly." The City Manager acknowledged mixed reviews of the Judge's work but urged that the Judge be reappointed, noting that "[i]t goes without saying the City cannot afford to lose any efficiency in our Courts, nor experience any decrease in our Fines and Forfeitures."

IV. FERGUSON LAW ENFORCEMENT PRACTICES VIOLATE THE LAW AND UNDERMINE COMMUNITY TRUST, ESPECIALLY AMONG AFRICAN AMERICANS

Ferguson's strategy of revenue generation through policing has fostered practices in the two central parts of Ferguson's law enforcement system—policing and the courts—that are themselves unconstitutional or that contribute to constitutional violations. In both parts of the system, these practices disproportionately harm African Americans. Further, the evidence indicates that this harm to African Americans stems, at least in part, from racial bias, including racial stereotyping. Ultimately, unlawful and harmful practices in policing and in the municipal court system erode police legitimacy and community trust, making policing in Ferguson less fair, less effective at promoting public safety, and less safe.

A. Ferguson's Police Practices

FPD's approach to law enforcement, shaped by the City's pressure to raise revenue, has resulted in a pattern and practice of constitutional violations. Officers violate the Fourth Amendment in stopping people without reasonable suspicion, arresting them without probable cause, and using unreasonable force. Officers frequently infringe on residents' First Amendment rights, interfering with their right to record police activities and making enforcement decisions based on the content of individuals' expression.

FPD's lack of systems to detect and hold officers responsible for misconduct reflects the department's focus on revenue generation at the expense of lawful policing and helps perpetuate the patterns of unconstitutional conduct we found. FPD fails to adequately supervise officers or review their enforcement actions. While FPD collects vehicle-stop data because it is required to do so by state law, it collects no reliable or consistent data regarding pedestrian stops, even though it has the technology to do so.[13] In Ferguson, officers will sometimes make an arrest without writing a report or even obtaining an incident number, and hundreds of reports can pile up for months without supervisors reviewing them. Officers' uses of force frequently go unreported, and are reviewed only laxly when reviewed at all. As a result of these deficient practices, stops, arrests, and uses of force that violate the law or FPD policy are rarely detected and often ignored when they are discovered.

1. FPD Engages in a Pattern of Unconstitutional Stops and Arrests in Violation of the Fourth Amendment

FPD's approach to law enforcement has led officers to conduct stops and arrests that violate the Constitution. We identified several elements to this pattern of misconduct. Frequently, officers stop people without reasonable suspicion or arrest them without probable cause. Officers rely heavily on the municipal "Failure to Comply" charge, which appears to be facially unconstitutional in part, and is frequently abused in practice. FPD also relies on a system of officer-generated arrest orders called "wanteds"

---

13 FPD policy states that "[o]fficers should document" all field contacts and field interrogation "relevant to criminal activity and identification of criminal suspects on the appropriate Department approved computer entry forms." FPD General Order 407.00. Policy requires that a "Field Investigation Report" be completed for persons and vehicles "in all instances when an officer feels" that the subject "may be in the area for a questionable or suspicious purpose." FPD General Order 422.01. In practice, however, FPD officers do not reliably document field contacts, particularly of pedestrians, and the department does not evaluate such field contacts.

that circumvents the warrant system and poses a significant risk of abuse. The data show, moreover, that FPD misconduct in the area of stops and arrests disproportionately impacts African Americans.

a. FPD Officers Frequently Detain People Without Reasonable Suspicion and Arrest People Without Probable Cause

The Fourth Amendment protects individuals from unreasonable searches and seizures. Generally, a search or seizure is unreasonable "in the absence of individualized suspicion of wrongdoing." *City of Indianapolis v. Edmond,* 531 U.S. 32, 37 (2000). The Fourth Amendment permits law enforcement officers to briefly detain individuals for investigative purposes if the officers possess reasonable suspicion that criminal activity is afoot. *Terry v. Ohio,* 392 U.S. 1, 21 (1968). Reasonable suspicion exists when an "officer is aware of particularized, objective facts which, taken together with rational inferences from those facts, reasonably warrant suspicion that a crime is being committed." *United States v. Givens,* 763 F.3d 987, 989 (8th Cir. 2014) (internal quotation marks omitted). In addition, if the officer reasonably believes the person with whom he or she is dealing is armed and dangerous, the officer may conduct a protective search or frisk of the person's outer clothing. *United States v. Cotter,* 701 F.3d 544, 547 (8th Cir. 2012). Such a search is not justified on the basis of "inchoate and unparticularized suspicion;" rather, the "issue is whether a reasonably prudent man in the circumstances would be warranted in the belief that his safety or that of others was in danger." *Id.* (quoting *Terry,* 392 U.S. at 27). For an arrest to constitute a reasonable seizure under the Fourth Amendment, it must be supported by probable cause, which exists only if "the totality of facts based on reasonably trustworthy information would justify a prudent person in believing the individual arrested had committed an offense at the time of the arrest." *Stoner v. Watlingten,* 735 F.3d 799, 803 (8th Cir. 2013).

Under Missouri law, when making an arrest, "[t]he officer must inform the defendant by what authority he acts, and must also show the warrant if required." Mo. Rev. Stat. § 544.180. In reviewing FPD records, we found numerous incidents in which—based on the officer's own description of the detention—an officer detained an individual without articulable reasonable suspicion of criminal activity or arrested a person without probable cause. In none of these cases did the officer explain or justify his conduct.

For example, in July 2013 police encountered an African-American man in a parking lot while on their way to arrest someone else at an apartment building. Police knew that the encountered man was not the person they had come to arrest. Nonetheless, without even reasonable suspicion, they handcuffed the man, placed him in the back of a patrol car, and ran his record. It turned out he was the intended arrestee's landlord. The landlord went on to help the police enter the person's unit to effect the arrest, but he later filed a complaint alleging racial discrimination and unlawful detention. Ignoring the central fact that they had handcuffed a man and put him in a police car despite having no reason to believe he had done anything wrong, a sergeant vigorously defended FPD's actions, characterizing the detention as "minimal" and pointing out that the car was air conditioned. Even temporary detention, however, constitutes a deprivation of liberty and must be justified under the Fourth Amendment. *Whren v. United States,* 517 U.S. 806, 809-10 (1996).

Many of the unlawful stops we found appear to have been driven, in part, by an officer's desire to check whether the subject had a municipal arrest warrant pending. Several incidents suggest that officers are more concerned with issuing citations and generating charges than with addressing community needs. In October 2012, police officers pulled over an African-American man who had lived in Ferguson for 16 years, claiming that his passenger-side brake light was broken. The driver happened to have replaced the light recently and knew it to be functioning properly. Nonetheless, according to the man's written complaint, one officer stated, "let's see how many tickets you're going to get," while a second officer tapped his Electronic Control Weapon ("ECW") on the roof of the man's car. The officers wrote the man a citation for "tail light/reflector/license plate light out." They refused to let the man show them that his car's equipment was in order, warning him, "don't you get out of that car until you get to your house." The man, who believed he had been racially profiled, was so upset that he went to the police station that night to show a sergeant that his brakes and license plate light worked.

At times, the constitutional violations are even more blatant. An African-American man recounted to us an experience he had while sitting at a bus stop near Canfield Drive. According to the man, an FPD patrol car abruptly pulled up in front of him. The officer inside, a patrol lieutenant, rolled down his window and addressed the man:

> Lieutenant: Get over here.
> Bus Patron: Me?
> Lieutenant: Get the f* * * over here. Yeah, you.
> Bus Patron: Why? What did I do?
> Lieutenant: Give me your ID.
> Bus Patron: Why?
> Lieutenant: Stop being a smart ass and give me your ID.

The lieutenant ran the man's name for warrants. Finding none, he returned the ID and said, "get the hell out of my face." These allegations are consistent with other, independent allegations of misconduct that we heard about this particular lieutenant, and reflect the routinely disrespectful treatment many African

Americans say they have come to expect from Ferguson police. That a lieutenant with supervisory responsibilities allegedly engaged in this conduct is further cause for concern.

This incident is also consistent with a pattern of suspicionless, legally unsupportable stops we found documented in FPD's records, described by FPD as "ped checks" or "pedestrian checks." Though at times officers use the term to refer to reasonable-suspicion-based pedestrian stops, or "*Terry* stops," they often use it when stopping a person with no objective, articulable suspicion. For example, one night in December 2013, officers went out and "ped. checked those wandering around" in Ferguson's apartment complexes. In another case, officers responded to a call about a man selling drugs by stopping a group of six African-American youths who, due to their numbers, did not match the facts of the call. The youths were "detained and ped checked." Officers invoke the term "ped check" as though it has some unique constitutional legitimacy. It does not. Officers may not detain a person, even briefly, without articulable reasonable suspicion. *Terry*, 392 U.S. at 21. To the extent that the words "ped check" suggest otherwise, the terminology alone is dangerous because it threatens to confuse officers' understanding of the law. Moreover, because FPD does not track or analyze pedestrian *Terry* stops—whether termed "ped checks" or something else—in any reliable way, they are especially susceptible to discriminatory or otherwise unlawful use.

As with its pattern of unconstitutional stops, FPD routinely makes arrests without probable cause. Frequently, officers arrest people for conduct that plainly does not meet the elements of the cited offense. For example, in November 2013, an officer approached five African-American young people listening to music in a car. Claiming to have smelled marijuana, the officer placed them under arrest for disorderly conduct based on their "gathering in a group for the purposes of committing illegal activity." The young people were detained and charged—some taken to jail, others delivered to their parents—despite the officer finding no marijuana, even after conducting an inventory search of the car. Similarly, in February 2012, an officer wrote an arrest notification ticket for Peace Disturbance for "loud music" coming from a car. The arrest ticket appears unlawful as the officer did not assert, and there is no other indication, that a third party was disturbed by the music—an element of the offense. *See* Ferguson Mun. Code § 29-82 (prohibiting certain conduct that "unreasonably and knowingly disturbs or alarms another person or persons"). Nonetheless, a supervisor approved it. These warrantless arrests violated the Fourth Amendment because they were not based on probable cause. *See Virginia v. Moore*, 553 U.S. 164, 173 (2008).

While the record demonstrates a pattern of stops that are improper from the beginning, it also exposes encounters that start as constitutionally defensible but quickly cross the line. For example, in the summer of 2012, an officer detained a 32-year-old African-American man who was sitting in his car cooling off after playing basketball. The officer arguably had grounds to stop and question the man, since his windows appeared more deeply tinted than permitted under Ferguson's code. Without cause, the officer went on to accuse the man of being a pedophile, prohibit the man from using his cell phone, order the man out of his car for a pat-down despite having no reason to believe he was armed, and ask to search his car. When the man refused, citing his constitutional rights, the officer reportedly pointed a gun at his head, and arrested him. The officer charged the man with eight different counts, including making a false declaration for initially providing the short form of his first name (e.g., "Mike" instead of "Michael") and an address that, although legitimate, differed from the one on his license. The officer also charged the man both with having an expired operator's license, and with having no operator's license in possession. The man told us he lost his job as a contractor with the federal government as a result of the charges.

b. FPD Officers Routinely Abuse the "Failure to Comply" Charge

One area of FPD activity deserves special attention for its frequency of Fourth Amendment violations: enforcement of Ferguson's Failure to Comply municipal ordinance.[14] Ferguson Mun. Code § 29-16. Officers rely heavily on this charge to arrest individuals who do not do what they ask, even when refusal is not a crime. The offense is typically charged under one of two subsections. One subsection prohibits disobeying a lawful order in a way that hinders an officer's duties, § 29-16(1); the other requires individuals to identify themselves, § 29-16(2). FPD engages in a pattern of unconstitutional enforcement with respect to both, resulting in many unlawful arrests.

i. Improper Enforcement of Code Provision Prohibiting Disobeying a Lawful Order

Officers frequently arrest individuals under Section 29-16(1) on facts that do not meet the provision's elements. Section 29-16(1) makes it unlawful to "[f]ail to comply with the lawful order or request of a police officer in the discharge of the officer's official duties where such failure interfered with, obstructed or hindered the officer in the performance of such duties." Many cases initiated under this provision begin with an officer ordering an individual to stop despite lacking objective indicia

---

14 FPD officers are not consistent in how they label this charge in their reports. They refer to violations of Section 29-16 as both "Failure to Comply" and "Failure to Obey." This report refers to all violations of this code provision as "Failure to Comply."

that the individual is engaged in wrongdoing. The order to stop is not a "lawful order" under those circumstances because the officer lacks reasonable suspicion that criminal activity is afoot. *See United States v. Brignoni-Ponce*, 422 U.S. 873, 882-83 (1975); *United States v. Jones*, 606 F.3d 964, 967-68 (8th Cir. 2010). Nonetheless, when individuals do not stop in those situations, FPD officers treat that conduct as a failure to comply with a lawful order, and make arrests. Such arrests violate the Fourth Amendment because they are not based on probable cause that the crime of Failure to Comply has been committed. *Dunaway v. New York*, 442 U.S. 200, 208 (1979).

FPD officers apply Section 29-16(1) remarkably broadly. In an incident from August 2010, an officer broke up an altercation between two minors and sent them back to their homes. The officer ordered one to stay inside her residence and the other not to return to the first's residence. Later that day, the two minors again engaged in an altercation outside the first minor's residence. The officer arrested both for Failure to Comply with the earlier orders. But Section 29-16(1) does not confer on officers the power to confine people to their homes or keep them away from certain places based solely on their verbal orders. At any rate, the facts of this incident do not satisfy the statute for another reason: there was no evidence that the failure to comply "interfered with, obstructed or hindered the officer in the performance" of official duties. § 29-16(1). The officer's arrest of the two minors for Failure to Comply without probable cause of all elements of the offense violated the Fourth Amendment.

*ii. Improper Enforcement of Code Provision
Requiring Individuals to Identify Themselves to a
Police Officer*

FPD's charging under Section 29-16(2) also violates the Constitution. Section 29-16(2) makes it unlawful to "[f]ail to give information requested by a police officer in the discharge of his/her official duties relating to the identity of such person." This provision, a type of "stop-and-identify" law, is likely unconstitutional under the void-for-vagueness doctrine. It is also unconstitutional as typically applied by FPD.

As the Supreme Court has explained, the void-for-vagueness doctrine "requires that a penal statute define the criminal offense with sufficient definiteness that ordinary people can understand what conduct is prohibited and in a manner that does not encourage arbitrary and discriminatory enforcement." *Kolender v. Lawson*, 461 U.S. 352, 357 (1983). In *Kolender*, the Supreme Court invalidated a California stop-and-identify law as unconstitutionally vague because its requirement that detained persons give officers "credible and reliable" identification provided no standard for what a suspect must do to comply with it. Instead, the law "vest[ed] complete discretion in the hands of the police" to determine whether a person had provided sufficient identity information, which created a "potential for arbitrarily suppressing First Amendment liberties" and "the constitutional right to freedom of movement." *Id.* at 358. The Eighth Circuit has applied the doctrine numerous times. In *Fields v. City of Omaha*, 810 F.2d 830 (8th Cir. 1987), the court struck down a city ordinance that required a person to "identify himself" because it did not make definite what would suffice for identification and thereby provided no "standard to guide the police officer's discretionary assessment" or "prevent arbitrary and discriminatory law enforcement." *Id.* at 833-34; *see also Stahl v. City of St. Louis*, 687 F.3d 1038, 1040 (8th Cir. 2012) (holding that an ordinance prohibiting conduct that would impede traffic was unconstitutionally vague under the Due Process Clause because it "may fail to provide the kind of notice that will enable ordinary people to understand what conduct it prohibits") (internal quotation marks omitted).

Under these binding precedents, Ferguson's stop-and-identify law appears to be unconstitutionally vague because the term "information ... relating to the identity of such person" in Section 29-16(2) is not defined. Neither the ordinance nor any court has narrowed that language. *Cf. Hiibel v. Sixth Judicial Dist. Ct. of Nevada,* 542 U.S. 177, 188-89 (2004) (upholding stop-and-identify law that was construed by the state supreme court to require only that a suspect provide his name). As a consequence, the average person has no understanding of precisely how much identity information, and what kind, he or she must provide when an FPD officer demands it; nor do officers. Indeed, we are aware of several people who were asked to provide their Social Security numbers, including one man who was arrested after refusing to do so. Given that the ordinance appears to lend itself to such arbitrary enforcement, Section 2916(2) is likely unconstitutional on its face.[15]

Even apart from the facial unconstitutionality of the statute, the evidence is clear that FPD's enforcement of Section 29-16(2) is unconstitutional in its application. Stop-and-identify laws stand in tension with the Supreme Court's admonition that a person approached by a police officer "need not answer any question put to him; indeed, he may decline to listen to the questions at all and may go on his way." *Florida v. Royer,* 460 U.S. 491, 497-98 (1983). For this reason, the Court has held that an officer cannot require a person to identify herself unless the officer first has reasonable suspicion to initiate

---

15 Other broad quality-of-life ordinances in the Ferguson municipal code, such as the disorderly conduct provision, may also be vulnerable to attack as unconstitutionally vague or overbroad. *See* Ferguson Mun. Code § 29-94 (defining disorderly conduct to include the conduct of "[a]ny person, while in a public place, who utters in a loud, abusive or threatening manner, any obscene words, epithets *or similar abusive language*") (emphasis added).

the stop. *See Brown v. Texas,* 443 U.S. 47, 52-53 (1979) (holding that the application of a Texas statute that criminalized refusal to provide a name and address to a peace officer violated the Fourth Amendment where the officer lacked reasonable suspicion of criminal activity); *see also Hiibel,* 542 U.S. at 184 (deeming the reasonable suspicion requirement a "constitutional limitation[]" on stop-and-identify statutes). FPD officers, however, routinely arrest individuals under Section 29-16(2) for failure to identify themselves despite lacking reasonable suspicion to stop them in the first place.

For example, in an October 2011 incident, an officer arrested two sisters who were backing their car into their driveway. The officer claimed that the car had been idling in the middle of the street, warranting investigation, while the women claim they had pulled up outside their home to drop someone off when the officer arrived. In any case, the officer arrested one sister for failing to provide her identification when requested. He arrested the other sister for getting out of the car after being ordered to stay inside. The two sisters spent the next three hours in jail. In a similar incident from December 2011, police officers approached two people sitting in a car on a public street and asked the driver for identification. When the driver balked, insisting that he was on a public street and should not have to answer questions, the officers ordered him out of the car and ultimately charged him with Failure to Comply.

In another case, from March 2013, officers responded to the police station to take custody of a person wanted on a state warrant. When they arrived, they encountered a different man—not the subject of the warrant—who happened to be leaving the station. Having nothing to connect the man to the warrant subject, other than his presence at the station, the officers nonetheless stopped him and asked that he identify himself. The man asserted his rights, asking the officers "Why do you need to know?" and declining to be frisked. When the man then extended his identification toward the officers, at their request, the officers interpreted his hand motion as an attempted assault and took him to the ground. Without articulating reasonable suspicion or any other justification for the initial detention, the officers arrested the man on two counts of Failure to Comply and two counts of Resisting Arrest.

In our conversations with FPD officers, one officer admitted that when he conducts a traffic stop, he asks for identification from all passengers as a matter of course. If any refuses, he considers that to be "furtive and aggressive" conduct and cites—and typically arrests—the person for Failure to Comply. The officer thus acknowledged that he regularly exceeds his authority under the Fourth Amendment by arresting passengers who refuse, as is their right, to provide identification. *See Hiibel*, 542 U.S. at 188 ("[A]n officer may not arrest a suspect for failure to identify himself if the request for identification is not reasonably related to the circumstances justifying the stop."); *Stufflebeam v. Harris*, 521 F.3d 884, 887-88 (8th Cir. 2008) (holding that the arrest of a passenger for failure to identify himself during a traffic stop violated the Fourth Amendment where the passenger was not suspected of other criminal activity and his identification was not needed for officer safety). Further, the officer told us that he was trained to arrest for this violation.

Good supervision would correct improper arrests by an officer before they became routine. But in Ferguson, the same dynamics that lead officers to make unlawful stops and arrests cause supervisors to conduct only perfunctory review of officers' actions—when they conduct any review at all. FPD supervisors are more concerned with the number of citations and arrests officers produce than whether those citations and arrests are lawful or promote public safety. Internal communications among command staff reveal that FPD for years has failed to ensure even that officers write their reports and first-line supervisors approve them. In 2010, a senior police official complained to supervisors that every week reports go unwritten, and hundreds of reports remain unapproved. "It is time for you to hold your officers accountable," he urged them. In 2014, the official had the same complaint, remarking on 600 reports that had not been approved over a six-month period. Another supervisor remarked that coding errors in the new records management system is set up "to hide, do away with, or just forget reports," creating a heavy administrative burden for supervisors who discover incomplete reports months after they are created. In practice, not all arrests are given incident numbers, meaning supervisors may never know to review them. These systemic deficiencies in oversight are consistent with an approach to law enforcement in which productivity and revenue generation, rather than lawful policing, are the priority. Thus, even as commanders exhort line supervisors to more closely supervise officer activity, they perpetuate the dynamics that discourage meaningful supervision.

c. FPD's Use of a Police-run "Wanted" System Circumvents Judicial Review and Poses the Risk of Abuse

FPD and other law enforcement agencies in St. Louis County use a system of "wanteds" or "stop orders" as a substitute for seeking judicial approval for an arrest warrant. When officers believe a person has committed a crime but are not able to immediately locate that person, they can enter a "wanted" into the statewide law enforcement database, indicating to all other law enforcement agencies that the person should be arrested if located. While wanteds are supposed to be based on probable cause, *see* FPD General Order 424.01, they operate as an end-run around the judicial system. Instead of swearing out a warrant and seeking judicial authorization from a neutral and detached magistrate, officers make the probable cause determination themselves and circumvent the courts. Officers use wanteds for serious state-level crimes and minor code violations alike, including traffic offenses.

FPD command staff express support for the wanted system, extolling the benefits of being able to immediately designate a person for detention. But this expedience carries constitutional risks. If officers enter wanteds into the system on less than probable cause, then the subsequent arrest would violate the Fourth Amendment. Our interviews with command staff and officers indicate that officers do not clearly understand the legal authority necessary to issue a wanted. For example, one veteran officer told us he will put out a wanted "if I do not have enough probable cause to arrest you." He gave the example of investigating a car theft. Upon identifying a suspect, he would put that suspect into the system as wanted "because we do not have probable cause that he stole the vehicle." Reflecting the muddled analysis officers may employ when deciding whether to issue a wanted, this officer concluded, "you have to have reasonable suspicion and some probable cause to put out a wanted."

At times, FPD officers use wanteds not merely in spite of a lack of probable cause, but *because* they lack probable cause. In December 2014, a Ferguson detective investigating a shooting emailed a county prosecutor to see if a warrant for a suspect could be obtained, since "a lot of state agencies won't act on a wanted." The prosecutor responded stating that although "[c]hances are" the crime was committed by the suspect, "we just don't have enough for a warrant right now." The detective responded that he would enter a wanted.

There is evidence that the use of wanteds has resulted in numerous unconstitutional arrests in Ferguson. Internal communications reveal problems with FPD officers arresting individuals on wanteds without first confirming that the wanteds are still valid. In 2010, for instance, an FPD supervisor wrote that "[a]s of late we have had subjects arrested that were wanted for other agencies brought in without being verified first. You guessed it, come to find out they were no longer wanted by the agencies and had to be released." The same supervisor told us that in 2014 he cleared hundreds of invalid wanteds from the system, some of them over ten years old, suggesting that invalid wanteds have been an ongoing problem.

Wanteds can also be imprecise, leading officers to arrest in violation of the Fourth Amendment. For example, in June 2011, officers arrested a man at gunpoint because the car he was driving had an active wanted "on the vehicle and its occupants" in connection with an alleged theft. In fact, the theft was alleged to have been committed by the man's brother. Nonetheless, according to FPD's files, the man was arrested solely on the basis of the wanted.

This system creates the risk that wanteds could be used improperly to develop evidence necessary for arrest rather than to secure a person against whom probable cause already exists. Several officers described wanteds as an investigatory tool. According to Chief Jackson, "a wanted allows us to get a suspect in for booking and potential interrogation." One purpose, he said, is "to conduct an interview of that person." While it is perfectly legitimate for officers to try to obtain statements from persons lawfully detained, it is unconstitutional for them to jail individuals on less than probable cause for that purpose. *Dunaway*, 442 U.S. at 216. One senior supervisor acknowledged that wanteds could be abused. He agreed that the potential exists, for example, for an officer to pressure a subject into speaking voluntarily to avoid being arrested. These are risks that the judicially-reviewed warrant process is meant to avoid.

Compounding our concern is the minimal training and supervision provided on when to issue a wanted, and the lack of any meaningful oversight to detect and respond to improperly issued wanteds. Some officers told us that they may have heard about wanteds in the training academy. Others said that they received no formal training on wanteds and learned about them from their field training officers. As for supervision, officers are supposed to get authorization from their supervisors before entering a wanted into a law enforcement database. They purportedly do this by providing the factual basis for probable cause to their supervisors, orally or in their written reports. However, several supervisors and officers we spoke with acknowledged that this supervisory review routinely does not happen. Further, the supervisors we interviewed told us that they had never declined to authorize a wanted.

Finally, a Missouri appellate court has highlighted the constitutional risks of relying on a wanted as the basis for an arrest. In *State v. Carroll*, 745 S.W.2d 156 (Mo. Ct. App. 1987), the court held that a robbery suspect was arrested without probable cause when Ferguson and St. Louis police officers picked him up on a wanted for leaving the scene of an accident. *Id.* at 158. The officers then interrogated him three times at two different police stations, and he eventually made incriminating statements. Despite the existence of a wanted, the court deemed the initial arrest unconstitutional because "[t]he record ... fail[ed] to show any *facts* known to the police at the time of the arrest to support a reasonable belief that defendant had committed a crime." *Id. Carroll* highlights the fact that wanteds do not confer an authority equal to a judicial arrest warrant. Rather, the *Carroll* court's holding suggests that wanteds may be of unknown reliability and thus insufficient to permit custodial detention under the Fourth Amendment. *See also* Steven J. Mulroy, *"Hold" On: The Remarkably Resilient, Constitutionally Dubious 48-Hour Hold,* 63 Case W. Res. L. Rev. 815, 823, 842-45 (2013) (observing that one problem with police "holds" is that, although they require probable cause, "in practice they often lack it").

We received complaints from FPD officers that the County prosecutor's office is too restrictive in granting warrant requests, and that this has necessitated the wanted practice. This investigation did not determine whether the St. Louis County prosecutor is overly restrictive or appropriately cautious in granting warrant requests. What is clear, however, is that current FPD practices have resulted in wanteds being issued and executed without legal basis.

2. FPD Engages in a Pattern of First Amendment Violations

FPD's approach to enforcement results in violations of individuals' First Amendment rights. FPD arrests people for a variety of protected conduct: people are punished for talking back to officers, recording public police activities, and lawfully protesting perceived injustices.

Under the Constitution, what a person says generally should not determine whether he or she is jailed. Police officers cannot constitutionally make arrest decisions based on individuals' verbal expressions of disrespect for law enforcement, including use of foul language. *Buffkins v. City of Omaha*, 922 F.2d 465, 472 (8th Cir. 1990) (holding that officers violated the Constitution when they arrested a woman for disorderly conduct after she called one an "asshole," especially since "police officers are expected to exercise greater restraint in their response than the average citizen"); *Copeland v. Locke*, 613 F.3d 875, 880 (8th Cir. 2010) (holding that the First Amendment prohibited a police chief from arresting an individual who pointed at him and told him "move the f*****g car," even if the comment momentarily distracted the chief from a routine traffic stop); *Gorra v. Hanson*, 880 F.2d 95, 100 (8th Cir. 1989) (holding that arresting a person in retaliation for making a statement "constitutes obvious infringement" of the First Amendment). As the Supreme Court has held, "the First Amendment protects a significant amount of verbal criticism and challenge directed at police officers."

City of Houston, Tex. v. Hill, 482 U.S. 451, 461 (1987) (striking down as unconstitutionally overbroad a local ordinance that criminalized interference with police by speech).

In Ferguson, however, officers frequently make enforcement decisions based on what subjects say, or how they say it. Just as officers reflexively resort to arrest immediately upon noncompliance with their orders, whether lawful or not, they are quick to overreact to challenges and verbal slights. These incidents—sometimes called "contempt of cop" cases—are propelled by officers' belief that arrest is an appropriate response to disrespect. These arrests are typically charged as a Failure to Comply, Disorderly Conduct, Interference with Officer, or Resisting Arrest.

For example, in July 2012, a police officer arrested a business owner on charges of Interfering in Police Business and Misuse of 911 because she objected to the officer's detention of her employee. The officer had stopped the employee for "walking unsafely in the street" as he returned to work from the bank. According to FPD records, the owner "became verbally involved," came out of her shop three times after being asked to stay inside, and called 911 to complain to the Police Chief. The officer characterized her protestations as interference and arrested her inside her shop.[16] The arrest violated the First Amendment, which "does not allow such speech to be made a crime." *Hill,* 482 U.S. at 462. Indeed, the officer's

---

16 The ordinance on interfering with arrest, detention, or stop, Ferguson Mun. Code § 29-17, does not actually permit arrest unless the subject uses or threatens violence, which did not occur here. Another code provision the officer may have relied on, § 29-19, is likely unconstitutionally overbroad because it prohibits obstruction of government operations "in any manner whatsoever." *See Hill,* 482 U.S. at 455, 462, 466 (invalidating ordinance that made it unlawful to "in any manner oppose, molest, abuse, or interrupt any policeman in the execution of his duty").

decision to arrest the woman after she tried to contact the Police Chief suggests that he may have been retaliating against her for reporting his conduct.

Officers in Ferguson also use their arrest power to retaliate against individuals for using language that, while disrespectful, is protected by the Constitution. For example, one afternoon in September 2012, an officer stopped a 20-year-old African-American man for dancing in the middle of a residential street. The officer obtained the man's identification and ran his name for warrants. Finding none, he told the man he was free to go. The man responded with profanities. When the officer told him to watch his language and reminded him that he was not being arrested, the man continued using profanity and was arrested for Manner of Walking in Roadway.

In February 2014, officers responded to a group of African-American teenage girls "play fighting" (in the words of the officer) in an intersection after school. When one of the schoolgirls gave the middle finger to a white witness who had called the police, an officer ordered her over to him. One of the girl's friends accompanied her. Though the friend had the right to be present and observe the situation—indeed, the offense reports include no facts suggesting a safety concern posed by her presence—the officers ordered her to leave and then attempted to arrest her when she refused. Officers used force to arrest the friend as she pulled away. When the first girl grabbed an officer's shoulder, they used force to arrest her, as well. Officers charged the two teenagers with a variety of offenses, including: Disorderly Conduct for giving the middle finger and using obscenities; Manner of Walking for being in the street; Failure to Comply for staying to observe; Interference with Officer; Assault on a Law Enforcement Officer; and Endangering the Welfare of a Child (themselves and their schoolmates) by resisting arrest and being involved in disorderly conduct. This incident underscores how officers' unlawful response to activity protected by the First Amendment can quickly escalate to physical resistance, resulting in additional force, additional charges, and increasing the risk of injury to officers and members of the public alike.

These accounts are drawn entirely from officers' own descriptions, recorded in offense reports. That FPD officers believe criticism and insolence are grounds for arrest, and that supervisors have condoned such unconstitutional policing, reflects intolerance for even lawful opposition to the exercise of police authority. These arrests also reflect that, in FPD, many officers have no tools for de-escalating emotionally charged scenes, even though the ability of a police officer to bring calm to a situation is a core policing skill.

FPD officers also routinely infringe on the public's First Amendment rights by preventing people from recording their activities. The First Amendment "prohibit[s] the government from limiting the stock of information from which members of the public may draw." *First Nat'l Bank v. Belloti,* 435 U.S. 765, 783 (1978). Applying this principle, the federal courts of appeal have held that the First Amendment "unambiguously" establishes a constitutional right to videotape police activities. *Glik v. Cunniffe,* 655 F.3d 78, 82 (1st Cir. 2011); *see also ACLU v. Alvarez,* 679 F.3d 583, 600 (7th Cir. 2012) (issuing a preliminary injunction against the use of a state eavesdropping statute to prevent the recording of public police activities); *Fordyce v. City of Seattle,* 55 F.3d 436, 439 (9th Cir. 1995) (recognizing a First Amendment right to film police carrying out their public duties); *Smith v. City of Cumming,* 212 F.3d 1332, 1333 (11th Cir. 2000) (recognizing a First Amendment right "to photograph or videotape police conduct"). Indeed, as the ability to record police activity has become more widespread, the role it can play in capturing questionable police activity, and ensuring that the activity is investigated and subject to broad public debate, has become clear. Protecting civilian recording of police activity is thus at the core of speech the First Amendment is intended to protect. *Cf. Branzburg v. Hayes*, 408 U.S. 665, 681 (1972) (First Amendment protects "news gathering"); *Mills v. Alabama*, 384 U.S. 214, 218 (1966) (news gathering enhances "free discussion of governmental affairs"). "In a democracy, public officials have no general privilege to avoid publicity and embarrassment by preventing public scrutiny of their actions." *Walker v. City of Pine Bluff*, 414 F.3d 989, 992 (8th Cir. 2005).

In Ferguson, however, officers claim without any factual support that the use of camera phones endangers officer safety. Sometimes, officers offer no rationale at all. Our conversations with community members and review of FPD records found numerous violations of the right to record police activity. In May 2014, an officer pulled over an African-American woman who was driving with her two sons. During the traffic stop, the woman's 16-year-old son began recording with his cell phone. The officer ordered him to put down the phone and refrain from using it for the remainder of the stop. The officer claimed this was "for safety reasons." The situation escalated, apparently due to the officer's rudeness and the woman's response. According to the 16 year old, he began recording again, leading the officer to wrestle the phone from him. Additional officers arrived and used force to arrest all three civilians under disputed circumstances that could have been clarified by a video recording.

In June 2014, an African-American couple who had taken their children to play at the park allowed their small children to urinate in the bushes next to their parked car. An officer stopped them, threatened to cite them for allowing the children to "expose themselves," and checked the father for warrants. When the mother asked if the officer had to detain the father in front of the children, the officer turned to the father and said, "you're going to jail because your wife keeps running her mouth." The mother then began recording the officer on her cell phone. The officer became irate, declaring, "you don't videotape me!" As the officer drove away with the father in custody for "parental neglect," the mother drove after them, continuing to record. The officer then pulled over and arrested her for traffic violations. When the father asked the officer to show mercy, he responded, "no more mercy, since she wanted to videotape," and declared "nobody videotapes me." The officer then took the phone, which the couple's daughter was holding. After posting bond, the couple found that the video had been deleted.

A month later, the same officer pulled over a truck hauling a trailer that did not have operating tail lights. The officer asked for identification from all three people inside, including a 54-year-old white man in the passenger seat who asked why. "You have to have a reason. This is a violation of my Fourth Amendment rights," he asserted. The officer, who characterized the man's reaction as "suspicious," responded, "the reason is, if you don't hand it to me, I'll arrest you." The man provided his identification. The officer then asked the man to move his cell phone from his lap to the dashboard, "for my safety." The man said, "okay, but I'm going to record this." Due to nervousness, he could not open the recording application and quickly placed the phone on the dash. The officer then announced that the man was under arrest for Failure to Comply. At the end of the traffic stop, the officer gave the driver a traffic citation, indicated at the other man, and said, "you're getting this ticket because of him." Upon bringing that man to the jail, someone asked the officer what offense the man had committed. The officer responded, "he's one of those guys who watches CNBC too much about his rights." The man did not say anything else, fearing what else the officer might be capable of doing. He later told us, "I never dreamed I could end up in jail for this. I'm scared of driving through Ferguson now."

The Ferguson Police Department's infringement of individuals' freedom of speech and right to record has been highlighted in recent months in the context of large-scale public protest. In November 2014, a federal judge entered a consent order prohibiting Ferguson officers from interfering with individuals' rights to lawfully and peacefully record public police activities. That same month, the City settled another suit alleging that it had abused its loitering ordinance, Mun. Code § 29-89, to arrest people who were protesting peacefully on public sidewalks.

Despite these lawsuits, it appears that FPD continues to interfere with individuals' rights to protest and record police activities. On February 9, 2015, several individuals were protesting outside the Ferguson police station on the six-month anniversary of Michael Brown's death. According to protesters, and consistent with several video recordings from that evening, the protesters stood peacefully in the police department's parking lot, on the sidewalks in front of it, and across the street. Video footage shows that two FPD vehicles abruptly accelerated from the police parking lot into the street. An officer announced, "everybody here's going to jail," causing the protesters to run. Video shows that as one man recorded the police arresting others, he was arrested for interfering with police action. Officers pushed him to the ground, began handcuffing him, and announced, "stop resisting or you're going to get tased." It appears from the video, however, that the man was neither interfering nor resisting. A protester in a wheelchair who was live streaming the protest was also arrested. Another officer moved several people with cameras away from the scene of the arrests, warning them against interfering and urging them to back up or else be arrested for Failure to Obey. The sergeant shouted at those filming that they would be arrested for Manner of Walking if they did not back away out of the street, even though it appears from the video recordings that the protesters and those recording were on the sidewalk at most, if not all, times. Six people were arrested during this incident. It appears that officers' escalation of this incident was unnecessary and in response to derogatory comments written in chalk on the FPD parking lot asphalt and on a police vehicle.

FPD's suppression of speech reflects a police culture that relies on the exercise of police power—however unlawful—to stifle unwelcome criticism. Recording police activity and engaging in public protest are fundamentally democratic enterprises because they provide a check on those "who are granted substantial discretion that may be misused to deprive individuals of their liberties." *Glik*, 655 F.3d at 82. Even profane backtalk can be a form of dissent against perceived misconduct. In the words of the Supreme Court, "[t]he freedom of individuals verbally to oppose or challenge police action without thereby risking arrest is one of the principal characteristics by which we distinguish a free nation from a police state." *Hill*, 482 U.S. at 463. Ideally, officers would not encounter verbal abuse. Communities would encourage mutual respect, and the police would likewise exhibit respect by treating people with dignity. But, particularly where officers engage in unconstitutional policing, they only exacerbate community opposition by quelling speech.

3. FPD Engages in a Pattern of Excessive Force in Violation of the Fourth Amendment

FPD engages in a pattern of excessive force in violation of the Fourth Amendment.

Many officers are quick to escalate encounters with subjects they perceive to be disobeying their orders or resisting arrest. They have come to rely on ECWs, specifically Tasers®, where less force—or no force at all—would do. They also release canines on unarmed subjects unreasonably and before attempting to use force less likely to cause injury. Some incidents of excessive force result from stops or arrests that have no basis in law. Others are punitive and retaliatory. In addition, FPD records suggest a tendency to use unnecessary force against vulnerable groups such as people with mental health conditions or cognitive disabilities, and juvenile students. Furthermore, as discussed in greater detail in Part III.C. of this report, Ferguson's pattern of using excessive force disproportionately harms African-American members of the community. The overwhelming majority of force—almost 90%—is used against African Americans.

The use of excessive force by a law enforcement officer violates the Fourth Amendment. *Graham v. Conner,* 490 U.S. 386, 394 (1989); *Atkinson v. City of Mountain View, Mo.,* 709 F.3d 1201, 1207-09 (8th Cir. 2013). The constitutionality of an officer's use of force depends on whether the officer's conduct was "'objectively reasonable' in light of the facts and circumstances," which must be assessed "from the perspective of a reasonable officer on the scene, rather than with the 20/20 vision of hindsight." *Graham,* 490 U.S. at 396. Relevant considerations include "the severity of the crime at issue, whether the suspect poses an immediate threat to the safety of the officers or others, and whether he is actively resisting arrest or attempting to evade arrest by flight." *Id.; Johnson v. Caroll,* 658 F.3d 819, 826 (8th Cir. 2011).

FPD also imposes limits on officers' use of force through department policies. The use-of-force policy instituted by Chief Jackson in 2010 states that "force may not be resorted to unless other reasonable alternatives have been exhausted or would clearly be ineffective under a particular set of circumstances." FPD General Order 410.01. The policy also sets out a use-of-force continuum, indicating the force options permitted in different circumstances, depending on the level of resistance provided by a suspect. FPD General Order 410.08.

FPD's stated practice is to maintain use-of-force investigation files for all situations in which officers use force. We reviewed the entire set of force files provided by the department for the period of January 1, 2010 to

September 8, 2014.[17] Setting aside the killing of animals (e.g., dogs, injured deer) and three instances in which the subject of the use of force was not identified, FPD provided 151 files. We also reviewed related documentation regarding canine deployments. Our finding that FPD force is routinely unreasonable and sometimes clearly punitive is drawn largely from FPD's documentation; that is, from officers' own words.

a. FPD's Use of Electronic Control Weapons Is
   Unreasonable

FPD's pattern of excessive force includes using ECWs in a manner that is unconstitutional, abusive, and unsafe. For example, in August 2010, a lieutenant used an ECW in drive-stun mode against an African-American woman in the Ferguson City Jail because she had refused to remove her bracelets.[18] The lieutenant resorted to his ECW even though there were five officers present and the woman posed no physical threat.

Similarly, in November 2013, a correctional officer fired an ECW at an African-American woman's chest because she would not follow his verbal commands to walk toward a cell. The woman, who had been arrested

---

17 This set, however, did not include any substantive information on the August 9, 2014 shooting of Michael Brown by Officer Darren Wilson. That incident is being separately investigated by the Criminal Section of the Civil Rights Division and the U.S. Attorney's Office for the Eastern District of Missouri.

18 ECWs have two modes. In dart mode, an officer fires a cartridge that sends two darts or prongs into a person's body, penetrating the skin and delivering a jolt of electricity of a length determined by the officer. In drive-stun mode, sometimes referred to as "pain compliance" mode, an officer presses the weapon directly against a person's body, pulling the trigger to activate the electricity. Many agencies strictly limit the use of ECWs in drive-stun mode because of the potential for abuse.

for driving while intoxicated, had yelled an insulting remark at the officer, but her conduct amounted to verbal noncompliance or passive resistance at most. Instead of attempting hand controls or seeking assistance from a state trooper who was also present, the correctional officer deployed the ECW because the woman was "not doing as she was told." When another FPD officer wrote up the formal incident report, the reporting officer wrote that the woman "approached [the correctional officer] in a threatening manner." This "threatening manner" allegation appears nowhere in the statements of the correctional officer or witness trooper. The woman was charged with Disorderly Conduct, and the correctional officer soon went on to become an officer with another law enforcement agency.

These are not isolated incidents. In September 2012, an officer drive-stunned an African-American woman who he had placed in the back of his patrol car but who had stretched out her leg to block him from closing the door. The woman was in handcuffs. In May 2013, officers drive-stunned a handcuffed African-American man who verbally refused to get out of the back seat of a police car once it had arrived at the jail. The man did not physically resist arrest or attempt to assault the officers. According to the man, he was also punched in the face and head. That allegation was neither reported by the involved officers nor investigated by their supervisor, who dismissed it.

FPD officers seem to regard ECWs as an all-purpose tool bearing no risk. But an ECW—an electroshock weapon that disrupts a person's muscle control, causing involuntary contractions—can indeed be harmful. The Eighth Circuit Court of Appeals has observed that ECW-inflicted injuries are "sometimes severe and unexpected." *LaCross v. City of Duluth*, 713 F.3d 1155, 1158 (8th Cir. 2013). Electroshock "inflicts a painful and frightening blow, which temporarily paralyzes the large muscles of the body, rendering the victim helpless." *Hickey v. Reeder*, 12 F.3d 754, 757 (8th Cir. 1993).

Guidance produced by the United States Department of Justice, Office of Community Oriented Policing Services, and the Police Executive Research Forum in 2011 warns that ECWs are "'less-lethal' and not 'nonlethal weapons'" and "have the potential to result in a fatal outcome." *2011 Electronic Control Weapon Guidelines* 12 (Police Executive Research Forum & U.S. Dep't of Justice Office of Community Oriented Policing Services, Mar. 2011) ("*2077 ECW Guidelines*").

FPD officers' swift, at times automatic, resort to using ECWs against individuals who typically have committed low-level crimes and who pose no immediate threat violates the Constitution. As the Eighth Circuit held in 2011, an officer uses excessive force and violates clearly established Fourth Amendment law when he deploys an ECW against an individual whose crime was minor and who is not actively resisting, attempting to flee, or posing any imminent danger to others. *Brown v. City of Golden Valley*, 574 F.3d 491, 497-99 (8th Cir. 2011) (upholding the denial of a qualified immunity claim made by an officer who drive-stunned a woman on her arm for two or three seconds when she refused to hang up her phone despite being ordered to do so twice); *cf. Hickey*, 12 F.3d at 759 (finding that the use of a stun gun against a prisoner for refusing to sweep his cell violated the more deferential Eighth Amendment prohibition against cruel and unusual punishment). Courts have found that even when a suspect resists but does so only minimally, the surrounding factors may render the use of an ECW objectively unreasonable. *See Mattos v. Agarano*, 661 F.3d 433, 444-46, 448-51 (9th Cir. 2011) (en banc) (holding in two consolidated cases that minimal defensive resistance—including stiffening the body to inhibit being pulled from a car, and raising an arm in defense—does not render using an ECW reasonable where the offense was minor, the subject did not attempt to flee, and the subject posed no immediate threat to officers); *Parker v. Gerrish*, 547 F.3d 1, 9-11 (1st Cir. 2008) (upholding a jury verdict of excessive use of force for an ECW use because the evidence supported a finding that the subject who had held his hands together was not actively resisting or posing an immediate threat); *Casey v. City of Fed. Heights*, 509 F.3d 1278, 1282-83 (10th Cir. 2007) (holding that the use of an ECW was not objectively reasonable when the subject pulled away from the officer but did not otherwise actively resist arrest, attempt to flee, or pose an immediate threat).

Indeed, officers' unreasonable ECW use violates FPD's own policies. The department prohibits the use of force unless reasonable alternatives have been exhausted or would clearly be ineffective. FPD General Order 410.01. A separate ECW policy describes the weapon as "designed to overcome active aggression or overt actions of assault." FPD General Order 499.00. The policy states that an ECW "will never be deployed punitively or for purposes of coercion. It is to be used as a way of averting a potentially injurious or dangerous situation." FPD General Order 499.04. Despite the existence of clearly established Fourth Amendment case law and explicit departmental policies in this area, FPD officers routinely engage in the unreasonable use of ECWs, and supervisors routinely approve their conduct.

It is in part FPD officers' approach to policing that leads them to violate the Constitution and FPD's own policies. Officers across the country encounter drunkenness, passive defiance, and verbal challenges. But in Ferguson, officers have not been trained or incentivized to use de-escalation techniques to avoid or minimize force in these situations. Instead, they respond with impatience, frustration, and disproportionate force. FPD's weak oversight of officer use of force, described in greater detail below, facilitates this abuse. Officers should be required to view the ECW as one tool among many, and "a weapon of need, not a tool of convenience." *2011 ECW Guidelines* at 11. Effective policing requires that officers not depend on ECWs, or any type of force, "at the expense of diminishing the fundamental skills of communicating with subjects and de-escalating tense encounters." *Id.* at 12.

b. FPD's Use of Canines on Low-level, Unarmed Offenders Is Unreasonable

FPD engages in a pattern of deploying canines to bite individuals when the articulated facts do not justify this significant use of force. The department's own records demonstrate that, as with other types of force, canine officers use dogs out of proportion to the threat posed by the people they encounter, leaving serious puncture wounds to nonviolent offenders, some of them children. Furthermore, in every canine bite incident for which racial information is available, the subject was African American. This disparity, in combination with the decision to deploy canines in circumstances with a seemingly low objective threat, suggests that race may play an impermissible role in officers' decisions to deploy canines.

FPD currently has four canines, each assigned to a particular canine officer. Under FPD policy, canines are to be used to locate and apprehend "dangerous offenders." FPD General Order 498.00. When offenders are hiding, the policy states, "handlers will not allow their K-9 to engage a suspect by biting if a lower level of force could reasonably be expected to control the suspect or allow for the apprehension." *Id.* at 498.06. The policy also permits the use of a canine, however, when any crime—not just a felony or violent crime—has been committed. *Id.* at 498.05. This permissiveness, combined with the absence of meaningful supervisory review and an apparent tendency to overstate the threat based on race, has resulted in avoidable dog bites to low-level offenders when other means of control were available.

In December 2011, officers deployed a canine to bite an unarmed 14-year-old African-American boy who was waiting in an abandoned house for his friends. Four

205

officers, including a canine officer, responded to the house mid-morning after a caller reported that people had gone inside. Officers arrested one boy on the ground level. Describing the offense as a burglary in progress even though the facts showed that the only plausible offense was trespassing, the canine officer's report stated that the dog located a second boy hiding in a storage closet under the stairs in the basement. The officer peeked into the space and saw the boy, who was 5'5" and 140 pounds, curled up in a ball, hiding. According to the officer, the boy would not show his hands despite being warned that the officer would use the dog. The officer then deployed the dog, which bit the boy's arm, causing puncture wounds.

According to the boy, with whom we spoke, he never hid in a storage space and he never heard any police warnings. He told us that he was waiting for his friends in the basement of the house, a vacant building where they would go when they skipped school. The boy approached the stairs when he heard footsteps on the upper level, thinking his friends had arrived. When he saw the dog at the top of the steps, he turned to run, but the dog quickly bit him on the ankle and then the thigh, causing him to fall to the floor. The dog was about to bite his face or neck but instead got his left arm, which the boy had raised to protect himself. FPD officers struck him while he was on the ground, one of them putting a boot on the side of his head. He recalled the officers laughing about the incident afterward.

The lack of sufficient documentation or a supervisory force investigation prevents us from resolving which version of events is more accurate. However, even if the officer's version of the force used were accurate, the use of the dog to bite the boy was unreasonable. Though described as a felony, the facts as described by the officer, and the boy, indicate that this was a trespass—kids hanging out in a vacant building. The officers had no factual predicate to believe the boy was armed. The offense reports document no attempt to glean useful information about the second boy from the first, who was quickly arrested. By the canine officer's own account, he saw the boy in the closet and thus had the opportunity to assess the threat posed by this 5'5" 14 year old. Moreover, there were no exigent circumstances requiring apprehension by dog bite. Four officers were present and had control of the scene.

There is a recurring pattern of officers claiming they had to use a canine to extract a suspect hiding in a closed space. The frequency with which this particular rationale is used to justify dog bites, alongside the conclusory language in the reports, provides cause for concern. In December 2012, a 16-year-old African-American boy suspected of stealing a car fled from an officer, jumped several fences, and ran into a vacant house. A second officer arrived with a canine, which reportedly located the suspect hiding in a closet. Without providing a warning outside the closet, the officer opened the door and sent in the dog, which bit the suspect and dragged him out by the legs. This force appears objectively unreasonable. *See Kuha v. City of Minnetonka,* 365 F.3d 590, 598 (8th Cir. 2004), abrogated on other grounds by *Szabla v. City of Brooklyn Park, Minn.,* 486 F.3d 385, 396 (8th Cir. 2007) (en banc) (holding that "a jury could find it objectively unreasonable to use a police dog trained in the bite and hold method without first giving the suspect a warning and opportunity for peaceful surrender"). The first officer, who was also on the scene by this point, deployed his ECW against the suspect three times as the suspect struggled with the dog, which was still biting him. The offense reports provide only minimal explanation for why apprehension by dog bite was necessary. The pursuing officer claimed the suspect had "reached into the front section of his waist area," but the report does not say that he relayed this information to the canine officer, and no weapon was found. Moreover, given the lack of a warning at the closet, the use of the dog and ECW at the same time, and the application of three ECW stuns in quick succession, the officers' conduct raises the possibility that the force was applied in retaliation for leading officers on a chase.

In November 2013, an officer deployed a canine to bite and detain a fleeing subject even though the officer knew the suspect was unarmed. The officer deemed the subject, an African-American male who was walking down the street, suspicious because he appeared to walk away when he saw the officer. The officer stopped him and frisked him, finding no weapons. The officer then ran his name for warrants. When the man heard the dispatcher say over the police radio that he had outstanding warrants—the report does not specify whether the warrants were for failing to appear in municipal court or to pay owed fines, or something more serious—he ran. The officer followed him and released his dog, which bit the man on both arms. The officer's supervisor found the force justified because the officer released the dog "fearing that the subject was armed," even though the officer had already determined the man was unarmed.

As these incidents demonstrate, FPD officers' use of canines to bite people is frequently unreasonable. Officers command dogs to apprehend by biting even when multiple officers are present. They make no attempt to slow situations down, creating time to resolve the situation with lesser force. They appear to use canines not to counter a physical threat but to inflict punishment. They act as if every offender has a gun, justifying their decisions based on what might be possible rather than what the facts indicate is likely. Overall, FPD officers' use of canines reflects a culture in which officers choose not to use the skills and tactics that could resolve a situation without injuries, and instead deploy tools and methods that are almost guaranteed to produce an injury of some type.

FPD's use of canines is part of its pattern of excessive force in violation of the Fourth Amendment. In addition, FPD's use of dog bites only against African-American subjects is evidence of discriminatory policing in violation of the Fourteenth Amendment and other federal laws.

c. FPD's Use of Force Is Sometimes Retaliatory and
   Punitive

Many FPD uses of force appear entirely punitive. Officers often use force in response to behavior that may be annoying or distasteful but does not pose a threat. The punitive use of force by officers is unconstitutional and, in many cases, criminal. *See, e.g., Gibson v. County of Washoe, Nev.,* 290 F.3d 1175, 1197 (9th Cir. 2002) ("The Due Process clause protects pretrial detainees from the use of excessive force that amounts to punishment."); *see also* 18 U.S.C. § 242 (making willful deprivation of rights under color of law, such as by excessive force, a federal felony punishable by up to ten years in prison).

We reviewed many incidents in which it appeared that FPD officers used force not to counter a physical threat but to inflict punishment. The use of canines and ECWs, in particular, appear prone to such abuse by FPD. In April 2013, for example, a correctional officer deployed an ECW against an African-American prisoner, delivering a five-second shock, because the man had urinated out of his cell onto the jail floor. The correctional officer observed the man on his security camera feed inside the booking office. When the officer came out, some of the urine hit his pant leg and, he said, almost caused him to slip. "Due to the possibility of contagion," the correctional officer claimed, he deployed his ECW "to cease the assault." The ECW prongs, however, both struck the prisoner in the back. The correctional officer's claim that he deployed the ECW to stop the ongoing threat of urine is not credible, particularly given that the prisoner was in his locked cell with his back to the officer at the time the ECW was deployed. Using less-lethal force to counter urination, especially when done punitively as appears to be the case here, is unreasonable. *See Shumate v. Cleveland,* 483 F.

App'x 112, 114 (6th Cir. 2012) (affirming denial of summary judgment on an excessive-force claim against an officer who punched a handcuffed arrestee in response to being spit on, when the officer could have protected himself from further spitting by putting the arrestee in the back of a patrol car and closing the door).

d. FPD Use of Force Often Results from Unlawful Arrest and Officer Escalation

A defining aspect of FPD's pattern of excessive force is the extent to which force results from unlawful stops and arrests, and from officer escalation of incidents. Too often, officers overstep their authority by stopping individuals without reasonable suspicion and arresting without probable cause. Officers frequently compound the harm by using excessive force to effect the unlawful police action. Individuals encountering police under these circumstances are confused and surprised to find themselves being detained. They decline to stop or try to walk away, believing it within their rights to do so. They pull away incredulously, or respond with anger. Officers tend to respond to these reactions with force.

In January 2013, a patrol sergeant stopped an African-American man after he saw the man talk to an individual in a truck and then walk away. The sergeant detained the man, although he did not articulate any reasonable suspicion that criminal activity was afoot. When the man declined to answer questions or submit to a frisk—which the sergeant sought to execute despite articulating no reason to believe the man was armed—the sergeant grabbed the man by the belt, drew his ECW, and ordered the man to comply. The man crossed his arms and objected that he had not done anything wrong. Video captured by the ECW's built-in camera shows that the man made no aggressive movement toward the officer. The sergeant fired the ECW, applying a five-second cycle of electricity and causing the man to fall to the ground. The sergeant almost immediately applied the ECW again, which he later justified in his report by claiming that the man tried to stand up. The video makes clear, however, that the man never tried to stand—he only writhed in pain on the ground. The video also shows that the sergeant applied the ECW nearly continuously for 20 seconds, longer than represented in his report. The man was charged with Failure to Comply and Resisting Arrest, but no independent criminal violation.

In a January 2014 incident, officers attempted to arrest a young African-American man for trespassing on his girlfriend's grandparents' property, even though the man had been invited into the home by the girlfriend. According to officers, he resisted arrest, requiring several officers to subdue him. Seven officers repeatedly struck and used their ECWs against the subject, who was 5'8" and 170 pounds. The young man suffered head lacerations with significant bleeding.

In the above examples, force resulted from temporary detentions or attempted arrests for which officers lacked legal authority. Force at times appeared to be used as punishment for non-compliance with an order that lacked legal authority. Even where FPD officers have legal grounds to stop or arrest, however, they frequently take actions that ratchet up tensions and needlessly escalate the situation to the point that they feel force is necessary. One illustrative instance from October 2012 began as a purported check on a pedestrian's well-being and ended with the man being taken to the ground, drive-stunned twice, and arrested for Manner of Walking in Roadway and Failure to Comply. In that case, an African-American man was walking after midnight in the outer lane of West Florissant Avenue when an officer asked him to stop. The officer reported that he believed the man might be under the influence of an "impairing substance." When the man, who was 5'5" and 135 pounds, kept walking, the officer grabbed his arm; when the man pulled away, the officer forced him to the ground. Then, for reasons not articulated in the officer's report, the officer decided to handcuff the man, applying his ECW in drive-stun mode twice, reportedly because the man would not provide his hand for cuffing. The man was arrested but there is no indication in the report that he was in fact impaired or indeed doing anything other than walking down the street when approached by the officer.

In November 2011, officers stopped a car for speeding. The two African-American women inside exited the car and vocally objected to the stop. They were told to get back in the car. When the woman in the passenger seat got out a second time, an officer announced she was under arrest for Failure to Comply. This decision escalated into a use of force. According to the officers, the woman swung her arms and legs, although apparently not at anyone, and then stiffened her body. An officer responded by drive-stunning her in the leg. The woman was charged with Failure to Comply and Resisting Arrest.

As these examples demonstrate, a significant number of the documented use-of-force incidents involve charges of Failure to Comply and Resisting Arrest only. This means that officers who claim to act based on reasonable suspicion or probable cause of a crime either are wrong much of the time or do not have an adequate legal basis for many stops and arrests in the first place. *Cf. Lewis v. City of New Orleans*, 415 U.S. 130, 136 (1974) (Powell, J., concurring) (cautioning that an overbroad code ordinance "tends to be invoked only where there is no other valid basis for arresting an objectionable or suspicious person" and that the "opportunity for abuse ... is self-evident"). This pattern is a telltale sign of officer escalation and a strong indicator that the use of force was avoidable.

e. FPD Officers Have a Pattern of Resorting to Force
   Too Quickly When Interacting with Vulnerable
   Populations

Another dimension of FPD's pattern of unreasonable
force is FPD's overreliance on force when interacting
with more vulnerable populations, such as people with
mental health conditions or intellectual disabilities and
juvenile students.

*i. Force Used Against People with Mental Health
Conditions or Intellectual Disabilities*

The Fourth Amendment requires that an individual's mental health condition or intellectual disability be
considered when determining the reasonableness of an
officer's use of force. *See Champion v. Outlook Nashville,
Inc.*, 380 F.3d 893, 904 (6th Cir. 2004) (explaining in case
concerning use of force against a detainee with autism
that "[t]he diminished capacity of an unarmed detainee
must be taken into account when assessing the amount of
force exerted"); *see also Phillips v. Community Ins. Corp.*,
678 F.3d 513, 526 (7th Cir. 2012); *Deorle v. Rutherford*,
272 F.3d 1272, 1283 (9th Cir. 2001); *Giannetti v. City of
Stillwater*, 216 F. App'x 756, 764 (10th Cir. 2007). This
is because people with such disabilities "may be physically unable to comply with police commands." *Phillips*,
678 F.3d at 526. Our review indicates that FPD officers
do not adequately consider the mental health or cognitive disability of those they suspect of wrongdoing when
deciding whether to use force.

Ferguson is currently in litigation against the estate
of a man with mental illness who died in September 2011
after he had an ECW deployed against him three times
for allegedly running toward an officer while swinging
his fist. *See Estate of Moore v. Ferguson Police Dep't*, No.
4:14-cv-01443 (E.D. Mo. filed Aug. 19, 2014). The man had
been running naked through the streets and pounding on

cars that morning while yelling "I am Jesus." The Eighth Circuit recently considered a similar set of allegations in *De Boise v. Taser Intern., Inc.*, 760 F.3d 892 (8th Cir. 2014). There, a man suffering from schizophrenia, who had run naked in and out of his house and claimed to be a god, died after officers used their ECWs against him multiple times because he would not stay on the ground. *Id.* at 897-98. Although the court resolved the case on qualified immunity grounds without deciding the excessive-force issue, the one judge who reached that issue opined that the allegations could be sufficient to establish a Fourth Amendment violation. *Id.* at 899-900 (Bye, J., dissenting).

In 2013, FPD stopped a man running with a shopping cart because he seemed "suspicious." According to the file, the man was "obviously mentally handicapped." Officers took the man to the ground and attempted to arrest him for Failure to Comply after he refused to submit to a pat-down. In the officers' view, the man resisted arrest by pulling his arms away. The officers drive-stunned him in the side of the neck. They charged him only with Failure to Comply and Resisting Arrest. In August 2011, officers used an ECW device against a man with diabetes who bit an EMT's hand without breaking the skin. The man had been having seizures when he did not comply with officer commands.

In August 2010, an officer responded to a call about an African-American man walking onto the highway and lying down on the pavement. Seeing that the man was sweating, acting jittery, and had dilated pupils, the officer believed he was on drugs. The man was cooperative at first but balked, pushing the officer back when the officer tried to handcuff him for safety reasons. The officer struck the man several times with his Asp® baton—including once in the head, a form of deadly force—causing significant bleeding. Two other officers then deployed their ECWs against the man a total of five times.

Jail staff have also reacted to people with mental health conditions by resorting to greater force than necessary. For example, in July 2011, a correctional officer used an ECW to drive-stun an African-American male inmate three times after he tried to hang himself with material torn from a medical dressing and banged his head on the cell wall. That same month, a correctional officer used an ECW against an African-American inmate with bipolar disorder who broke the overhead glass light fixture and tried to use it to cut his wrists. According to the correctional officer, the glass was "safety glass" and could not be used to cut the skin.

These incidents indicate a pattern of insufficient sensitivity to, and training about, the limitations of those with mental health conditions or intellectual disabilities. Officers view mental illness as narcotic intoxication, or worse, willful defiance. They apply excessive force to such subjects, not accounting for the possibility that the subjects may not understand their commands or be able to comply with them. And they have been insufficiently trained on tactics that would minimize force when dealing with individuals who are in mental health crisis or who have intellectual disabilities.

ii. Force Used Against Students

FPD's approach to policing impacts how its officers interact with students, as well, leading them to treat routine discipline issues as criminal matters and to use force when communication and de-escalation techniques would likely resolve the conflict.

FPD stations two School Resource Officers in the Ferguson-Florissant School District,[19] one at Ferguson

---

19 The Ferguson-Florissant School District serves over 11,000 students, about 80% of whom are African American. *See* Ferguson-Florissant District Demographic Data 2014 & 2015, Mo. Dep't of Elementary & Secondary Educ., http://mcds.dese.mo.gov/

Middle School and one at McCluer South-Berkeley High School. The stated mission of the SRO program, according to the memorandum of understanding between FPD and the school district, is to provide a safe and secure learning environment for students. But that agreement does not clearly define the SROs' role or limit SRO involvement in cases of routine discipline or classroom management. Nor has FPD established such guidance for its SROs or provided officers with adequate training on engaging with youth in an educational setting. The result of these failures, combined with FPD's culture of unreasonable enforcement actions more generally, is police action that is unreasonable for a school environment.

For example, in November 2013, an SRO charged a ninth grade girl with several violations after she refused to follow his orders to walk to the principal's office. The student and a classmate, both 15-year-old African-American girls, had gotten into a fight during class. When the officer responded, school staff had the two girls separated in a hallway. One refused the officer's order to walk to the principal's office, instead trying to push past staff toward the other girl. The officer pushed her backward toward a row of lockers and then announced that she was under arrest for Failure to Comply. Although the officer agreed not to handcuff her when she agreed to walk to the principals' office, he forwarded charges of Failure to Comply, Resisting Arrest, and Peace Disturbance to the county family court. The other student was charged with Peace Disturbance.

FPD officers respond to misbehavior common among students with arrest and force, rather than reserving arrest for cases involving safety threats. As one SRO told us, the arrests he made during the 2013-14 school year overwhelmingly involved minor offenses—Disorderly Conduct, Peace Disturbance, and Failure to Comply with

guidedinquiry/Pages/District-and-School-Information.aspx (last visited Feb. 26, 2015).

instructions. In one case, an SRO decided to arrest a 14-year-old African-American student at the Ferguson Middle School for Failure to Comply when the student refused to leave the classroom after getting into a trivial argument with another student. The situation escalated, resulting in the student being drive-stunned with an ECW in the classroom and the school seeking a 180-day suspension for the student. SROs' propensity for arresting students demonstrates a lack of understanding of the negative consequences associated with such arrests. In fact, SROs told us that they viewed increased arrests in the schools as a positive result of their work. This perspective suggests a failure of training (including training in mental health, counseling, and the development of the teenage brain); a lack of priority given to de-escalation and conflict resolution; and insufficient appreciation for the negative educational and long-term outcomes that can result from treating disciplinary concerns as crimes and using force on students. *See* Dear Colleague Letter on the Nondiscriminatory Administration of School Discipline, U.S. Dep't of Justice & U.S. Dep't of Education, http://www.justice.gov/crt/about/edu/documents/dcl. pdf (2014) (citing research and providing guidance to public schools on how to comply with federal nondiscrimination law).

f. FPD's Weak Oversight of Use of Force Reflects its Lack of Concern for Whether Officer Conduct Is Consistent with the Law or Promotes Police Legitimacy

FPD's use-of-force review system is particularly ineffectual. Force frequently is not reported. When it is, there is rarely any meaningful review. Supervisors do little to no investigation; either do not understand or choose not to follow FPD's use-of-force policy in analyzing officer conduct; rarely correct officer misconduct when they find it; and do not see the patterns of abuse that are evident when viewing these incidents in the aggregate.

While Chief Jackson implemented new department policies when he joined FPD in 2010, including on use-of-force reporting and review, these policies are routinely ignored. Under FPD General Order 410.00, when an officer uses or attempts to use any force, a supervisor must respond to the scene to investigate. The supervisor must complete a two-page use-of-force report assessing whether the use of force complied with FPD's force policy. Additional forms are required for ECW uses and vehicle pursuits. According to policy and our interviews with Chief Jackson, a use-of-force packet is assembled—which should include the use-of-force report and supplemental forms, all police reports, any photographs, and any other supporting materials—and forwarded up the chain of command to the Chief. The force reporting and review system is intended to "help identify trends, improve training and officer safety, and provide timely information for the department addressing use-of-force issues with the public." FPD General Order 410.07. The policy even requires that a professional standards officer conduct an annual review of all force incidents. *Id.* These requirements are not adhered to in practice.

Perhaps the greatest deviation from FPD's use-of-force policies is that officers frequently do not report the force they use at all. There are many indications that this underreporting is widespread. First, we located information in FPD's internal affairs files indicating instances of force that were not included in the force files provided by FPD. Second, in reviewing randomly selected reports from FPD's records management system, we found several offense reports that described officers using force with no corresponding use-of-force report. Third, we found evidence that force had been used but not documented in officers' workers compensation claims. Of the nine cases between 2010 and 2014 in which officers claimed injury sustained from using force on the job, three had no corresponding use-of-force paperwork. Fourth, the set of force investigations provided by FPD contains lengthy gaps, including six stretches of time ranging from two to four months in which no incidents of force are reported. Otherwise, the files typically reflect between two and six force incidents per month. Fifth, we heard from community members about uses of force that do not appear within FPD's records, and we learned of many uses of force that were never officially reported or investigated from reviewing emails between FPD supervisors. Finally, FPD's force files reflect an overrepresentation of ECW uses—a type of force that creates a physical record (a spent ECW cartridge with discharged confetti) and that requires a separate form be filled out. It is much easier for officers to use physical blows and baton strikes without documenting them. Thus, the evidence indicates that a significant amount of force goes unreported within FPD. This in turn raises the possibility that the pattern of unreasonable force is even greater than we found.

Even when force is reported, the force review process falls so short of FPD's policy requirements that it is ineffective at improving officer safety or ensuring that force is used properly. First, and most significantly, supervisors almost never actually investigate force incidents. In almost every case, supervisors appear to view force investigations as a ministerial task, merely summarizing the involved officers' version of events and sometimes relying on the officers' offense report alone. The supervisory review starts and ends with the presumption that the officer's version of events is truthful and that the force was reasonable. As a consequence, though contrary to policy, supervisors almost never interview non-police witnesses, such as the arrestee or any independent witnesses. They do not review critical evidence even when it is readily available. For example, a significant portion of the documented uses of force occurs at the Ferguson jail, which employs surveillance cameras to monitor the area. Yet FPD records provide no indication that a supervisor has ever sought to review the footage for a jail incident. Nor do supervisors examine ECW camera video, even though it is available in FPD's newer model ECWs. Sometimes, supervisors provide no remarks on the use-of-force report, indicating simply, "see offense report."

Our review found the record to be replete with examples of this lack of meaningful supervisory review of force. For example, the use-of-force report for a May 2013 incident states that a suspect claims he had an ECW deployed against him and that he was punched in the head and face. The supervisor concludes simply, "other than the drive stun, no use of force was performed by the officers." The report does not clarify what investigation the supervisor did, if any, to assess the suspect's allegations, or how he determined that the allegations were false. Supervisors also fail to provide recommendations for how to ensure officer safety and minimize the need for force going forward. In January 2014, for instance, a correctional officer used force to subdue an inmate who tried to escape while the correctional officer was moving the inmate's cellmate to another cell without assistance. The supervisor missed the opportunity to recommend that correctional officers not act alone in such risky situations.

Second, supervisors either do not understand or choose not to follow FPD's use-of-force policy. As discussed above, in many of the force incidents we reviewed, it is clear from the officers' offense reports that the force used was, at the very least, contrary to FPD policy. Nonetheless, based on records provided by FPD, it appears that first-line supervisors and the command staff found all but one of the 151 incidents we reviewed to be within policy. This includes the instances of unreasonable ECW use discussed above. FPD policy advises that ECWs are to be used to "overcome active aggression or overt actions of assault." FPD General Order 499.00. They are to be used to "avert[] a potentially injurious or dangerous situation," and never "punitively or for purposes of coercion." FPD General Order 499.04. Simply referring back to these policies should have made clear to supervisors that the many uses of ECWs against subjects who were merely argumentative or passively resistant violated policy.

For example, in April 2014, an intoxicated jail detainee climbed up on the bars in his cell and refused to get down when ordered to by the arresting officer and the correctional officer on duty. The correctional officer then fired an ECW at him, from outside the closed cell door, striking the detainee in the chest and causing him to fall to the ground. In addition to being excessive, this force violated explicit FPD policy that "[p]roper consideration and care should be taken when deploying the X26 TASER on subjects who are in an elevated position or in other circumstance where a fall may cause substantial injury or death." FPD General Order 499.04. The reviewing supervisor deemed the use of force within policy.

Supervisors seem to believe that any level of resistance justifies any level of force. They routinely rely on boilerplate language, such as the statement that the subject took "a fighting stance," to justify force. Such language is not specific enough to understand the specific behavior the officer encountered and thus to determine whether the officer's response was reasonable. Indeed, a report from September 2010 shows how such terms may obscure what happened. In that case, the supervisor wrote that the subject "turned to [the officer] in a fighting stance" even though the officer's report makes clear that he chased and tackled the subject as the subject fled. That particular use of force may have been reasonable, but the use-of-force report reveals how little attention supervisors give to their force investigations. Another common justification, frequently offered by officers who use ECWs to subdue individuals who do not readily put their hands behind their back after being put on the ground, is to claim that a subject's hands were near his waist, where he might have a weapon. Supervisors tend to accept this justification without question.

Third, the review process breaks down even further when officers at the sergeant level or above use force. Instead of reporting their use of force to an official higher up the chain, who could evaluate it objectively, they complete the use-of-force investigation themselves. We found several examples of supervisors investigating their own conduct. When force investigations are conducted by the very officers involved in the incidents, the department is less likely to identify policy and constitutional violations, and the public is less likely to trust the department's commitment to policing itself.

Fourth, the failure of supervisors to investigate and the absence of analysis from their use-of-force reports frustrate review up the chain of command. Lieutenants, the assigned captain, and the Police Chief typically receive at most a one- or two-paragraph summary from supervisors; no witness statements, photographs, or video footage that should have been obtained during the investigation is included. These reviewers are left to rely only on the offense report and the sergeant's cursory summary. To take one example, 21 officers responded to a fight at the high school in March 2013, and several of them used force to take students into custody. FPD records contain only one offense report, which does not describe the actions of all officers who used force. The use-of-force report identifies the involved officers as "multiple" (without names) and provides only a one-paragraph summary stating that students "were grabbed, handcuffed, and restrained using various techniques of control." The offense report reflects that officers collected video from the school's security cameras, but the supervisor apparently never reviewed it. Further, while the offense report contains witness statements, those statements relate to the underlying fight, not the officer use of force, and there appear to be no statements from any of the 21 officers who responded to the fight. It is not possible for higher-level supervisors to adequately assess uses of force with so little information.

In fact, although a use-of-force packet is supposed to include all related documents, in practice only the two-page use-of-force report, that is, the supervisor's brief summary of the incident, goes to the Chief. In the example from the high school, then, the Chief would have known only that there was a fight at the school and that force was used—not which officers used force, what type of force was used, or what the students did to warrant the use of force. Offense reports are available in FPD's records management system, but Chief Jackson told us he rarely retrieves them when reviewing uses of force. The Chief also told us that he has never overturned a supervisor's determination of whether a use of force fell within FPD policy.

Finally, FPD does not perform any comprehensive review of force incidents sufficient to detect patterns of misconduct by a particular officer or unit, or patterns regarding a particular type of force. Indeed, FPD does not keep records in a manner that would allow for such a review. Within FPD's paper storage system, the two-page use-of-force reports (which are usually handwritten) are kept separately from all other documentation, including ECW and pursuit forms for the same incidents. Offense reports are attached to some use-of-force reports but not others. Some use-of-force reports have been removed from FPD's set of force files because the incidents became the subjects of an internal investigation or a lawsuit. As a consequence, when FPD provided us what it considers to be its force files—which, as described above, we have reason to believe do not capture all actual force incidents—a majority of those files were missing a critical document, such as an offense report, ECW report, or the use-of-force report itself. We had to make repeated requests for documents to construct force files amenable to fair review. There were some documents that FPD was unable to locate, even after repeated requests.

With its records incomplete and scattered, the department is unable to implement an early intervention system to identify officers who tend to use excessive force or the need for more training or better equipment—goals explicitly set out by FPD policy. It appears that no annual review of force incidents is conducted, as required by FPD General Order 410.07; indeed, a meaningful annual audit would be impossible. These recordkeeping problems also explain why Chief Jackson told us he could not remember ever imposing discipline for an improper use of force or ordering further training based on force problems.

These deficiencies in use-of-force review can have serious consequences. They make it less likely that officers will be held accountable for excessive force and more likely that constitutional violations will occur. They create potentially devastating liability for the City for failing to put in place systems to ensure officers operate within the bounds of the law. And they result in a police department that does not give its officers the supervision they need to do their jobs safely, effectively, and constitutionally.

B. Ferguson's Municipal Court Practices

The Ferguson municipal court handles most charges brought by FPD, and does so not with the primary goal of administering justice or protecting the rights of the accused, but of maximizing revenue. The impact that revenue concerns have on court operations undermines the court's role as a fair and impartial judicial body.[20]

---

20 The influence of revenue on the court, described both in Part II and in Part III.B. of this Report, may itself be unlawful. *See Ward v. Vill. of Monroeville*, 409 U.S. 57, 58-62 (1972) (finding a violation of the due process right to a fair and impartial trial where

Our investigation has uncovered substantial evidence that the court's procedures are constitutionally deficient and function to impede a person's ability to challenge or resolve a municipal charge, resulting in unnecessarily prolonged cases and an increased likelihood of running afoul of court requirements. At the same time, the court imposes severe penalties when a defendant fails to meet court requirements, including added fines and fees and arrest warrants that are unnecessary and run counter to public safety. These practices both reflect and reinforce an approach to law enforcement in Ferguson that violates the Constitution and undermines police legitimacy and community trust.

Ferguson's municipal court practices combine to cause significant harm to many individuals who have cases pending before the court. Our investigation has found overwhelming evidence of minor municipal code violations resulting in multiple arrests, jail time, and payments that exceed the cost of the original ticket many times over. One woman, discussed above, received two parking tickets for a single violation in 2007 that then totaled $151 plus fees. Over seven years later, she still owed Ferguson $541—after already paying $550 in fines and fees, having multiple arrest warrants issued against her, and being arrested and jailed on several occasions. Another woman told us that when she went to court to try to pay $100 on a $600 outstanding balance, the Court Clerk refused to take the partial payment, even though the woman explained that she was a single mother and could not afford to pay more that month. A 90-year-old man had a warrant issued for his arrest after he failed to timely pay the five citations FPD issued to him during a single traffic stop in 2013. An 83-year-old man had a warrant issued against him when he failed to timely resolve

---

a town mayor served as judge and was also responsible for the town's finances, which were substantially dependent on "fines, forfeitures, costs, and fees" collected by the court).

his Derelict Auto violation. A 67-year-old woman told us she was stopped and arrested by a Ferguson police officer for an outstanding warrant for failure to pay a trash-removal citation. She did not know about the warrant until her arrest, and the court ultimately charged her $1,000 in fines, which she continues to pay off in $100 monthly increments despite being on a limited, fixed income. We have heard similar stories from dozens of other individuals and have reviewed court records documenting many additional instances of similarly harsh penalties, often for relatively minor violations.

Our review of police and court records suggests that much of the harm of Ferguson's law enforcement practices in recent years is attributable to the court's routine use of arrest warrants to secure collection and compliance when a person misses a required court appearance or payment. In a case involving a moving violation, procedural failures also result in the suspension of the defendant's license. And, until recently, the court regularly imposed a separate Failure to Appear charge for missed appearances and payments; that charge resulted in an additional fine in the amount of $75.50, plus $26.50 in court costs. *See* Ferguson Mun. Code § 13-58 (repealed Sept. 23, 2014). During the last three years, the court imposed roughly one Failure to Appear charge per every two citations or summonses issued by FPD. Since at least 2010, the court has collected more revenue for Failure to Appear charges than for any other charge. This includes $442,901 in fines for Failure to Appear violations in 2013, which comprised 24% of the total revenue the court collected that year. While the City Council repealed the Failure to Appear ordinance in September 2014, many people continue to owe fines and fees stemming from that charge. And the court continues to issue arrest warrants in every case where that charge previously would have been applied. License suspension practices are similarly unchanged. Once issued, arrest warrants can, and frequently do, lead to arrest and time in jail, despite the fact that the underlying offense did not result in a penalty of imprisonment.[21]

Thus, while the municipal court does not generally deem the code violations that come before it as jail-worthy, it routinely views the failure to appear in court to remit payment to the City as jail-worthy, and commonly issues warrants to arrest individuals who have failed to make timely payment. Similarly, while the municipal court does not have any authority to impose a *fine* of over $1,000 for any offense, it is not uncommon for individuals to pay more than this amount to the City of Ferguson—in forfeited bond payments, additional Failure to Appear charges, and added court fees—for what may have begun as a simple code violation. In this way, the penalties that the court imposes are driven not by public safety needs, but by financial interests. And despite the harm imposed by these needless penalties, until recently, the City and court did little to respond to the increasing frequency of Failure to Appear charges, and in many respects made court practices more opaque and difficult to navigate.

1. Court Practices Impose Substantial and Unnecessary Barriers to the Challenge or Resolution of Municipal Code Violations

It is a hallmark of due process that individuals are entitled to adequate notice of the allegations made against them and to a meaningful opportunity to be heard. *See Cole v. Arkansas,* 333 U.S. 196, 201 (1948); *see also Ward v. Vill. of Monroeville,* 409 U.S. 57, 58-62 (1972)

---

21 As with many of the problematic court practices that we identify in this report, other municipalities in St. Louis County also have imposed a separate Failure to Appear charge, fine, and fee for missed court appearances and payments. Many continue to do so.

(applying due process requirements to case adjudicated by municipal traffic court). As documented below, however, Ferguson municipal court rules and procedures often fail to provide these basic protections, imposing unnecessary barriers to resolving a citation or summons and thus increasing the likelihood of incurring the severe penalties that result if a code violation is not quickly resolved.

We have concerns not only about the obstacles to resolving a charge even when an individual chooses not to contest it, but also about the trial processes that apply in the rare occasion that a person does attempt to challenge a charge. While it is "axiomatic that a fair trial in a fair tribunal is a basic requirement of due process," *Caperton v. A.T. Massey Coal Co., Inc.*, 556 U.S. 868, 876 (2009), the adjudicative tribunal provided by the Ferguson municipal court appears deficient in many respects.[22] Attempts to raise legal claims are met with retaliatory conduct. In an August 2012 email exchange, for instance, the Court Clerk asked what the Prosecuting Attorney does when an attorney appears in a red light camera case, and the Prosecuting Attorney responded: "I usually dismiss them if the attorney merely requests a recommendation. If the attorney goes off on all of the constitutional stuff, then I tell the attorney to come ... and argue in front [of] the judge—after that, his client can pay the ticket." We have found evidence of similar adverse action taken against litigants attempting to fulsomely argue a case at trial. The man discussed above who was cited after allowing

---

22 As discussed in Part II of this report, City officials have acknowledged several of these procedural deficiencies. In 2012, a City Councilmember, citing specific examples, urged against reappointing Judge Brockmeyer because he "often times does not listen to the testimony, does not review the reports or the criminal history of defendants, and doesn't let all the pertinent witnesses testify before rendering a verdict."

his child to urinate in a bush attempted to challenge his charges. The man retained counsel who, during trial, was repeatedly interrupted by the court during his cross-examination of the officer. When the attorney objected to the interruptions, the judge told him that, if he continued on this path, "I will hold you in contempt and I will incarcerate you," which, as discussed below, the court has done in the past to others appearing before it. The attorney told us that, believing no line of questioning would alter the outcome, he tempered his defense so as not to be jailed. Notably, at that trial, even though the testifying officer had previously been found untruthful during an official FPD investigation, the prosecuting attorney presented his testimony without informing defendant of that fact, and the court credited that testimony.[23] The

---

23 This finding of untruthfulness by a police officer constitutes impeachment evidence that must be disclosed in any trial in which the officer testifies for the City. Under the Fourteenth Amendment, the failure to disclose evidence that is "favorable to an accused" violates due process "where the evidence is material either to guilt or to punishment, irrespective of the good faith or bad faith of the prosecution." *Brady v. Maryland,* 373 U.S. 83, 87 (1963). This duty applies to impeachment evidence, *United States v. Bagley,* 473 U.S. 667, 676 (1985), and it applies even if the defendant does not request the evidence, *United States v. Agurs,* 427 U.S. 97, 107 (1976). The duty encompasses, furthermore, information that should be known to the prosecutor, including information known solely by the police department. *Kyles v. Whitley,* 514 U.S. 419, 437 (1995). This constitutional duty to disclose appears to extend to municipal court cases, which can result in jail terms of up to three months under Section 29-2 of Ferguson's municipal code. *See City of Kansas City v. Oxley,* 579 S.W.2d 113, 114 (Mo. 1979) (en banc) (holding that the due process standard of proof beyond a reasonable doubt applied in a municipal court speeding case because "the violation has criminal overtones"); *see also City of Cape Girardeau v. Jones,* 725 S.W.2d 904, 907-09 (Mo. Ct.

evidence thus suggests substantial deficiencies in the manner in which the court conducts trials.

Even where defendants opt not to challenge their charges, a number of court processes make resolving a case exceedingly difficult. City officials and FPD officers we spoke with nearly uniformly asserted that individuals' experiences when they become embroiled in Ferguson's municipal code enforcement are due not to any failings in Ferguson's law enforcement practices, but rather to those individuals' lack of "personal responsibility." But these statements ignore the barriers to resolving a case that court practices impose, including: 1) a lack of transparency regarding rights and responsibilities; 2) requiring in-person appearance to resolve most municipal charges; 3) policies that exacerbate the harms of Missouri's law requiring license suspension where a person fails to appear on a moving violation charge; 4) basic access deficiencies that frustrate a person's ability to resolve even those charges that do not require in-court appearance; and 5) legally inadequate fine assessment methods that do not appropriately consider a person's ability to pay and do not provide alternatives to fines for those living in or near poverty. Together, these barriers impose considerable hardship. We have heard repeated reports, and found evidence in court records, of people appearing in court many times—in some instances on more than ten occasions—to try to resolve a case but being unable to do so, and subsequently having additional fines, fees, and arrest warrants issued against them.

App. 1987) (explaining that reasonable doubt standard applied to municipal trespass prosecution because municipal ordinance violations are "quasi-criminal," and reversing two convictions based on privilege against self-incrimination). We are aware of at least two cases, from January 2015, in which the City called this officer as a witness without disclosing the finding of untruthfulness to the defense.

a. Court Practices and Procedural Deficiencies Create a Lack of Transparency R3egarding Rights and Responsibilities

It is often difficult for an individual who receives a municipal citation or summons in Ferguson to know how much is owed, where and how to pay the ticket, what the options for payment are, what rights the individual has, and what the consequences are for various actions or oversights. The initial information provided to people who are cited for violating Ferguson's municipal code is often incomplete or inconsistent. Communication with municipal court defendants is haphazard and known by the court to be unreliable. And the court's procedures and operations are ambiguous, are not written down, and are not transparent or even available to the public on the court's website or elsewhere.

The rules and procedures of the court are difficult for the public to discern. Aside from a small number of exceptions, the Municipal Judge issues rules of practice and procedure verbally and on an ad hoc basis. Until recently, on the rare occasion that the Judge issued a written order that altered court practices, those orders were not distributed broadly to court and other FPD officials whose actions they affect and were not readily accessible to the public. Further, Ferguson, unlike other courts in the region, does not include *any* information about its operations on its website other than inaccurate instructions about how to make payment.[24] Court staff

---

24 *See City Courts*, City of Ferguson, http://www.fergusoncity. com/60/The-City-Of-Ferguson-Municipal-Courts (last visited Feb. 26, 2015). By contrast, the neighboring municipality of Normandy operates a court website with an entire page containing information regarding fine due dates, methods of payment, and different payment options, including the availability of payment plans for those who cannot afford to pay a fine in full. *See How Do I Pay a Ticket / Fine?*, City of Normandy, http://www.cityofnormandy. gov/index.aspx?NID=570 (last visited Feb. 26, 2015).

acknowledged during our investigation that the public would benefit from increased information about how to resolve cases and about court practices and procedures. Yet neither the court nor other City officials have undertaken efforts to make court operations more transparent in order to ensure that litigants understand their rights or court procedures, or to enable the public to assess whether the court is operating in a fair manner.

Current court practices fail to provide adequate information even to those who are charged with a municipal violation. The lack of clarity about a person's rights and responsibilities often begins from the moment a person is issued a citation. For some offenses, FPD uses state of Missouri uniform citations, and typically indicates on the ticket the assigned court date for the offense. Many times, however, FPD officers omit critical information from the citation, which makes it impossible for a person to determine the specific nature of the offense charged, the amount of the fine owed, or whether a court appearance is required or some alternative method of payment is available. In some cases, citations fail to indicate the offense charged altogether; in November 2013, for instance, court staff wrote FPD patrol to "see what [a] ticket was for" because it "does not have a charge on it." In other cases, a ticket will indicate a charge but omit other crucial information. For example, speeding tickets often fail to indicate the alleged speed observed, even though both the fine owed and whether a court appearance is mandatory depends upon the specific speed alleged. Evidence shows that in some of these cases, a person has appeared in court but been unable to resolve the citation because of the missing information. In June 2014, for instance, a court clerk wrote to an FPD officer: "The above ticket ... does not have a speed in it. The guy came in and we had to send him away. Can you email me the speed when you get time." Separate and apart from the difficulties these omissions create for people, the fact that the court staff routinely add the speed to tickets weeks after they are issued raises concerns about the accuracy and reliability of officers' assertions in official records.

We have also found evidence that in issuing citations, FPD officers frequently provide people with incorrect information about the date and time of their assigned court session. In November 2012, court staff emailed the two patrol lieutenants asking: "Would you please be so kind to tell your squads to check their ct. dates and times. We are getting quite a few wrong dates and times [on tickets]." In December 2012, a court clerk emailed an FPD officer to inform him that while he had been putting 6:00 p.m. on his citations that month, the scheduled court session was actually a morning session. More recently, in March 2014, an officer wrote a court clerk because the officer had issued a citation that listed the court date as ten days later than the actual court date assigned. Some of these emails indicate that court staff planned to send a letter to the person who was cited. As noted below, however, such letters often are returned to the court as undeliverable. It is thus unsurprising that, on one occasion, a City employee who works in the building where court was held wrote the Court Clerk to tell her that "[a] few people stopped by tonight looking for court and I referred them to you." The email notes that one person insisted on providing her information so the employee could "vouch for her appearance for Night Court." The email does not identify any other individual who showed up for court that night, nor does it state that any steps were taken to ensure that those assigned the incorrect court date did not have Failure to Appear charges and fines imposed, arrest warrants issued against them, or their licenses suspended.

Even if the citation a person receives has been properly filled out, it is often unclear whether a court appearance is required or if some other method of resolving a case is available. Ferguson has a schedule that establishes fixed fines for a limited number of violations that do not require court appearance. Nonetheless, this list—called the "TVB" or "Traffic Violations Bureau" list—is incomplete and does not provide sufficient clarity regarding whether a court appearance is mandatory. Court staff members have themselves informed us that there are certain offenses for which they will sometimes require a court appearance and other times not, depending on their own assessment of whether an appearance should be required in a given case. That information, however, is not reliably communicated to the person who has been given the citation.

Although the City of Ferguson frequently bears responsibility for giving people misinformation about when they must appear in court, Ferguson does little to ensure that persons who have missed a court date are properly notified of the consequences that result from an additional missed appearance, such as arrest or losing their driver's licenses, or that those consequences have already been levied. If a person misses a required appearance, it is the purported practice of court staff to send a letter that sets a new court date and informs the defendant that missing the next appearance will result in an arrest warrant being issued. But court staff do not even claim to send these letters before issuing warrants if an individual is on a payment plan and misses a payment, or if a person already has an outstanding warrant on a different offense; in those cases, the court issues a warrant after a single missed payment or appearance. Further, even for the cases in which the court says it does send such letters prior to issuing a warrant, court records suggest that those letters are often not actually sent. Even where a letter is sent, some are returned to court, and court staff told us that in those cases, they make no additional effort to notify the individual of the new court date or the consequences of non-appearance. Court staff and staff from other municipal courts have informed us that defendants in poverty are more likely not to receive such a letter from court because they frequently change residence.

If an individual misses a second court date, an arrest warrant is issued, without any confirmation that the individual received notice of that second court date. In the past, when the court issued a warrant it would also send notice to the individual that a warrant was issued against them and telling them to appear at the police department to resolve the matter. This notice did not provide the basis of the arrest warrant or describe how it might be resolved. In any case, Ferguson stopped providing even this incomplete notice in 2012. In explaining the decision to stop sending this warrant notice, the Court Clerk wrote in a June 2011 email to Chief Jackson that "this will save the cost of warrant cards and postage" and "it is not necessary to send out these cards." Some court employees, however, told us that the notice letter had been useful—at least for those who received it—and that they believe it should still be sent. That the court discontinued what little notice it was providing to people in advance of issuing a warrant is particularly troubling given that, during our investigation, we spoke with several individuals who were arrested without ever knowing that a warrant was outstanding.[25]

---

25 Prior to September 2014, a second missed court appearance (or a single missed payment) would result not only in a warrant being issued, but also the imposition of an additional Failure to Appear *charge*. This charge was imposed automatically. It does not appear that there was any attempt by the court to inform individuals that a failure to appear could be excused upon a showing of good cause, or to provide individuals with an opportunity to make such a showing. Additionally, just as the court does not currently send any notice informing a defendant that an arrest warrant has been issued, the court did not send any notice that this additional Failure to Appear charge had been brought.

Once a warrant is issued, a person can clear the warrant by appearing at the court window in the police department and paying a pre-determined bond. However, that process is itself not communicated to the public and, in any case, is only useful if an individual knows there is a warrant for her or his arrest. Court clerks told us that in some cases they deem sympathetic in their own discretion, they will cancel the warrant without a bond. Further, it appears that if a person is aware of an outstanding warrant but believes that the warrant was issued in error, that person can petition the Municipal Judge to cancel the warrant only after the bond is paid in full. If a person cannot afford to pay the bond, there is no opportunity to seek recourse from the court.

If a person is arrested on an outstanding warrant—or as the result of an encounter with FPD—it is often difficult to secure release with a bond payment, not only because of the inordinately high bond amounts discussed below, but also because of procedural obstacles. In practice, bond procedures depart from those articulated in official policy, and are arbitrary and confusing. FPD staff have told us that correctional officers have at times tried to find a warrant in the court's files to determine the bond amount owed, but have been unable to do so. This is unsurprising given the existence of what has been described to us as "drawers and drawers of warrants." In some cases, people have attempted to pay a bond to secure the release of a family member in FPD custody, but were not even seen by FPD staff. On one occasion, an FPD staff member reported to an FPD captain that a person "came to the station last night and waited to post bond for [a detainee], from 1:00 until 3:30. No one ever came up to get her money and no one informed her that she was going to have to wait that long."

b. Needlessly Requiring In-Court Appearances for Most Code Violations Imposes Unnecessary Obstacles to Resolving Cases

Ferguson requires far more defendants to appear in court than is required under state law. Under Missouri Supreme Court rules, there is a short list of violations that require the violator's appearance in court: any violation resulting in personal injury or property damage; driving while intoxicated; driving without a proper license; and attempting to elude a police officer. *See* Mo. Sup. Ct. R. 37.49. The municipal judge of each court has the discretion to expand this list of "must appears," and Ferguson's municipal court has expanded it exponentially: of 376 actively charged municipal offenses, court staff informed us that approximately 229 typically require an appearance in court before the fine can be paid, including Dog Creating Nuisance, Equipment Violations, No Passing Zone, Housing—Overgrown Vegetation, and Failure to Remove Leaf Debris. Ferguson requires these court appearances regardless of whether the individual is contesting the charges.

Requiring an individual to appear at a specific place and time to pay a citation makes it far more likely that the individual will fail to appear or pay the citation on time, quickly resulting, in Ferguson, in an arrest warrant and a suspended license. Even setting aside the fact that people often receive inaccurate information about when they must appear in court, the in-person appearance requirement imposes particular difficulties on low-wage workers, single parents, and those with limited access to reliable transportation. Requiring an individual to appear in court also imposes particular burdens on those with jobs that have set hours that may conflict with an assigned court session. Court sessions are sometimes set during the workday and sometimes in the early evening. Additionally, while court dates can be set for several months after the citation was issued, in some cases they can also be issued as early as a week after a citation is received. For example, court staff have instructed FPD officers that derelict auto violations must be set for the "very next court date even if it is just a week ... or so away." This can add an additional obstacle for those with firmly established employment schedules.

There are also historical reasons, of which the City is well-aware, that many Ferguson residents may not appear in court. Some individuals fear that if they cannot immediately pay the fines they owe, they will be arrested and sent to jail. Ferguson court staff members told us that they believe the high number of missed court appearances in their court is attributable, in part, to this popular belief. These fears are well founded. While Judge Brockmeyer has told us that he has never sentenced someone to jail time for being unable to pay a fine, we have found evidence that the Judge has held people appearing in court for contempt on account of their unwillingness to answer questions and sentenced those individuals to jail time. In December 2013, the FPD officer assigned to provide security at a court session directly emailed the City Manager to provide notice that "Judge Brockmeyer ordered [a defendant] arrested tonight after [he] refused to answer any questions and told the Judge that he had no jurisdiction. This happened on two separate occasions and with the second occasion when [the defendant] continued with his refusal to answer the Judge, he was order[ed] to be arrested and held for 10 days."[26] We also

---

26 The email reports that the defendant, a black male, was booked into jail. This email does not provide the full context of the circumstances that led to the 10-day jail sentence and further information is required to assess the appropriateness of that order. Nonetheless, the email suggests that the court jailed a defendant for refusing to answer questions, which raises significant Fifth Amendment concerns. There is also no indication as to whether the defendant was represented or, if not, was allowed or afforded

spoke with a woman who told us that, after asking questions in court, FPD officers arrested her for Contempt of Court at the instructions of the Court Clerk. Moreover, we have also received a report of an FPD officer arresting an individual at court for an outstanding warrant. In that instance, which occurred in April 2014, the individual—who was in court to make a fine payment—was approached by an FPD officer, asked to step outside of the court session, and was immediately arrested. In addition, as Ferguson's Municipal Judge confirmed, it is not uncommon for him to add charges and assess additional fines when a defendant challenges the citation that brought the defendant into court. Appearing in court in Ferguson also requires waits that can stretch into hours, sometimes outdoors in inclement weather. Many individuals report being treated dismissively, or worse, by court staff and the Municipal Judge.

Further, as Ferguson officials have told us, many people have experience with the numerous other municipal courts in St. Louis County that informs individuals' expectations about the Ferguson municipal court. Our investigation shows that other municipalities in the area have engaged in a number of practices that have the effect of discouraging people from attending court sessions. For instance, court clerks from other municipalities have told us that they have seen judges order people arrested if they appear in court with an outstanding warrant but are unable to pay the fine owed or post the bond amount listed on the warrant. Indeed, one municipal judge from a neighboring municipality told us that this practice has resulted in what he believes to be a widespread belief that those who attend court but cannot pay will be immediately arrested—a view that municipal judge says is "entirely the municipal courts' fault" for perpetuating because they have not taken steps to correct it. Recent

---

representation to defend against the contempt charge and 10-day sentence.

reports have documented other problematic practices. For example, a June 2014 letter from Presiding Circuit Court Judge Maura McShane to municipal court judges in the region discussed troubling and possibly unlawful practices of municipal courts in St. Louis County that served to prevent the public from attending court sessions. These practices included not allowing children in court. Indeed, as late as October 2014, the municipal court website in the neighboring municipality of Bel Ridge—where Judge Brockmeyer serves as prosecutor—stated that children are not allowed in court. While it appears that Ferguson's court has always allowed children, we talked with people who assumed it did not because of their experiences in other courts. One man told us he was aggressively questioned by FPD officers after he left his child outside court with a friend because of this assumption. Thus, even though Ferguson might not engage in some of these practices, and while it may even be the case that other municipalities have themselves implemented reforms, the long history of these practices continues to shape community members' views of what might happen to them if they attend court.

Court officials have told us that Ferguson's expansive list of "must appear" offenses is not driven by any public safety need. That is underscored by the fact that, in some cases, attorneys are allowed to resolve such offenses over the phone without making any appearance in court. Nonetheless, despite the acknowledged obstacles to appearing in person in court and the lack of any articulated need to appear in court in all but a few instances, Ferguson has taken few, if any, steps to reduce the number of cases that require a court appearance.

c. Driver's License Suspensions Mandated by State Law and Unnecessarily Prolonged by Ferguson Make It Difficult to Resolve a Case and Impose Substantial Hardship

For many who have already had a warrant issued against them for failing to either appear or make a required payment, appearing in court is made especially difficult by the fact that their warrants likely resulted in the suspension of their driver's licenses. Pursuant to Missouri state law, anyone who fails to pay a traffic citation for a moving violation on time, or who fails to appear in court regarding a moving traffic violation, has his or her driver's license suspended. Mo. Rev. Stat. § 302.341.1. Thus, by virtue of having their licenses suspended, those who have already missed a required court appearance are more likely to fail to meet subsequent court obligations if they require physically appearing in court—fostering a cycle of missed appearances that is difficult to end. That is particularly so given what some City officials from Ferguson and surrounding communities have called substandard public transportation options. We spoke with one woman who had her license suspended because she received a Failure to Appear charge in Ferguson and so had to rely on a friend to drive her to court. When her friend canceled, she had no other means of getting to court on time, missed court, and had another Failure to Appear charge and arrest warrant issued against her—adding to the charges that required resolution before her license could be reinstated.[27]

To be clear, responsibility for the hardship imposed by automatically suspending a person's license for failing to appear in a traffic case rests largely with this state

---

[27] While Missouri provides a process to secure a temporary waiver of a license suspension, we have heard from many that this process can be difficult and, in any case, is only available in certain circumstances.

law. Notably, however, Ferguson's own discretionary practices amplify and prolong that law's impact. A temporary suspension can be lifted with a compliance letter from the municipal court, but the Ferguson municipal court does not issue compliance letters unless a person has satisfied the *entire fine* pending on the charge that caused the suspension. This rule is not mandated by state law, which instead provides a municipality with the authority to decide when to issue a compliance letter. *See* Mo. Rev. Stat. § 302.341.1 ("Such suspension shall remain in effect until the court with the subject pending charge requests setting aside the noncompliance suspension pending final disposition."). Indeed, Ferguson court staff told us that they will issue compliance letters before full payment has been made for cases that they determine, in their unguided discretion, to be sympathetic.

This rule and the Ferguson practices that magnify its impact underscore how missed court appearances can have broad ramifications for individuals' ability to maintain a job and care for their families. We spoke with one woman who received three citations during a single incident in 2013 in which she pulled to the side of the road to allow a police car to pass, was confronted by the officer for doing so, and was cited for obstructing traffic, failing to signal, and not wearing a seatbelt. The woman appeared in court to challenge those citations, was told a new trial date would be mailed to her, and instead received notice from the Missouri Department of Revenue several months later that her license was suspended. Upon informing the Court Clerk that she never received notice of her court date, the Clerk told her the trial date had passed two weeks earlier and that there was now a warrant for her arrest pending.[28] Given that

---

28 By initiating the license suspension procedure after a single missed appearance and without first providing notice or an opportunity to remedy the missed appearance, the court appears to

the woman's license was suspended only two weeks after her trial date, it appears the court did not send a warning letter before entering a warrant and suspending the license, contrary to purported policy. Court records likewise do not indicate a letter being sent. The woman asked to see the Municipal Judge to explain the situation, but court staff informed her that she could only see the Judge if she was issued a new court date and that she would only be issued a new court date if she paid her $200 bond. With no opportunity to further petition the court, she wrote to Mayor Knowles about her situation, stating:

> Although I feel I have been harassed, wronged and unjustly done by Ferguson ... [w]hat I am upset and concerned about is my driver's license being suspended. I was told that I may not be able to [be] reinstate[d] until the tickets are taken care of. I am a hard working mother of two children and I cannot by any means take care of my family or work with my license being suspended and being unable to drive. I have to have [a] valid license to keep my job because I transport clients that I work with not to mention I drive my children back and forth to school, practices and rehearsals on a daily basis. I am writing this letter because no one has been able to help me and I am really hoping that I can get some help getting this issue resolved expediently.

---

have violated Missouri law. *See* Mo. Rev. Stat. § 302.341.1 (providing that after a missed appearance associated with a moving violation, a court "shall within ten days ... inform the defendant by ordinary mail at the last address shown on the court records that the court will order the director of revenue to suspend the defendant's driving privileges if the charges are not disposed of and fully paid within thirty days from the date of mailing").

It appears that, at the Mayor's request, the court entered "Not Guilty" dispositions on her cases, several months after they first resulted in the license suspension.

d. Court Operations Impose Obstacles to Resolving Even Those Offenses that Do Not Require In-Person Court Appearance

The limited number of code violations that do not require an in-person court appearance can likewise be difficult to resolve, even if a person can afford to do so. The court has accepted mailed payments for some time and has recently begun to accept online payments, but the court's website suggests that in-person payment is required and provides no information that payment online or by mail is an option. As a result, many people try to remit payment to the court window within the police department. But community members have informed us that the court window often closes earlier than the posted hours indicate. Indeed, during our investigation, we observed the court window close at 4:30 p.m. on days where an evening court session was not being held, despite the fact that both the Ferguson City website and the Missouri Courts website state that the window closes at 5:00 p.m.[29] On one such occasion, we observed two different sets of people arrive after 4:30 p.m. but before 5:00 p.m. One man told us his ticket payment was due that day. Another woman arrived in the rain with her small child, unsuccessfully attempted to call someone to the window, and left. Even when the court window is technically open, we have seen people standing at the window waiting for a response to their knocks for long periods

---

29 *See City Courts*, City of Ferguson, http://www.fergusoncity. com/60/The-City-Of-Ferguson-Municipal-Courts (last visited Feb. 26, 2015); *Ferguson Municipal Court*, Your Missouri Courts, http://www.courts.mo.gov/page.jsp?id=8862 (last visited Feb. 26, 2015).

of time, sometimes in inclement weather—even as court staff sat inside the police department tending to their normal duties.

As noted above, documents we reviewed showed that even where individuals are successful in talking with court staff about a citation, FPD-issued citations are sometimes so deficient that court staff are unable to determine what the fine, or even charge, is supposed to be. Evidence also shows that court staff have at times been unable to even find a person's case file, often because the FPD officer who issued the ticket failed to properly file a copy. In these cases, a person is left unable to resolve her or his citation.

e. High Fines, Coupled with Legally Inadequate Ability-to-Pay Determinations and Insufficient Alternatives to Immediate Payment, Impose a Significant Burden on People Living In or Near Poverty

It is common for a single traffic stop or other encounter with FPD to give rise to fines in amounts that a person living in poverty is unable to immediately pay. This fact is attributable in part to FPD's practice of issuing multiple citations—frequently three or more—on a single stop. This fact is also attributable to the fine assessment practices of the Ferguson municipal court, including not only the high fine amounts imposed, but also the inadequate process available for those who cannot afford to pay a fine. Even setting aside cases where additional fines and fees were imposed for Failure to Appear violations, our investigation found instances in which the court charged $302 for a single Manner of Walking violation; $427 for a single Peace Disturbance violation; $531 for High Grass and Weeds; $777 for Resisting Arrest; and $792 for Failure to Obey, and $527 for Failure to Comply, which officers appear to use interchangeably.

For many, the hardship of the fine amounts imposed is exacerbated by the fact that they owe similar fines in other, neighboring municipalities. We spoke with one woman who, in addition to owing several hundred dollars in fines to Ferguson, also owed fines to the municipal courts in Jennings and Edmundson. In total, she owed over $2,500 in fines and fees, even after already making over $1,000 in payments and clearing cases in several other municipalities. This woman's case is not unique. We have heard reports from many individuals and even City officials that, in light of the large number of municipalities in the area immediately surrounding Ferguson, most of which have their own police departments and municipal courts, it is common for people to face significant fines from many municipalities.

City officials have extolled that the Ferguson preset fine schedule establishes fines that are "at or near the top of the list" compared with other municipalities across a large number of offenses. A more recent comparison of the preset fines of roughly 70 municipal courts in the region confirms that Ferguson's fine amounts are above regional averages for many offenses, particularly discretionary offenses such as non-speeding-related traffic offenses. That comparison also shows that Ferguson imposes the highest fine of any of those roughly 70 municipalities for the offense of Failing to Provide Proof of Insurance; Ferguson charges $375, whereas the average fine imposed is $186 and the median fine imposed is $175. In 2013 alone, the Ferguson court collected over $286,000 in fines for that offense—more than any other offense except Failure to Appear.

The fines that the court imposes for offenses without preset fines are more difficult to evaluate precisely because they are imposed on a case-by-case basis. Typically, however, in imposing fines for non-TVB offenses during court sessions, the Municipal Judge adopts the fine recommendations of the Prosecuting Attorney—who also serves as the Ferguson City Attorney. As discussed above, court staff have communicated with the Municipal

Judge regarding the need to ensure that the prosecutor's recommended fines are sufficiently high because "[w]e need to keep up our revenue." We were also told of at least one incident in which an attorney received a fine recommendation from the prosecutor for his client, but when the client went to court to pay the fine, a clerk refused payment, informing her that there was an additional $100 owed beyond the fine recommended by the prosecutor.

The court imposes these fines without providing any process by which a person can seek a fine reduction on account of financial incapacity. The court does not provide any opportunity for a person unable to pay a preset TVB fine to seek a modification of the fine amount. Nor does the court consider a person's financial ability to pay in determining how much of a fine to impose in cases without preset fines. The Ferguson court's failure to assess a defendant's ability to pay stands in direct tension with Missouri law, which instructs that in determining the amount and the method of payment of a fine, a court "shall, insofar as practicable, proportion the fine to the burden that payment will impose in view of the financial resources of an individual." Mo. Rev. Stat. § 560.026.

In lieu of proportioning a fine to a particular individual's ability to pay or allowing a process by which a person could petition the court for a reduction, the court offers payment plans to those who cannot afford to immediately pay in full. But such payment plans do not serve as a substitute for an ability-to-pay determination, which, properly employed, can enable a person in some cases to pay in full and resolve the case. Moreover, the court's rules regarding payment plans are themselves severe. Unlike some other municipalities that require a $50 monthly payment, Ferguson's standard payment plan requires payments of $100 per month, which remains a difficult amount for many to pay, especially those who are also making payments to other municipalities.

Further, the court treats a single missed, partial, or untimely payment as a missed appearance. In such a case, the court immediately issues an arrest warrant without any notice or opportunity to explain why a payment was missed—for example, because the person was sick, or the court closed its doors early that day. The court reportedly has softened this rule during the course of our investigation by allowing a person who has missed a payment to go to court to seek leave for not paying the full amount owed. However, even this softened rule provides minimal relief, as making this request requires a person to appear in court the first Wednesday of the month at 11:00 a.m. If a person misses that session, the court immediately issues an arrest warrant.

Before the court provided this Wednesday morning court session for those on payment plans, court staff frequently rejected requests from payment plan participants to reduce or continue monthly payments—leaving individuals unable to make the required payment with no recourse besides incurring a Failure to Appear charge, receiving additional fines, and having an arrest warrant issued. In July 2014, an assistant court clerk wrote in an email that she rejected a defendant's request for a reduced monthly payment on account of inability to pay and told the defendant, "everyone says [they] can't pay." This is consistent with earlier noted statements by the acting Ferguson prosecutor that he stopped granting "needless requests for continuances from the payment docket." Another defendant who owed $1,002 in fines and fees stemming from a Driving with a Revoked License charge wrote to a City official that he would be unable to make his required monthly payment but hoped to avoid having a warrant issued. He explained that he was unemployed, that the court had put him on a payment plan only a week before his first payment was due, and that he did not have enough time to gather enough money. He implored the City to provide "some kind of community service to work off the fines/fees," stating that "I want to pay you guys what I owe" and "I have been trying to scrape up what I can," but that "with warrants it's hard to get a job." The City official forwarded the request to a court clerk, who noted that the underlying charge dated back to 2007, that five Failure to Appear charges had been levied, and that no payments had yet been made. The clerk responded: "In this certain case [the defendant] will go to warrant." Records show that, only a week earlier, this same clerk asked a court clerk from another municipality to clear a ticket for former Ferguson Police Chief Moonier as a "courtesy." And, only a month later, that same clerk also helped the Ferguson Collector of Revenue clear two citations issued by neighboring municipalities.

Ferguson does not typically offer community service as an alternative to fines. City officials have emphasized to us that Ferguson is one of only a few municipalities in the region to provide *any* form of a community service program, and that the program that is available is well run. But the program, which began in February 2014, is only available on a limited basis, mostly to certain defendants who are 19 years old or younger.[30] We have heard directly from individuals who could not afford to pay their fines—and thus accumulated additional charges and fines and had warrants issued against them—that they requested a community service alternative to monetary payment but were told no such alternative existed. One man who still owes $1,100 stemming from a speeding and seatbelt violation from 2000 told us that

---

30 Recently, the court has allowed some individuals over age 19 to resolve fines through community service, but that remains a rarity. *See City of Ferguson Continues Court Reform Initiative by Offering Community Service Program,* City of Ferguson (Dec. 15, 2014), http://www.fergusoncity.com/CivicAlerts. aspx?AID=370&ARC=699 (stating community service program was launched in partnership with Ferguson Youth Initiative in February 2014 "to assist teenagers and certain other defendants").

he has been arrested repeatedly in connection with the fines he cannot afford to pay, and that "no one is willing to work with him to find an alternative solution." City officials have recognized the need to provide a meaningful community service option. In August 2013, one City Councilmember wrote to the City Manager and the Mayor that, "[f]or a few years now we have talked about offering community service to those who can't afford to pay their fines, but we haven't actually made it happen." The Councilmember noted the benefits of such a program, including that it would "keep those people that simply don't have the money to pay their fines from constantly being arrested and going to jail, only to be released and do it all over again."

2. The Court Imposes Unduly Harsh Penalties for Missed Payments or Appearances

The procedural deficiencies identified above work together to make it exceedingly difficult to resolve a case and exceedingly easy to run afoul of the court's stringent and confusing rules, particularly for those living in or near poverty. That the court is at least in part responsible for causing cases to protract and result in technical violations has not prevented it from imposing significant penalties when those violations occur. Although Ferguson's court—unlike many other municipal courts in the region—has ceased imposing the Failure to Appear charge, the court continues to routinely issue arrest warrants for missed appearances and missed payments. The evidence we have found shows that these arrest warrants are used almost exclusively for the purpose of compelling payment through the threat of incarceration. The evidence also shows that the harms of the court's warrant practices are exacerbated by the court's bond procedures, which impose unnecessary obstacles to clearing a warrant or securing release after being arrested on a warrant and often function to further prolong a case and a person's involvement in the municipal justice system. These practices—together with the consequences to individuals and communities that result—raise significant due process and equal protection concerns.

a. The Ferguson Municipal Court Uses Arrest Warrants
   Primarily as a Means of Securing Payment

Ferguson uses its police department in large part as a collection agency for its municipal court. Ferguson's municipal court issues arrest warrants at a rate that police officials have called, in internal emails, "staggering." According to the court's own figures, as of December 2014, over 16,000 people had outstanding arrest warrants that had been issued by the court. In fiscal year 2013 alone, the court issued warrants to approximately 9,007 people. Many of those individuals had warrants issued on multiple charges, as the 9,007 warrants applied to 32,975 different offenses.

In the wake of several news accounts indicating that the Ferguson municipal court issued over 32,000 warrants in fiscal year 2013, court staff determined that it had mistakenly reported to the state of Missouri the number of charged offenses that had warrants (32,975), not the number of people who had warrants outstanding (9,007). Our investigation indicates that is the case. In any event, it is probative of FPD's enforcement practices that those roughly 9,000 warrants were issued for over 32,000 offenses. Moreover, for those against whom a warrant is issued, the number of offenses included within the warrant has tremendous practical importance. As discussed below, the bond amount a person must pay to clear a warrant before an arrest occurs, or to secure release once a warrant has been executed, is often dependent on the number of offenses to which the warrant applies. And, that the court issued warrants for the arrest of roughly 9,000 people is itself not insignificant; even under that calculation, Ferguson has one of the highest warrant totals in the region.

The large number of warrants issued by the court, by any count, is due exclusively to the fact that the court uses arrest warrants and the threat of arrest as its primary tool for collecting outstanding fines for municipal code violations. With extremely limited exceptions, every warrant issued by the Ferguson municipal court was issued because: 1) a person missed consecutive court appearances, or 2) a person missed a single required fine payment as part of a payment plan. Under current court policy, the court issues a warrant in every case where either of those circumstances arises—regardless of the severity of the code violation that the case involves. Indeed, the court rarely issues a warrant for any other purpose. FPD does not request arrest or any other kind of warrants from the Ferguson municipal court; in fact, FPD officers told us that they have been instructed not to file warrant applications with the municipal court because the court does not have the capacity to consider them.

While issuing municipal warrants against people who have not appeared or paid their municipal code violation fines is sometimes framed as addressing the failure to abide by court rules, in practice, it is clear that warrants are primarily issued to coerce payment.[31] One municipal judge from a neighboring municipality told us that the use of the Failure to Appear charge "provides cushion for judges against the attack that the court is operating as a debtor's prison." And the Municipal Judge in Ferguson

---

31 As stated in the Missouri Municipal Court Handbook produced by the Circuit Court: "Defendants who fail or refuse to pay their fines and costs can be extremely difficult to deal with, but if there is a credible threat of incarceration if they do not pay, the job of collection becomes much easier." Mo. Mun. Benchbook, Cir. Ct., Mun. Divs. § 13.6 (2010).

has acknowledged repeatedly that the warrants the court issues are not put in place for public safety purposes. Indeed, once a warrant issues, there is no urgency within FPD to actually execute it. Court staff reported that they typically take weeks, if not months, to enter warrants into the system that enables patrol officers to determine if a person they encounter has an outstanding warrant. As of December 2014, for example, some warrants issued in September 2014 were not yet detectable to officers in the field. Court staff also informed us that no one from FPD has ever commented on that lag or prioritized closing it. Nor does there seem to be any public safety obstacle to eliminating failure to appear warrants altogether. The court has, in fact, adopted a temporary "warrant recall program" that allows individuals who show up to court to immediately have their warrants recalled and a new court date assigned. And, under longstanding practice, once an attorney makes an appearance in a case, the court automatically discharges any pending warrants.

That the primary role of warrants is not to protect public safety but rather to facilitate fine collection is further evidenced by the fact that the warrants issued by the court are overwhelmingly issued in non-criminal traffic cases that would not themselves result in a penalty of imprisonment. From 2010 to December 2014, the offenses (besides Failure to Appear ordinance violations) that most often led to a municipal warrant were: Driving While License Is Suspended, Expired License Plates, Failure to Register a Vehicle, No Proof of Insurance, and Speed Limit violations. These offenses comprised the majority of offenses that led to a warrant not because they are more severe than other offenses, but rather because every missed appearance or payment on any charge results in a warrant, and these were some of the most common charges brought by FPD during that period.

Even though these underlying code violations would not on their own result in a penalty of imprisonment, arrest and detention are not uncommon once a warrant enters on a case. We have found that FPD officers frequently check individuals for warrants, even when the person is not reasonably suspected of engaging in any criminal activity, and, if a municipal warrant exists, will often make an arrest. City officials have told us that the decision to arrest a person for an outstanding warrant is "highly discretionary" and that officers will frequently not arrest unless the person is "ignorant." Records show, however, that officers do arrest individuals for outstanding municipal warrants with considerable frequency. Jail records are poorly managed, and data on jail bookings is only available as of April 2014. But during the roughly six-month period from April to September 2014, 256 people were booked into the Ferguson City Jail after being arrested at least in part for an outstanding warrant—96% of whom were African American. Of these individuals, 28 were held for longer than two days, and 27 of these 28 people were black.

Similarly, data collected during vehicle stops shows that, during a larger period of time between October 2012 and October 2014, FPD arrested roughly 460 individuals following a vehicle stop *solely* because they had outstanding warrants. This figure is likely a significant underrepresentation of the total number of people arrested for outstanding warrants during that period, as it does not include those people arrested on outstanding warrants not during traffic stops; nor does it include those people arrested during traffic stops for multiple reasons, but who might not have been stopped, much less arrested, without the officer performing a warrant check on the car and finding an outstanding warrant. Even among this limited pool, the data shows the disparate impact these arrests have on African Americans. Of the 460 individuals arrested during traffic stops solely for outstanding warrants, 443 individuals—or 96%—were African American.

That data also does not include those people arrested by *other* municipal police departments on the basis of an outstanding warrant issued by Ferguson. As has been widely reported in recent months, many municipal police departments in the region identify people with warrants pending in other towns and then arrest and hold those individuals on behalf of those towns. FPD's records show that it routinely arrests individuals on warrants issued by other jurisdictions. And, although we did not review the records of other departments, we have heard reports of many individuals who were arrested for a Ferguson-issued warrant by police officers outside of Ferguson. On some occasions, Ferguson will decline to pick up a person arrested in a different municipality for a Ferguson warrant and, after however long it takes for that decision to be made, the person will be released, sometimes after being required to pay bond. On other occasions, Ferguson will send an officer to retrieve the person for incarceration in the Ferguson City Jail; FPD supervisors have in fact instructed officers to do so "regardless of the charge or the bond amount, or the number of prisoners we have in custody." We found evidence of FPD officers traveling more than 200 miles to retrieve a person detained by another agency on a Ferguson municipal warrant.

Because of the large number of municipalities in the region, many of which have warrant practices similar to Ferguson, it is not unusual for a person to be arrested by one department, have outstanding warrants pending in other police departments, and be handed off from one department to another until all warrants are cleared. We have heard of individuals who have run out of money during this process—referred to by many as the "muni shuffle"—and as a result were detained for a week or longer.

The large number of municipal court warrants being issued, many of which lead to arrest, raises significant due process and equal protection concerns. In particular,

Ferguson's practice of automatically treating a missed payment as a failure to appear—thus triggering an arrest warrant and possible incarceration—is directly at odds with well-established law that prohibits "punishing a person for his poverty." *Bearden v. Georgia*, 461 U.S. 660, 671 (1983); *see also Tate v. Short*, 401 U.S. 395, 398 (1971). In *Bearden*, the Supreme Court found unconstitutional a state's decision to revoke probation and sentence a defendant to prison because the defendant was unable to pay a required fine. *Bearden*, 461 U.S. at 672-73. The Court held that before imposing imprisonment, a court must first inquire as to whether the missed payment was attributable to an inability to pay and, if so, "consider alternate measures of punishment other than imprisonment." *Id.* at 672; *see also Martin v. Solem*, 801 F.2d 324, 332 (8th Cir. 1986) (noting that the state court had failed to adequately determine, as required by *Bearden*, whether the defendant had "made sufficient bona fide efforts legally to acquire the resources to pay," but nonetheless denying habeas relief because the defendant's failure to pay was due not to indigency but his "willful refusal to pay").

The Ferguson court, however, has in the past routinely issued arrest warrants when a person is unable to make a required fine payment without any ability-to-pay determination. While the court does not *sentence* a defendant to jail in such a case, the result is often equivalent to what *Bearden* proscribes: the incarceration of a defendant solely because of an inability to pay a fine. In response to concerns about issuing warrants in such cases, Ferguson officials have told us that without issuing warrants and threatening incarceration, they have no ability to secure payment. But the Supreme Court rejected that argument, finding that states are "not powerless to enforce judgments against those financially unable to pay a fine," and noting that—especially in cases like those at issue here in which the court has already made a determination that penological interests do *not* demand incarceration—a court can "establish a reduced fine or alternate public service in lieu of a fine that adequately serves the state's goals of punishment and deterrence, given the defendant's diminished financial resources."[32] *Id.* As discussed above, however, Ferguson has not established any such alternative.[33]

Finally, in light of the significant portion of municipal charges that lead to an arrest warrant, as well as the substantial number of arrest warrants that lead to arrest and detention, we have considerable concerns regarding whether individuals facing charges in Ferguson municipal court are entitled to, and being unlawfully denied, the right to counsel.

---

32 Ferguson officials have also told us that the arrest warrant is issued not because of the missed payment per se, but rather because the person missing the payment failed to abide by the court's rules. But the Supreme Court has rejected that contention, too. In *Bearden,* the Court noted that the sentencing court's stated concern "was that the petitioner had disobeyed a prior court order to pay the fine," but found that the sentence nonetheless "is no more than imprisoning a person solely because he lacks funds" to pay. *Bearden,* 461 U.S. at 674.

33 Additionally, Ferguson's municipal code provides: "When a sentence for violation of any provision of this Code or other ordinance of the city ... includes a fine and such fine is not paid, or if the costs of prosecution adjudged against an offender are not paid, the person under sentence shall be imprisoned one day for every ten dollars ($10.00) of any such unpaid fine or costs ... not to exceed a total of four (4) months." Ferguson Mun. Code § 1-16. Our investigation did not uncover any evidence that the court has sentenced anyone to imprisonment pursuant to this statute in the past several years. Nonetheless, it is concerning that this statute, which unconstitutionally sanctions imprisonment for failing to pay a fine, remains in effect. *Cf. Bearden v. Georgia,* 461 U.S. 660, 671 (1983).

b. Ferguson's Bond Practices Impose Undue Hardship on Those Seeking to Secure Release from the Ferguson City Jail

Our investigation found substantial deficiencies in the way Ferguson police and court officials set, accept, refund, and forfeit bond payments. Recently, in response to concerns raised during our investigation, the City implemented several changes to its bond practices, most of which apply to those detained after a warrantless arrest.[34] These changes represent positive developments, but many deficiencies remain.[35] Given the high number of arrest warrants issued by the municipal court—and given that in many cases a person can only clear a pending warrant or secure release from detention by posting bond—the deficiencies identified below impose significant harm to individuals in Ferguson.

---

34 In December 2014, the court set forth a bond schedule for warrantless arrests, which provides that, for all but 14 code violations, a person arrested pursuant to a municipal code violation and brought to Ferguson City Jail shall be issued a citation or summons and released on his or her own recognizance without any bond payment required. For those 14 code violations requiring a bond, the court has set "fixed" bond amounts, although these are subject to the court's discretion to raise or lower those amounts at the request of the City or the detained individual. The court's recent order further provides that, even if an individual does not pay the bond required, he or she shall in any case be released after 12 hours, rather than the previous 72-hour limit.

35 For example, the recent orders fail to specify that, in considering whether to adjust the bond imposed, the court shall make an assessment of an individual's ability to pay, and assign bond proportionately. *Cf. Pugh v. Rainwater*, 572 F.2d 1053, 1057 (5th Cir. 1978) (en banc) (noting that the incarceration of those who cannot afford to meet the requirements of a fixed bond schedule "without meaningful consideration of other possible alternatives" infringes on due process and equal protection requirements).

Current bond practices are unclear and inconsistent. Information provided by the City reveals a haphazard bond system that results in people being erroneously arrested, and some people paying bond but not getting credit for having done so. Documents describe officers finding hundred dollar bills in their pockets that were given to them for bond payment and not remembering which jail detainee provided them; bond paperwork being found on the floor; and individuals being arrested after their bonds had been accepted because the corresponding warrants were never cancelled. At one point in 2012, Ferguson's Court Clerk called such issues a "daily problem." The City's practices for receiving and tracking bond payments have not changed appreciably since then.

The practices for setting bond are similarly erratic. The Municipal Judge advised us that he sets all bonds upon issuing an arrest warrant. We found, however, that bond amounts are mostly set by court staff, and are rarely even reviewed by the Judge. While court staff told us that the current bond schedule requires a bond of $200 for up to four traffic offenses, $100 for every traffic offense thereafter, $100 for every Failure to Appear charge, and $300 for every criminal offense, FPD's own policy includes a bond schedule that departs from these figures. In practice, bond amounts vary widely. *See* FPD General Order 421.02. Our review of a random sample of warrants indicates that bond is set in a manner that often departs from both the schedule referenced by court staff and the schedule found in FPD policy. In a number of these cases, the bond amount far exceeded the amount of the underlying fine.

The court's bond practices, including the fact that the court often imposes bonds that exceed the amount owed to the court, do not appear to be grounded in any public safety need. In a July 2014 email to Chief Jackson and other police officials, the Court Clerk reported that "[s]tarting today we are going to reduce anyone's bond that calls and is in warrant[] to half the amount," explaining that "[t]his may bring in some extra monies this way." The email identifies no public safety obstacle or other reason not to implement the bond reduction. Notably, the email also states that "[w]e will only do this between the hours of 8:30 to 4" and that no half-bond will be accepted after those hours unless the Court Clerk approves it.[36] Thus, as a result of this policy, an individual able to appear at the court window during business hours would pay half as much to clear a warrant as an individual who is actually arrested on a warrant after hours. That Ferguson's bond practices do not appear grounded in public safety is underscored by the fact that the court will typically cancel outstanding warrants without requiring the posting of *any* bond for people who have an attorney enter an appearance on their behalf. Records show that this practice is also applied haphazardly, and there do not appear to be any rules that govern the apparent discretion court staff have to waive or require bond following an attorney's appearance.

It is not uncommon for an individual charged with only a minor violation to be arrested on a warrant, be unable to afford bond, and have no recourse but to await release. Longstanding court rules provide for a person arrested pursuant to an arrest warrant to be held up to 72 hours before being released without bond, and the court's recent orders do not appear to change this. Records show that individuals are routinely held for 72 hours. FPD's records management system only began capturing meaningful jail data in April 2014; but from April to September 2014 alone, 77 people were detained in the jail for longer than two days, and many of those detentions neared, reached, or exceeded the 72-hour mark. Of those 77 people, 73, or 95%, were black. Many

---

36 The court's website states that the court window is open from 8:30 a.m. to 5:00 p.m., not 4:00 p.m. *See City Courts,* City of Ferguson, http://www.fergusoncity.com/60/The-City-Of-Ferguson-Municipal-Courts (last visited Feb. 26, 2015).

people, including the woman described earlier who was charged with two parking code violations, have reported being held up until the 72-hour limit—despite having no ability to pay.

Indeed, many others report being held for far longer, and documentary evidence is consistent with these reports. In April 2010, for example, the Chief of Police wrote an email to the Captain of the Patrol Division stating that the "intent is that when the watch commander / street supervisor gets the census from the jail he asks who will come up on 72 hrs.," and, if there is any such person, "he can have them given the next available court date and released, or authorize they remain in jail, since he will be the designate." The email continues: "If someone has already been there more than 72 hours, it may be assumed their continued hold was previously authorized." Further, as noted above, while comprehensive jail records do not exist for detentions prior to April 2014, records do show several recent instances in which FPD detained a person for longer than the purported 72-hour limit.

Despite the fact that those arrested by FPD for outstanding municipal warrants can be held for several days if unable to post bond, the Ferguson municipal court does not give credit for time served. As a result, there have been many cases in which a person has been arrested on a warrant, detained for 72 hours or more, and released owing the same amount as before the arrest was made. Court records do not even track the total amount of time a person has spent in jail as part of a case. When asked why this is not tracked, a member of court staff told us: "It's only three days anyway."

These prolonged detentions for those who cannot afford bond are alarming, and raise considerable due process and equal protection concerns. The prolonged detentions are especially concerning given that there is no public safety need for those who receive municipal warrants to be jailed at all. The Ferguson Municipal

Judge has acknowledged that for most code violations, it is "probably a good idea to do away with jail time."

Further, there are many circumstances in which court practices preclude a person from making payment against the underlying fine owed—and thus resolving the case, or at least moving the case toward resolution—and instead force the person to pay a bond. If, for example, an individual is jailed on a "must appear" charge and has not yet appeared in court to have the fine assessed, the individual will not be allowed to make payment on the underlying charge. Rather, the person must post bond, receive a new court date, appear in court, and start the process anew. Even when the underlying fine has been assessed, a person in jail may still be forced to make a bond payment instead of a fine payment to secure release if court staff are unavailable to determine the amount the person owes. And when a person attempts to resolve a warrant before they end up arrested, a bond payment will typically be required unless the person can afford to pay the underlying fine in full, as, by purported policy, the court does not accept partial payment of fines outside of a court-sanctioned payment plan.

Bond forfeiture procedures also raise significant due process concerns. Under current practice, the first missed appearance or missed payment following a bond payment results in a warning letter being sent; after the second missed appearance or payment, the court initiates a forfeiture action (and issues another arrest warrant). As with "warrant warning letters" described above, our investigation has been unable to verify that the court *consistently* sends bond forfeiture warning letters. And, as with warrant warning letters, bond forfeiture warning letters are sometimes returned to the court, but court staff members do not appear to make any further attempt to contact the intended recipient.

Upon a bond being forfeited, the court directs the bond money into the City's account and does not apply the amount to the individual's underlying fine. For example, if a person owes a $200 fine payment, is arrested on a warrant, and posts a bond of $200, the forfeiture of the bond will result in the fine remaining $200 and an arrest warrant being issued. If, instead, Ferguson were to allow this $200 to go toward the underlying fine, this would resolve the matter entirely, obviating the need for any warrant or subsequent court appearance. Not applying a forfeited bond to the underlying fine is especially troubling considering that this policy does not appear to be clearly communicated to those paying bonds. Particularly in cases where the bond is set at an amount near the underlying fine owed—which we have found to be common—it is entirely plausible that a person paying bond would mistakenly believe that payment resolves the case.

When asked why the forfeited bond is not applied to the underlying fine, court staff asserted that applicable law prohibits them from doing so without the bond payer's consent.[37] That explanation is grounded in an incorrect view of the law. In *Perry v. Aversman,* 168 S.W.3d 541 (Mo. Ct. App. 2005), the Missouri Court of Appeals explicitly upheld a rule requiring that forfeited bonds be applied to pending fines of the person who paid bond and found that such practices are acceptable so long as the court provides sufficient notice. *Id.* at 543-46. In light of the fact that applicable law permits forfeited bonds to be applied to pending fines, Ferguson's longstanding

---

[37] Critically, however, when a person attends court after paying a bond and is assessed a fine, court staff members *do* automatically apply the bond already paid to the fine owed, and in fact require application of the bond to the fine regardless of the defendant's wishes. Thus, the court has simultaneously asserted that it *can* apply a bond to a fine without a defendant's consent when the bond would otherwise be returned to the defendant, but that it *cannot* apply a bond to a fine without a defendant's consent when the bond would otherwise be forfeited into the City's own accounts.

practice of directing forfeited bond money to the City's general fund is troubling. In fiscal year 2013 alone, the City collected forfeited bond amounts of $177,168, which could instead have been applied to the fines of those making the payments.

Ferguson's rules and procedures for *refunding* bond payments upon satisfaction of the underlying fine raise similar concerns. Ferguson requires that when a person pays the underlying fine to avoid bond forfeiture, he or she must pay in person and provide photo identification. Yet, where the underlying fine is less than the bond amount—a common occurrence—the City does not immediately refund the difference to the individual. Rather, pursuant to a directive issued by the current City Finance Director approximately four years ago, bond refunds *cannot* be made in person, and instead must be sent via mail. According to Ferguson's Court Clerk, it is not entirely uncommon for these refund checks to be returned as undeliverable and become "unclaimed property."

C. Ferguson Law Enforcement Practices Disproportionately Harm Ferguson's African-American Residents and Are Driven in Part by Racial Bias

Ferguson's police and municipal court practices disproportionately harm African Americans. Further, our investigation found substantial evidence that this harm stems in part from intentional discrimination in violation of the Constitution.

African Americans experience disparate impact in nearly every aspect of Ferguson's law enforcement system. Despite making up 67% of the population, African Americans accounted for 85% of FPD's traffic stops, 90% of FPD's citations, and 93% of FPD's arrests from 2012 to 2014. Other statistical disparities, set forth in detail below, show that in Ferguson:

- African Americans are 2.07 times more likely to be searched during a vehicular stop but are 26% less likely to have contraband found on them during a search. They are 2.00 times more likely to receive a citation and 2.37 times more likely to be arrested following a vehicular stop.
- African Americans have force used against them at disproportionately high rates, accounting for 88% of all cases from 2010 to August 2014 in which an FPD officer reported using force. In all 14 uses of force involving a canine bite for which we have information about the race of the person bitten, the person was African American.
- African Americans are more likely to receive multiple citations during a single incident, receiving four or more citations on 73 occasions between October 2012 and July 2014, whereas non-African Americans received four or more citations only twice during that period.
- African Americans account for 95% of Manner of Walking charges; 94% of all Fail to Comply charges; 92% of all Resisting Arrest charges; 92% of all Peace Disturbance charges; and 89% of all Failure to Obey charges.[38]
- African Americans are 68% less likely than others to have their cases dismissed by the Municipal Judge, and in 2013 African Americans accounted for 92% of cases in which an arrest warrant was issued.
- African Americans account for 96% of known arrests made exclusively because of an outstanding municipal warrant.

---

38 As noted above, FPD charges violations of Municipal Code Section 29-16 as both Failure to Obey and Failure to Comply. Court data carries forward this inconsistency.

These disparities are not the necessary or unavoidable results of legitimate public safety efforts. In fact, the practices that lead to these disparities in many ways undermine law enforcement effectiveness. *See, e.g.,* Jack Glaser, *Suspect Race: Causes and Consequence of Racial Profiling* 96-126 (2015) (because profiling can increase crime while harming communities, it has a "high risk" of contravening the core police objectives of controlling crime and promoting public safety). The disparate impact of these practices thus violates federal law, including Title VI and the Safe Streets Act.

The racially disparate impact of Ferguson's practices is driven, at least in part, by intentional discrimination in violation of the Equal Protection Clause of the Fourteenth Amendment. Racial bias and stereotyping is evident from the facts, taken together. This evidence includes: the consistency and magnitude of the racial disparities throughout Ferguson's police and court enforcement actions; the selection and execution of police and court practices that disproportionately harm African Americans and do little to promote public safety; the persistent exercise of discretion to the detriment of African Americans; the apparent consideration of race in assessing threat; and the historical opposition to having African Americans live in Ferguson, which lingers among some today. We have also found explicit racial bias in the communications of police and court supervisors and that some officials apply racial stereotypes, rather than facts, to explain the harm African Americans experience due to Ferguson's approach to law enforcement. "Determining whether invidious discriminatory purpose was a motivating factor demands a sensitive inquiry into such circumstantial and direct evidence of intent as may be available." *Vill. of Arlington Heights v. Metro. Hous. Dev. Corp.,* 429 U.S. 252, 266 (1977). Based on this evidence as a whole, we have found that Ferguson's law enforcement activities stem in part from a discriminatory purpose and thus deny African Americans equal protection of the laws in violation of the Constitution.

1. Ferguson's Law Enforcement Actions Impose a Disparate Impact on African Americans that Violates Federal Law

African Americans are disproportionately represented at nearly every stage of Ferguson law enforcement, from initial police contact to final disposition of a case in municipal court. While FPD's data collection and retention practices are deficient in many respects, the data that is collected by FPD is sufficient to allow for meaningful and reliable analysis of racial disparities. This data—collected directly by police and court officials—reveals racial disparities that are substantial and consistent across a wide range of police and court enforcement actions.

African Americans experience the harms of the disparities identified below as part of a comprehensive municipal justice system that, at each juncture, enforces the law more harshly against black people than others. The disparate impact of Ferguson's enforcement actions is compounding: at each point in the enforcement process there is a higher likelihood that an African American will be subjected to harsher treatment; accordingly, as the adverse consequences imposed by Ferguson grow more and more severe, those consequences are imposed more and more disproportionately against African Americans. Thus, while 85% of FPD's vehicle stops are of African Americans, 90% of FPD's citations are issued to African Americans, and 92% of all warrants are issued in cases against African Americans. Strikingly, available data shows that of those subjected to one of the most severe actions this system routinely imposes—actual arrest for an outstanding municipal warrant—96% are African American.

a. Disparate Impact of FPD Practices

i. Disparate Impact of FPD Enforcement Actions Arising from Vehicular Stops

Pursuant to Missouri state law on racial profiling, Mo. Rev. Stat. § 590.650, FPD officers are required to collect race and other data during every traffic stop. While some law enforcement agencies collect more comprehensive data to identify and stem racial profiling, this information is sufficient to show that FPD practices exert a racially disparate impact along several dimensions.

FPD reported 11,610 vehicle stops between October 2012 and October 2014. African Americans accounted for 85%, or 9,875, of those stops, despite making up only 67% of the population. White individuals made up 15%, or 1,735, of stops during that period, despite representing 29% of the population. These differences indicate that FPD traffic stop practices may disparately impact black drivers.[39] Even setting aside the question of

---

39 While there are limitations to using basic population data as a benchmark when evaluating whether there are racial disparities in vehicle stops, it is sufficiently reliable here. In fact, in Ferguson, black drivers might account for *less* of the driving pool than would be expected from overall population rates because a lower proportion of blacks than whites is at or above the minimum driving age. *See 2009-2013 5-Year American Community Survey*, U.S. Census Bureau (2015) (showing higher proportion of black population in under-15 and under-19 age categories than white population). Ferguson officials have told us that they believe that black drivers account for *more* of the driving pool than their 67% share of the population because the driving pool also includes drivers traveling from neighboring municipalities—many of which have higher black populations than Ferguson. Our investigation casts doubt upon that claim. An analysis of zip-code data from the 53,850 summonses FPD issued from January 1, 2009 to October 14, 2014, shows that the African-American makeup for

whether there are racial disparities in FPD's traffic *stop* practices, however, the data collected during those stops reliably shows statistically significant racial disparities in the *outcomes* people receive *after* being stopped. Unlike with vehicle stops, assessing the disparate impact of post-stop outcomes—such as the rate at which stops result in citations, searches, or arrests—is not dependent on population data or on assumptions about differential offending rates by race; instead, the enforcement actions imposed against stopped black drivers are compared directly to the enforcement actions imposed against stopped white drivers.

In Ferguson, traffic stops of black drivers are more likely to lead to searches, citations, and arrests than are stops of white drivers. Black people are significantly more likely to be searched during a traffic stop than white people. From October 2012 to October 2014, 11% of stopped black drivers were searched, whereas only 5% of stopped white drivers were searched.

Despite being searched at higher rates, African Americans are 26% *less* likely to have contraband found on them than whites: 24% of searches of African Americans resulted in a contraband finding, whereas 30% of searches of whites resulted in a contraband finding. This disparity exists even after controlling for the type of search conducted, whether a search incident to arrest, a consent search, or a search predicated on reasonable suspicion. The lower rate at which officers find contraband when searching African Americans indicates either that officers' suspicion of criminal wrongdoing is less likely to be accurate when interacting with African Americans or that officers are more likely to search

---

all zip codes receiving a summons—weighted by population size and the number of summonses received by people from that zip code—is 63%. Thus, there is substantial reason to believe that the share of drivers in Ferguson who are black is in fact *lower* than population data suggests.

African Americans without any suspicion of criminal wrongdoing. Either explanation suggests bias, whether explicit or implicit.[40] This lower hit rate for African Americans also underscores that this disparate enforcement practice is ineffective.

Other, more subtle indicators likewise show meaningful disparities in FPD's search practices: of the 31 *Terry* stop searches FPD conducted during this period between October 2012 to October 2014, 30 were of black individuals; of the 103 times FPD asked both the driver and passenger to exit a vehicle during a search, the searched individuals were black in 95 cases; and, while only one search of a white person lasted more than half an hour (1% of all searches of white drivers), 59 searches of African Americans lasted that long (5% of all searches of black drivers).

Of all stopped black drivers, 91%, or 8,987, received citations, while 87%, or 1,501, of all stopped white drivers received a citation.[41] 891 stopped black drivers—10% of all stopped black drivers—were arrested as a result of the stop, whereas only 63 stopped white drivers—4% of all stopped white drivers—were arrested. This disparity

---

40 Assessing contraband or "hit rates" is a generally accepted practice in the field of criminology to "operationaliz[e] the concept of 'intent to discriminate.'" The test shows "bias against a protected group if the success rate of searches on that group is lower than on another group." Nicola Persico & Petra Todd, *The Hit Rates Test for Racial Bias in Motor-Vehicle Searches*, 25 Justice Quarterly 37, 52 (2008). Indeed, as noted below, in assessing whether racially disparate impact is motivated by discriminatory intent for Equal Protection Clause purposes, disparity can itself provide probative evidence of discriminatory intent.

41 As noted above, African Americans received 90% of all citations issued by FPD from October 2012 to July 2014. This data shows that 86% of people receiving citations following an FPD traffic stop between October 2012 and October 2014 were African American.

is explainable in large part by the high number of black individuals arrested for outstanding municipal warrants issued for missed court payments and appearances. As we discuss below, African Americans are more likely to have warrants issued against them than whites and are more likely to be arrested for an outstanding warrant than their white counterparts. Notably, on 14 occasions FPD listed the only reason for an arrest following a traffic stop as "resisting arrest." In all 14 of those cases, the person arrested was black.

These disparities in the outcomes that result from traffic stops remain even after regression analysis is used to control for non-race-based variables, including driver age; gender; the assignment of the officer making the stop; disparities in officer behavior; and the stated reason the stop was initiated. Upon accounting for differences in those variables, African Americans remained 2.07 times more likely to be searched; 2.00 times more likely to receive a citation; and 2.37 times more likely to be arrested than other stopped individuals. Each of these disparities is statistically significant and would occur by chance less than one time in 1,000.[42] The odds of these disparities occurring by chance together are significantly lower still.

ii. Disparate Impact of FPD's Multiple Citation Practices

The substantial racial disparities that exist within the data collected from traffic stops are consistent with the disparities found throughout FPD's practices. As discussed above, our investigation found that FPD officers frequently make discretionary choices to issue multiple citations during a single incident. Setting aside the fact

---

42 It is generally accepted practice in the field of statistics to consider any result that would occur by chance less than five times out of 100 to be statistically significant.

that, in some cases, citations are redundant and impose duplicative penalties for the same offense, the issuance of multiples citations also disproportionately impacts African Americans. In 2013, for instance, more than 50% of all African Americans cited received multiple citations during a single encounter with FPD, whereas only 26% of non-African Americans did. Specifically, 26% of African Americans receiving a citation received two citations at once, whereas only 17% of white individuals received two citations at once. Those disparities are even greater for incidents that resulted in more than two citations: 15% of African Americans cited received three citations at the same time, whereas 6% of cited whites received three citations; and while 10% of cited African Americans received four or more citations at once, only 3% of cited whites received that many during a single incident. Each of these disparities is statistically significant, and would occur by chance less than one time in 1,000. Indeed, related data from an overlapping time period shows that, between October 2012 to July 2014, 38 black individuals received four citations during a single incident, compared with only two white individuals; and while 35 black individuals received five or more citations at once, not a single white person did.[43]

iii. Disparate Impact of Other FPD Charging Practices

From October 2012 to July 2014, African Americans accounted for 85%, or 30,525, of the 35,871 *total* charges brought by FPD—including traffic citations, summonses, and arrests. Non-African Americans accounted for 15%,

---

43 Similar to the post-stop outcome disparities—which show disparities in FPD practices after an initial stop has been made—these figures show disparities in FPD practices after a decision to issue a citation has been made. Thus, these disparities are not based in any part on population data.

or 5,346, of all charges brought during that period.[44] These rates vary somewhat across different offenses. For example, African Americans represent a relatively low proportion of those charged with Driving While Intoxicated and Speeding on State Roads or Highways. With respect to speeding offenses for all roads, African Americans account for 72% of citations based on radar or laser, but 80% of citations based on other or unspecified methods. Thus, as evaluated by radar, African Americans violate the law at lower rates than as evaluated by FPD officers. Indeed, controlling for other factors, the disparity in speeding tickets between African Americans and non-African Americans is 48% larger when citations are issued not on the basis of radar or laser, but by some other method, such as the officer's own visual assessment. This difference is statistically significant.

Data on charges issued by FPD from 2011-2013 shows that, for numerous municipal offenses for which FPD officers have a high degree of discretion in charging, African Americans are disproportionately represented relative to their representation in Ferguson's population. While African Americans make up 67% of Ferguson's population, they make up 95% of Manner of Walking in Roadway charges; 94% of Failure to Comply charges; 92% of Resisting Arrest charges; 92% of Peace Disturbance

---

44 Although the state-mandated racial profiling data collected during traffic stops captures ethnicity in addition to race, most other FPD reports capture race only. As a result, these figures for non-African Americans include not only whites, but also non-black Latinos. That FPD's data collection methods do not consistently capture ethnicity does not affect this report's analysis of the disparate impact imposed on African Americans, but it has prevented an analysis of whether FPD practices also disparately impact Latinos. In 2010, Latinos comprised 1% of Ferguson's population. *See 2010 Census*, U.S. Census Bureau (2010), *available at* http://factfinder.census.gov/bkmk/table/1.0/en/DEC/10_SF1/QTP3/1600000US2923986 (last visited Feb. 26, 2015).

charges; and 89% of Failure to Obey charges. Because these non-traffic offenses are more likely to be brought against persons who actually live in Ferguson than are vehicle stops, census data here does provide a useful benchmark for whether a pattern of racially disparate policing appears to exist. These disparities mean that African Americans in Ferguson bear the overwhelming burden of FPD's pattern of unlawful stops, searches, and arrests with respect to these highly discretionary ordinances.

iv. Disparate Impact of FPD Arrests for Outstanding Warrants

FPD records show that once a warrant issues, racial disparities in FPD's warrant execution practices make it exceedingly more likely for a black individual with an outstanding warrant to be arrested than a white individual with an outstanding warrant. Arrest data captured by FPD often fails to identify when a person is arrested *solely* on account of an outstanding warrant. Nonetheless, the data FPD collects during traffic stops pursuant to Missouri state requirements does capture information regarding when arrests are made for no other reason than that an arrest warrant was pending. Based upon that data, from October 2012 to October 2014, FPD arrested 460 individuals exclusively because the person had an outstanding arrest warrant. Of those 460 people arrested, 443, or 96%, were black. That African Americans are disproportionately impacted by FPD's warrant execution practices is also reflected in the fact that, during the roughly six-month period from April to September 2014, African Americans accounted for 96% of those booked into the Ferguson City Jail at least *in part* because they were arrested for an outstanding municipal warrant.

v. Concerns Regarding Pedestrian Stops

Although available data enables an assessment of the disparate impact of many FPD practices, many other practices cannot be assessed statistically because of FPD's inadequate data collection. FPD does not reliably collect or track data regarding pedestrian stops, or FPD officers' conduct during those stops. Given this lack of data, we are unable to determine whether African Americans are disproportionately the subjects of pedestrian stops, or the rate of searches, arrests, or other post-pedestrian stop outcomes. We note, however, that during our investigation we have spoken with not only black community members who have been stopped by FPD officers, but also non-black community members and employees of local businesses who have observed FPD conduct pedestrian stops of others, all of whom universally report that pedestrian stops in Ferguson almost always involve African-American youth. Even though FPD does not specifically track pedestrian stops, other FPD records are consistent with those accounts. Arrest and other incident reports sometimes describe encounters that begin with pedestrian stops, almost all of which involve African Americans.

b. Disparate Impact of Court Practices

Our investigation has also found that the rules and practices of the Ferguson municipal court also exert a disparate impact on African Americans. As discussed above, once a charge is filed in Ferguson municipal court, a number of procedural barriers imposed by the court combine to make it unnecessarily difficult to resolve the charge. Data created and maintained by the court show that black defendants are significantly more likely to be adversely impacted by those barriers. An assessment of every charge filed in Ferguson municipal court in 2011 shows that, over time, black defendants are more likely to have their cases persist for longer durations, more likely to face a higher number of mandatory court appearances and other requirements, and more likely to have a warrant issued against them for failing to meet those requirements.[45]

In light of the opaque court procedures previously discussed, the likelihood of running afoul of a court requirement increases when a case lasts for a longer period of time and results in more court encounters. Court cases involving black individuals typically last longer than those involving white individuals. Of the 2,369 charges filed against white defendants in 2011, over 63% were closed after six months. By contrast, only 34% of the 10,984 charges against black defendants were closed within that time period. 10% of black defendants, however, resolved their case between six months and a year from when it was filed, while 9% of white defendants required that much time to secure resolution. And, while 17% of black defendants resolved their charge over a year after it was brought against them, only 9% of white defendants required that much time. Each of these cases was ultimately resolved, in most instances by satisfying debts owed to the court; but this data shows substantial disparities between blacks and whites regarding how long it took to do so.

On average, African Americans are also more likely to have a high number of "events" occur before a case is resolved. The court's records track all activities that occur in a case—from payments and court appearances to continuances and Failure to Appear charges. 11% of cases involving African Americans had three "events," whereas 10% of cases involving white defendants had

---

45 The universe of cases in this and subsequent analyses consisted of cases filed in 2011 because, given that some cases endure for years, a more recent sample would have excluded a greater amount of data from case events that have not yet occurred.

three events. 14% of cases involving black defendants had four to five events, compared with 9% of cases involving white defendants. Those disparities increase as the recorded number of events per case increases. Data show that there are ten or more events in 17% of cases involving black defendants but only 5% of cases involving white defendants. Given that an "event" can represent a variety of different kinds of occurrences, these particular disparities are perhaps less probative; nonetheless, they strongly suggest that black defendants have, on average, more encounters with the court during a single case than their white peers.

Given the figures above, it is perhaps unsurprising that the municipal court's practice of issuing warrants to compel fine payments following a missed court appearance or missed payment has a disparate impact on black defendants. 92% of all warrants issued in 2013 were issued in cases involving an African-American defendant. This figure is disproportionate to the representation of African Americans in the court's docket. Although the proportion of court cases involving black defendants has increased in recent years—81% of all cases filed in 2009, compared with 85% of all cases filed in 2013—that proportion remains substantially below the proportion of warrants issued to African Americans.

These disparities are consistent with the evidence discussed above that African Americans are often unable to resolve municipal charges despite taking appropriate steps to do so, and the evidence discussed below suggesting that court officials exercise discretion in a manner that disadvantages the African Americans that appear before the court.

Notably, the evidence suggests that African Americans are not only disparately impacted by court procedures, but also by the court's discretionary rulings in individual cases. Although court data did not enable a comprehensive assessment of disparities in fines that the court imposes, we did review fine data regarding ten different offenses and offense categories, including the five highly discretionary offenses disproportionately brought against African Americans noted above.[46] That analysis suggests that there may be racial disparities in the court's fine assessment practices. In analyzing the initial fines assessed for those ten offenses for each year from 2011-2013—30 data points in total—the average fine assessment was higher for African Americans than others in 26 of the 30 data points. For example, among the 53 Failure to Obey charges brought in 2013 that did not lead to added Failure to Appear fines—44 of which involved an African-American defendant—African Americans were assessed an average fine of $206, whereas the average fine for others was $147. The magnitude of racial disparities in fine amounts varied across the 30 yearly offense averages analyzed, but those disparities consistently disfavored African Americans.

Further, an evaluation of dismissal rates throughout the life of a case shows that, on average, an African-American defendant is 68% less likely than other defendants to have a case dismissed. In addition to cases that are "Dismissed," court records also show cases that are "Voided" altogether. There are only roughly 400 cases listed as Voided from 2011-2013, but the data that is available for that relatively small number of Voided cases shows that African Americans are three times less likely to receive the Voided outcome than others.

---

46 The ten offenses or offense categories analyzed include: 1) Manner of Walking in Roadway; 2) Failure to Comply; 3) Resisting Arrest; 4) Peace Disturbance; 5) Failure to Obey; 6) High Grass and Weeds; 7) One Headlight; 8) Expired License Plate; 9) aggregated data for 14 different parking violation offenses; and 10) aggregated data for four different headlight offenses, including: One Headlight; Defective Headlights; No Headlights; and Failure to Maintain Headlights.

c. Ferguson's Racially Disparate Practices Violate Federal Law

This data shows that police and court practices impose a disparate impact on black individuals that itself violates the law. Title VI and the Safe Streets Act prohibit law enforcement agencies that receive federal financial assistance, such as FPD, from engaging in law enforcement activities that have an unnecessary disparate impact based on race, color, or national origin. 42 U.S.C. § 2000d. Title VI's implementing regulations prohibit law enforcement agencies from using "criteria or methods of administration" that have an unnecessary disparate impact based on race, color, or national origin. 28 C.F.R. § 42.104(b)(2); *see also Alexander v. Sandoval*, 532 U.S. 275, 281-82 (2001). Similarly, the Safe Streets Act applies not only to intentional discrimination, but also to any law enforcement practices that unnecessarily disparately impact an identified group based on the enumerated factors. 28 C.F.R. § 42.203. *Cf. Charleston Housing Authority v. USDA*, 419 F.3d 729, 741-42 (8th Cir. 2005) (finding in the related Fair Housing Act context that where official action imposes a racially disparate impact, the action can only be justified through a showing that it is necessary to non-discriminatory objectives).

Thus, under these statutes, the discriminatory impact of Ferguson's law enforcement practices—which is both unnecessary and avoidable—is unlawful regardless of whether it is intentional or not. As set forth below, these practices also violate the prohibitions against intentional discrimination contained within Title VI, the Safe Streets Act, and the Fourteenth Amendment.

2. Ferguson's Law Enforcement Practices Are Motivated in Part by Discriminatory Intent in Violation of the Fourteenth Amendment and Other Federal Laws

The race-based disparities created by Ferguson's law enforcement practices cannot be explained by chance or by any difference in the rates at which people of different races adhere to the law. These disparities occur, at least in part, because Ferguson law enforcement practices are directly shaped and perpetuated by racial bias. Those practices thus operate in violation of the Fourteenth Amendment's Equal Protection Clause, which prohibits discriminatory policing on the basis of race. *Whren*, 517 U.S. at 813; *Johnson v. Crooks*, 326 F.3d 995, 999 (8th Cir. 2003).[47]

An Equal Protection Clause violation can occur where, as here, the official administration of facially neutral laws or policies results in a discriminatory effect that is motivated, at least in part, by a discriminatory purpose. *See Washington v. Davis*, 426 U.S. 229, 239-40 (1976). In assessing whether a given practice stems from a discriminatory purpose, courts conduct a "sensitive inquiry into such circumstantial and direct evidence of intent as may be available," including historical background, contemporaneous statements by decision makers, and substantive departures from normal procedure. *Vill. of Arlington Heights*, 429 U.S. at 266; *United States v. Bell*, 86 F.3d 820, 823 (8th Cir. 1996). To violate the Equal Protection Clause, official action need not rest *solely* on racially discriminatory purposes; rather, official action violates the Equal Protection Clause if it is motivated,

---

47 Ferguson's discriminatory practices also violate Title VI and the Safe Streets Act, which, in addition to prohibiting some forms of unintentional conduct that has a disparate impact based on race, also prohibit intentionally discriminatory conduct that has a disparate impact. *See* 42 U.S.C. § 2000d; 42 U.S.C. § 3789d.

at least in part, by discriminatory purpose. *Personnel Adm'r of Mass. v. Feeney*, 442 U.S. 256, 279 (1979).

We have uncovered significant evidence showing that racial bias has impermissibly played a role in shaping the actions of police and court officials in Ferguson. That evidence, detailed below, includes: 1) the consistency and magnitude of the racial disparities found throughout police and court enforcement actions; 2) direct communications by police supervisors and court officials that exhibit racial bias, particularly against African Americans; 3) a number of other communications by police and court officials that reflect harmful racial stereotypes; 4) the background and historic context surrounding FPD's racially disparate enforcement practices; 5) the fact that City, police, and court officials failed to take any meaningful steps to evaluate or address the race-based impact of its law enforcement practices despite longstanding and widely reported racial disparities, and instead consistently reapplied police and court practices known to disparately impact African Americans.

a. Consistency and Magnitude of Identified Racial Disparities

In assessing whether an official action was motivated in part by discriminatory intent, the actual impact of the action and whether it "bears more heavily on one race or another" may "provide an important starting point." *Vill. of Arlington Heights*, 429 U.S. at 266 (internal citations and quotation marks omitted). Indeed, in rare cases, statistical evidence of discriminatory impact may be sufficiently probative to itself establish discriminatory intent. *Hazelwood School Dist. v. United States*, 433 U.S. 299, 307-08 (1977) (noting in the Title VII context that where "gross statistical disparities can be shown, they alone may in a proper case constitute prima facie proof of a pattern or practice of discrimination").

The race-based disparities we have found are not isolated or aberrational; rather, they exist in nearly every aspect of Ferguson police and court operations. As discussed above, statistical analysis shows that African Americans are more likely to be searched but less likely to have contraband found on them; more likely to receive a citation following a stop and more likely to receive multiple citations at once; more likely to be arrested; more likely to have force used against them; more likely to have their case last longer and require more encounters with the municipal court; more likely to have an arrest warrant issued against them by the municipal court; and more likely to be arrested solely on the basis of an outstanding warrant. As noted above, many of these disparities would occur by chance less than one time in 1000.

These disparities provide significant evidence of discriminatory intent, as the "impact of an official action is often probative of why the action was taken in the first place since people usually intend the natural consequences of their actions." *Reno v. Bossier Parish Sch. Bd.*, 520 U.S. 471, 487 (1997); *see also Davis*, 426 U.S. at 242 ("An invidious discriminatory purpose may often be inferred from the totality of the relevant facts, including the fact, if it is true, that the [practice] bears more heavily on one race than another."). These disparities are unexplainable on grounds other than race and evidence that racial bias, whether implicit or explicit, has shaped law enforcement conduct.[48]

---

48 Social psychologists have long recognized the influence of implicit racial bias on decision making, and law enforcement experts have similarly acknowledged the impact of implicit racial bias on law enforcement decisions. *See, e.g.*, R. Richard Banks, Jennifer L. Eberhardt, & Lee Ross, *Discrimination and Implicit Bias in a Racially Unequal Society*, 94 Cal. L. Rev. 1169 (2006); Tracey G. Gove, *Implicit Bias and Law Enforcement*, The Police Chief (October 2011).

b. Direct Evidence of Racial Bias

Our investigation uncovered direct evidence of racial bias in the communications of influential Ferguson decision makers. In email messages and during interviews, several court and law enforcement personnel expressed discriminatory views and intolerance with regard to race, religion, and national origin. The content of these communications is unequivocally derogatory, dehumanizing, and demonstrative of impermissible bias.

We have discovered evidence of racial bias in emails sent by Ferguson officials, all of whom are current employees, almost without exception through their official City of Ferguson email accounts, and apparently sent during work hours. These email exchanges involved several police and court supervisors, including FPD supervisors and commanders. The following emails are illustrative:

- A November 2008 email stated that President Barack Obama would not be President for very long because "what black man holds a steady job for four years."
- A March 2010 email mocked African Americans through speech and familial stereotypes, using a story involving child support. One line from the email read: "I be so glad that dis be my last child support payment! Month after month, year after year, all dose payments!"
- An April 2011 email depicted President Barack Obama as a chimpanzee.
- A May 2011 email stated: "An African-American woman in New Orleans was admitted into the hospital for a pregnancy termination. Two weeks later she received a check for $5,000. She phoned the hospital to ask who it was from. The hospital said, 'Crimestoppers.'"

- A June 2011 email described a man seeking to obtain "welfare" for his dogs because they are "mixed in color, unemployed, lazy, can't speak English and have no frigging clue who their Daddies are."
- An October 2011 email included a photo of a bare-chested group of dancing women, apparently in Africa, with the caption, "Michelle Obama's High School Reunion."
- A December 2011 email included jokes that are based on offensive stereotypes about Muslims.

Our review of documents revealed many additional email communications that exhibited racial or ethnic bias, as well as other forms of bias. Our investigation has not revealed any indication that any officer or court clerk engaged in these communications was ever disciplined. Nor did we see a single instance in which a police or court recipient of such an email asked that the sender refrain from sending such emails, or any indication that these emails were reported as inappropriate. Instead, the emails were usually forwarded along to others.[49]

Critically, each of these email exchanges involved supervisors of FPD's patrol and court operations.[50]

---

49 We did find one instance in 2012 in which the City Manager forwarded an email that played upon stereotypes of Latinos, but within minutes of sending it, sent another email to the recipient in which he stated he had not seen the offensive part of the email and apologized for the "inappropriate and offensive" message. Police and court staff took no such corrective action, and indeed in many instances expressed amusement at the offensive correspondence.

50 We were able to review far more emails from FPD supervisors than patrol officers. City officials informed us that, while many FPD supervisors have their email accounts on hard drives in the police department, most patrol officers use a form of webmail that does not retain messages once they are deleted.

FPD patrol supervisors are responsible for holding officers accountable to governing laws, including the Constitution, and helping to ensure that officers treat all people equally under the law, regardless of race or any other protected characteristic. The racial animus and stereotypes expressed by these supervisors suggest that they are unlikely to hold an officer accountable for discriminatory conduct or to take any steps to discourage the development or perpetuation of racial stereotypes among officers.

Similarly, court supervisors have significant influence and discretion in managing the court's operations and in processing individual cases. As discussed in Parts I and III.B of this report, our investigation has found that a number of court rules and procedures are interpreted and applied entirely at the discretion of the court clerks. These include: whether to require a court appearance for certain offenses; whether to grant continuances or other procedural requests; whether to accept partial payment of an owed fine; whether to cancel a warrant without a bond payment; and whether to provide individuals with documentation enabling them to have a suspended driver's license reinstated before the full fine owed has been paid off. Court clerks are also largely responsible for setting bond amounts. The evidence we found thus shows not only racial bias, but racial bias by those with considerable influence over the outcome of any given court case.

This documentary evidence of explicit racial bias is consistent with reports from community members indicating that some FPD officers use racial epithets in dealing with members of the public. We spoke with one African-American man who, in August 2014, had an argument in his apartment to which FPD officers responded, and was immediately pulled out of the apartment by force. After telling the officer, "you don't have a reason to lock me up," he claims the officer responded: "N * * * * *,

I can find something to lock you up on." When the man responded, "good luck with that," the officer slammed his face into the wall, and after the man fell to the floor, the officer said, "don't pass out motherf* * * *r because I'm not carrying you to my car." Another young man described walking with friends in July 2014 past a group of FPD officers who shouted racial epithets at them as they passed.

Courts have widely acknowledged that direct statements exhibiting racial bias are exceedingly rare, and that such statements are not necessary for establishing the existence of discriminatory purpose. *See, e.g., Hayden v. Paterson*, 594 F.3d 150, 163 (2d Cir. 2010) (noting that "discriminatory intent is rarely susceptible to direct proof"); *see also Thomas v. Eastman Kodak Co.*, 183 F.3d 38, 64 (1st Cir. 1999) (noting in Title VII case that "[t]here is no requirement that a plaintiff ... must present direct, 'smoking gun' evidence of racially biased decision making in order to prevail"); *Robinson v. Runyon*, 149 F.3d 507, 513 (6th Cir. 1998) (noting in Title VII case that "[r]arely will there be direct evidence from the lips of the defendant proclaiming his or her racial animus"). Where such evidence does exist, however, it is highly probative of discriminatory intent. That is particularly true where, as here, the communications exhibiting bias are made by those with considerable decision-making authority. *See Doe v. Mamaroneck*, 462 F. Supp. 2d 520, 550 (S.D.N.Y. 2006); *Eberhart v. Gettys*, 215 F. Supp. 2d 666, 678 (M.D.N.C. 2002).

c. Evidence of Racial Stereotyping

Several Ferguson officials told us during our investigation that it is a lack of "personal responsibility" among African-American members of the Ferguson community that causes African Americans to experience disproportionate harm under Ferguson's approach to law enforcement. Our investigation suggests that this explanation is at odd with the facts. While there are people of all races who may lack personal responsibility, the harm of Ferguson's approach to law enforcement is largely due to the myriad systemic deficiencies discussed above. Our investigation revealed African Americans making extraordinary efforts to pay off expensive tickets for minor, often unfairly charged, violations, despite systemic obstacles to resolving those tickets. While our investigation did not indicate that African Americans are disproportionately irresponsible, it did reveal that, as the above emails reflect, some Ferguson decision makers hold negative stereotypes about African Americans, and lack of personal responsibility is one of them. Application of this stereotype furthers the disproportionate impact of Ferguson's police and court practices. It causes court and police decision makers to discredit African Americans' explanations for not being able to pay tickets and allows officials to disown the harms of Ferguson's law enforcement practices.

The common practice among Ferguson officials of writing off tickets further evidences a double standard grounded in racial stereotyping. Even as Ferguson City officials maintain the harmful stereotype that black individuals lack personal responsibility—and continue to cite this lack of personal responsibility as the cause of the disparate impact of Ferguson's practices—white City officials condone a striking lack of personal responsibility among themselves and their friends. Court records and emails show City officials, including the Municipal Judge, the Court Clerk, and FPD supervisors assisting friends, colleagues, acquaintances, and themselves in eliminating citations, fines, and fees. For example:

- In August 2014, the Court Clerk emailed Municipal Judge Brockmeyer a copy of a Failure to Appear notice for a speeding violation issued by the City of Breckenridge, and asked: "[FPD patrol supervisor] came to me this morning, could you please take [care] of this for him in Breckenridge?" The Judge replied: "Sure." Judge Brockmeyer also serves as Municipal Judge in Breckenridge.

- In October 2013, Judge Brockmeyer sent Ferguson's Prosecuting Attorney an email with the subject line "City of Hazelwood vs. Ronald Brockmeyer." The Judge wrote: "Pursuant to our conversation, attached please find the red light camera ticket received by the undersigned. I would appreciate it if you would please see to it that this ticket is dismissed." The Prosecuting Attorney, who also serves as prosecuting attorney in Hazelwood, responded: "I worked on red light matters today and dismissed the ticket that you sent over. Since I entered that into the system today, you may or may not get a second notice—you can just ignore that."

- In August 2013, an FPD patrol supervisor wrote an email entitled "Oops" to the Prosecuting Attorney regarding a ticket his relative received in another municipality for traveling 59 miles per hour in a 40 miles-per-hour zone, noting "[h]aving it dismissed would be a blessing." The Prosecuting Attorney responded that the prosecutor of that other municipality promised to nolle pros the ticket. The supervisor responded with appreciation, noting that the dismissal "[c]ouldn't have come at a better time."

- Also in August 2013, Ferguson's Mayor emailed the Prosecuting Attorney about a parking ticket received by an employee of a non-profit day camp for which the Mayor sometimes volunteers. The Mayor wrote that the person "shouldn't have left his car unattended there, but it was an honest mistake" and stated, "I would hate for him to have to pay for this, can you help?" The Prosecuting Attorney forwarded the email to the Court Clerk, instructing her to "NP [nolle prosequi, or not prosecute] this parking ticket."

- In November 2011, a court clerk received a request from a friend to "fix a parking ticket" received by the friend's coworker's wife. After the ticket was faxed to the clerk, she replied: "It's gone baby!"

- In March 2014, a friend of the Court Clerk's relative emailed the Court Clerk with a scanned copy of a ticket asking if there was anything she could do to help. She responded: "Your ticket of $200 has magically disappeared!" Later, in June 2014, the same person emailed the Court Clerk regarding two tickets and asked: "Can you work your magic again? It would be deeply appreciated." The Clerk later informed him one ticket had been dismissed and she was waiting to hear back about the second ticket.

These are just a few illustrative examples. It is clear that writing off tickets between the Ferguson court staff and the clerks of other municipal courts in the region is routine. Email exchanges show that Ferguson officials secured or received ticket write-offs from staff in a number of neighboring municipalities. There is evidence that the Court Clerk and a City of Hazelwood clerk "fixed" at least 12 tickets at each other's request, and that the Court Clerk successfully sought help with a ticket from a clerk in St. Ann. And in April 2011, a court administrator in the City of Pine Lawn emailed the Ferguson Court Clerk to have a warrant recalled for a person applying for a job with the Pine Lawn Police Department. The court administrator explained that "[a]fter he gets the job, he will have money to pay off his fines with Ferguson." The

Court Clerk recalled the warrant and issued a new court date for more than two months after the request was made.

City officials' application of the stereotype that African Americans lack "personal responsibility" to explain why Ferguson's practices harm African Americans, even as these same City officials exhibit a lack of personal—and professional—responsibility in handling their own and their friends' code violations, is further evidence of discriminatory bias on the part of decision makers central to the direction of law enforcement in Ferguson.

d. Historical Background

Until the 1960s, Ferguson was a "sundown town" where African Americans were banned from the City after dark. The City would block off the main road from Kinloch, which was a poor, all-black suburb, "with a chain and construction materials but kept a second road open during the day so housekeepers and nannies could get from Kinloch to jobs in Ferguson."[51] During our investigative interviews, several older African-American residents recalled this era in Ferguson and recounted that African Americans knew that, for them, the City was "off-limits."

The Ferguson of half a century ago is not the same Ferguson that exists today. We heard from many residents—black and white—who expressed pride in their community, especially with regard to the fact that Ferguson is one of the most demographically diverse communities in the area. Pride in this aspect of Ferguson is well founded; Ferguson is more diverse than most of the United States, and than many of its surrounding

---

51 Richard Rothstein, *The Making of Ferguson*, Econ. Policy Inst. (Oct. 2014), *available at* http://www.epi.org/publication/making-ferguson/.

cities. It is clear that many Ferguson residents of different races genuinely embrace that diversity.

But we also found evidence during our investigation that some within Ferguson still have difficulty coming to terms with Ferguson's changing demographics and seeing Ferguson's African American and white residents as equals in civic life. While total population rates have remained relatively constant over the last three decades, the portion of Ferguson residents who are African American has increased steadily but dramatically, from 25% in 1990 to 67% in 2010. Some individuals, including individuals charged with discretionary enforcement decisions in either the police department or the court, have expressed concerns about the increasing number of African Americans that have moved to Ferguson in recent years. Similarly, some City officials and residents we spoke with explicitly distinguished Ferguson's African-American residents from Ferguson's "normal" residents or "regular" people. One white third-generation Ferguson resident told us that in many ways Ferguson is "progressive and quite vibrant," while in another it is "typical—trying to hang on to its 'whiteness.'"

On its own, Ferguson's historical backdrop as a racially segregated community that did not treat African Americans equally under the law does not demonstrate that law enforcement practices today are motivated by impermissible discriminatory intent. It is one factor to consider, however, especially given the evidence that, among some in Ferguson, these attitudes persist today. As courts have instructed, the historical background of an official practice that leads to discriminatory effects is, together with other evidence, probative as to whether that practice is grounded in part in discriminatory purposes. *See Vill. of Arlington Heights,* 429 U.S. at 267; *see also Rogers v. Lodge,* 458 U.S. 613, *passim* (1982).

e. Failure to Evaluate or Correct Practices that Have
   Long Resulted in a Racially Disparate Impact

That the discriminatory effect of Ferguson's law
enforcement practices is the result of intentional discrimination is further evidenced by the fact that City,
police, and court officials have consistently failed to
evaluate or reform—and in fact appear to have redou-
bled their commitment to—the very practices that have
plainly and consistently exerted a disparate impact on
African Americans.

The disparities we have identified appear to be longstanding. The statistical analysis performed as part of
our investigation relied upon police and court data from
recent years, but FPD has collected data related to vehicle stops pursuant to state requirements since 2000.
Each year, that information is gathered by FPD, sent to
the office of the Missouri Attorney General, and published on the Missouri Attorney General's webpage.[52]
The data show disparate impact on African Americans
in Ferguson for as long as that data has been reported.
Based on that racial profiling data, Missouri publishes
a "Disparity Index" for each reporting municipality, calculated as the percent of stops of a certain racial group
compared with that group's local population rate. In
each of the last 14 years, the data show that African
Americans are "over represented" in FPD's vehicular
stops.[53] That data also shows that in most years, FPD officers searched African Americans at higher rates than

---

52 *See Missouri Vehicle Stops Report,* Missouri Attorney General,
http://ago.mo.gov/VehicleStops/Reports.php?lea=161 (last visited Feb. 13, 2015).

53 Data for the entire state of Missouri shows an even higher
"Disparity Index" for those years than the disparity index present
in Ferguson. This raises, by the state's own metric, considerable
concerns about policing outside of Ferguson as well.

others, but found contraband on African Americans at lower rates.

In 2001, for example, African Americans comprised about the same proportion of the population as whites, but while stops of white drivers accounted for 1,495 stops, African Americans accounted for 3,426, more than twice as many. While a white person stopped that year was searched in 6% of cases, a black person stopped was searched in 14% of cases. That same year, searches of whites resulted in a contraband finding in 21% of cases, but searches of African Americans only resulted in a contraband finding in 16% of cases. Similar disparities were identified in most other years, with varying degrees of magnitude. In any event, the data reveals a pattern of racial disparities in Ferguson's police activities. That pattern appears to have been ignored by Ferguson officials.

That the extant racial disparities are intentional is also evident in the fact that Ferguson has consistently returned to the unlawful practices described in Parts III.A. and B. of this Report knowing that they impose a persistent disparate impact on African Americans. City officials have continued to encourage FPD to stop and cite aggressively as part of its revenue generation efforts, even though that encouragement and increased officer discretion has yielded disproportionate African-American representation in FPD stops and citations. Until we recommended it during our investigation, FPD officials had not restricted officer discretion to issue multiple citations at once, even though the application of that discretion has led officers to issue far more citations to African Americans at once than others, on average, and even though only black individuals (35 in total) ever received five or more citations at once over a three-year period. FPD has not provided further guidance to constrain officer discretion in conducting searches, even though FPD officers have, for years, searched African Americans at higher rates than others but found contraband during those searches less often than in searches of individuals of other races.

Similarly, City officials have not taken any meaningful steps to contain the discretion of court clerks to grant continuances, clear warrants, or enable driver's license suspensions to be lifted, even though those practices have resulted in warrants being issued and executed at highly disproportionate rates against African Americans. Indeed, until the City of Ferguson repealed the Failure to Appear statute in September 2014—after this investigation began—the City had not taken meaningful steps to evaluate or reform any of the court practices described in this Report, even though the implementation of those practices has plainly exerted a disparate impact on African Americans.

FPD also has not significantly altered its use-of-force tactics, even though FPD records make clear that current force decisions disparately impact black suspects, and that officers appear to assess threat differently depending upon the race of the suspect. FPD, for example, has not reviewed or revised its canine program, even though available records show that canine officers have exclusively set their dogs against black individuals, often in cases where doing so was not justified by the danger presented. In many incidents in which officers used significant levels of force, the facts as described by the officers themselves did not appear to support the force used, especially in light of the fact that less severe tactics likely would have been equally effective. In some of these incidents, law enforcement experts with whom we consulted could find no explanation other than race to explain the severe tactics used.

During our investigation, FPD officials told us that their police tactics are responsive to the scenario at hand. But records suggest that, where a suspect or group of suspects is white, FPD applies a different calculus, typically resulting in a more measured law enforcement response. In one 2012 incident, for example, officers reported responding to a fight in progress at a local bar that involved white suspects. Officers reported encountering "40-50 people actively fighting, throwing bottles and glasses, as well as chairs." The report noted that "one subject had his ear bitten off." While the responding officers reported using force, they only used "minimal baton and flashlight strikes as well as fists, muscling techniques and knee strikes." While the report states that "due to the amount of subjects fighting, no physical arrests were possible," it notes also that four subjects were brought to the station for "safekeeping." While we have found other evidence that FPD later issued a wanted for two individuals as a result of the incident, FPD's response stands in stark contrast to the actions officers describe taking in many incidents involving black suspects, some of which we earlier described.

Based on this evidence, it is apparent that FPD requires better training, limits on officer discretion, increased supervision, and more robust accountability systems, not only to ensure that officers act in accordance with the Fourth Amendment, but with the Fourteenth Amendment as well. FPD has failed to take any such corrective action, and instead has actively endorsed and encouraged the perpetuation of the practices that have led to such stark disparities. This, together with the totality of the facts that we have found, evidences that those practices exist, at least in part, on account of an unconstitutional discriminatory purpose. *See Feeney*, 442 U.S. at 279 n.24 (noting that the discriminatory intent inquiry is "practical," because what "any official entity is 'up to' may be plain from the results its actions achieve, or the results they avoid").

D. Ferguson Law Enforcement Practices Erode Community Trust, Especially Among Ferguson's African-American Residents, and Make Policing Less Effective, More Difficult, and Less Safe

The unlawful police misconduct and court practices described above have generated great distrust of Ferguson law enforcement, especially among African Americans.[54] As described below, other FPD practices further contribute to distrust, including FPD's failure to hold officers accountable for misconduct, failure to implement community policing principles, and the lack of diversity within FPD. Together, these practices severely damaged the relationship between African Americans and the Ferguson Police Department long before Michael Brown's shooting death in August 2014. This divide has made policing in Ferguson less effective, more difficult, and more likely to discriminate.

1. Ferguson's Unlawful Police and Court Practices Have Led to Distrust and Resentment Among Many in Ferguson

The lack of trust between a significant portion of Ferguson's residents, especially its African-American residents, and the Ferguson Police Department has become, since August 2014, undeniable. The causes of this distrust and division, however, have been the subject of debate. City and police officials, and some other Ferguson residents, have asserted that this lack of meaningful

---

54 Although beyond the scope of this investigation, it appears clear that individuals' experiences with other law enforcement agencies in St. Louis County, including with the police departments in surrounding municipalities and the County Police, in many instances have contributed to a general distrust of law enforcement that impacts interactions with the Ferguson police and municipal court.

connection with much of Ferguson's African-American community is due to the fact that they are "transient" renters; that they do not appreciate how much the City of Ferguson does for them; that "pop-culture" portrays alienating themes; or because of "rumors" that the police and municipal court are unyielding because they are driven by raising revenue.

Our investigation showed that the disconnect and distrust between much of Ferguson's African-American community and FPD is caused largely by years of the unlawful and unfair law enforcement practices by Ferguson's police department and municipal court described above. In the documents we reviewed, the meetings we observed and participated in, and in the hundreds of conversations Civil Rights Division staff had with residents of Ferguson and the surrounding area, many residents, primarily African-American residents, described being belittled, disbelieved, and treated with little regard for their legal rights by the Ferguson Police Department. One white individual who has lived in Ferguson for 48 years told us that it feels like Ferguson's police and court system is "designed to bring a black man down ... [there are] no second chances." We heard from African-American residents who told us of Ferguson's "long history of targeting blacks for harassment and degrading treatment," and who described the steps they take to avoid this—from taking routes to work that skirt Ferguson to moving out of state. An African-American minister of a church in a nearby community told us that he doesn't allow his two sons to drive through Ferguson out of "fear that they will be targeted for arrest."

African Americans' views of FPD are shaped not just by *what* FPD officers do, but by *how* they do it. During our investigation, dozens of African Americans in Ferguson told us of verbal abuse by FPD officers during routine interactions, and these accounts are consistent with complaints people have made about FPD for years. In December 2011, for example, an African-American man alleged that as he was standing outside of Wal-Mart, an officer called him a "stupid motherf****r" and a "bastard." According to the man, a lieutenant was on the scene and did nothing to reproach the officer, instead threatening to arrest the man. In April 2012, officers allegedly called an African-American woman a "bitch" and a "mental case" at the jail following an arrest. In June 2011, a 60-year-old man complained that an officer verbally harassed him while he stood in line to see the judge in municipal court. According to the man, the officer repeatedly ordered him to move forward as the line advanced and, because he did not advance far enough, turned to the other court-goers and joked, "he is hooked on phonics."

Another concern we heard from many African-American residents, and saw in the files we reviewed, was of casual intimidation by FPD officers, including threats to draw or fire their weapons, often for seemingly little or no cause. In September 2012, a 28-year resident of Ferguson complained to FPD about a traffic stop during which a lieutenant approached with a loud and confrontational manner with his hand on his holstered gun. The resident, who had a military police background, noted that the lieutenant's behavior, especially having his hand on his gun, ratcheted up the tension level, and he questioned why the lieutenant had been so aggressive. In another incident captured on video and discussed below in more detail, an officer placed his gun on a wall or post and pointed it back and forth to each of two store employees as he talked to them while they took the trash out late one night. In another case discussed above, a person reported that an FPD officer removed his ECW during a traffic stop and continuously tapped the ECW on the roof of the person's car. These written complaints reported to FPD are consistent with complaints we heard from community members during our investigation about officers casually threatening to hurt or even shoot them.

It appears that many police and City officials were unaware of this distrust and fear of Ferguson police among African Americans prior to August 2014. Ferguson's Chief, for example, told us that prior to the Michael Brown shooting he thought community-police relations were good. During our investigation, however, City and police leadership, and many officers of all ranks, acknowledged a deep divide between police and some Ferguson residents, particularly black residents. Mayor Knowles acknowledged that there is "clearly mistrust" of FPD by many community members, including a "systemic problem" with youth not wanting to work with police. One FPD officer estimated that about a quarter of the Ferguson community distrusts the police department.

A growing body of research, alongside decades of police experience, is consistent with what our investigation found in Ferguson: that when police and courts treat people unfairly, unlawfully, or disrespectfully, law enforcement loses legitimacy in the eyes of those who have experienced, or even observed, the unjust conduct. *See, e.g.,* Tom R. Tyler & Yuen J. Huo, *Trust in the Law: Encouraging Public Cooperation with the Police and Courts* (2002). Further, this loss of legitimacy makes individuals more likely to resist enforcement efforts and less likely to cooperate with law enforcement efforts to prevent and investigate crime. *See, e.g.,* Jason Sunshine & Tom R. Tyler, *The Role of Procedural Justice and Legitimacy in Shaping Public Support for Policing,* 37 Law & Soc'y Rev. 513, 534-36 (2003); *Promoting Cooperative Strategies to Reduce Racial Profiling* 20-21 (U.S. Dep't of Justice, Office of Community Oriented Policing Services, 2008) ("Being viewed as fair and just is critical to successful policing in a democracy. When the police are perceived as unfair in their enforcement, it will undermine their effectiveness."); Ron Davis et al., *Exploring the Role of the Police in Prisoner Reentry* 13-14 (Nat'l Inst. of Justice, New Perspectives in Policing, July

2012) ("Increasingly, research is supporting the notion that legitimacy is an important factor in the effectiveness of law, and the establishment and maintenance of legitimacy are particularly important in the context of policing.") (citations omitted). To improve community trust and police effectiveness, Ferguson must ensure not only that its officers act in accord with the Constitution, but that they treat people fairly and respectfully.

2. FPD's Exercise of Discretion, Even When Lawful, Often Undermines Community Trust and Public Safety

Even where lawful, many discretionary FPD enforcement actions increase distrust and significantly decrease the likelihood that individuals will seek police assistance even when they are victims of crime, or that they will cooperate with the police to solve or prevent other crimes. Chief Jackson told us "we don't get cooperating witnesses" from the apartment complexes. Consistent with this statement, our review of documents and our conversations with Ferguson residents revealed many instances in which they are reluctant to report being victims of crime or to cooperate with police, and many instances in which FPD imposed unnecessary negative consequences for doing so.

In one instance, for example, a woman called FPD to report a domestic disturbance. By the time the police arrived, the woman's boyfriend had left. The police looked through the house and saw indications that the boyfriend lived there. When the woman told police that only she and her brother were listed on the home's occupancy permit, the officer placed the woman under arrest for the permit violation and she was jailed. In another instance, after a woman called police to report a domestic disturbance and was given a summons for an occupancy permit violation, she said, according to the officer's report, that she "hated the Ferguson Police Department and will never call again, even if she is being killed."

In another incident, a young African-American man was shot while walking on the road with three friends. The police department located and interviewed two of the friends about the shooting. After the interview, they arrested and jailed one of these cooperating witnesses, who was 19 years old, on an outstanding municipal warrant.

We also reviewed many instances in which FPD officers arrested individuals who sought to care for loved ones who had been hurt. In one instance from May 2014, for example, a man rushed to the scene of a car accident involving his girlfriend, who was badly injured and bleeding profusely when he arrived. He approached and tried to calm her. When officers arrived they treated him rudely, according to the man, telling him to move away from his girlfriend, which he did not want to do. They then immediately proceeded to handcuff and arrest him, which, officers assert, he resisted. EMS and other officers were not on the scene during this arrest, so the accident victim remained unattended, bleeding from her injuries, while officers were arresting the boyfriend. Officers charged the man with five municipal code violations (Resisting Arrest, Disorderly Conduct, Assault on an Officer, Obstructing Government Operations, and Failure to Comply) and had his vehicle towed and impounded. In an incident from 2013, a woman sought to reach her fiancé, who was in a car accident. After she refused to stay on the sidewalk as the officer ordered, she was arrested and jailed. While it is sometimes both essential and difficult to keep distraught family from being in close proximity to their loved ones on the scene of an accident, there is rarely a need to arrest and jail them rather than, at most, detain them on the scene.

Rather than view these instances as opportunities to convey their compassion for individuals at times of crisis even as they maintain order, FPD appears instead to view these and similar incidents we reviewed as opportunities to issue multiple citations and make arrests. For very little public safety benefit, FPD loses opportunities to build community trust and respect, and instead further alienates potential allies in crime prevention.

3. FPD's Failure to Respond to Complaints of Officer Misconduct Further Erodes Community Trust

Public trust has been further eroded by FPD's lack of any meaningful system for holding officers accountable when they violate law or policy. Through its system for taking, investigating, and responding to misconduct complaints, a police department has the opportunity to demonstrate that officer misconduct is unacceptable and unrepresentative of how the law enforcement agency values and treats its constituents. In this way, a police department's internal affairs process provides an opportunity for the department to restore trust and affirm its legitimacy. Similarly, misconduct investigations allow law enforcement the opportunity to provide community members who have been mistreated a constructive, effective way to voice their complaints. And, of course, effective internal affairs processes can be a critical part of correcting officer behavior, and improving police training and policies.

Ferguson's internal affairs system fails to respond meaningfully to complaints of officer misconduct. It does not serve as a mechanism to restore community members' trust in law enforcement, or correct officer behavior. Instead, it serves to contrast FPD's tolerance for officer misconduct against the Department's aggressive enforcement of even minor municipal infractions, lending credence to a sentiment that we heard often from Ferguson residents: that a "different set of rules" applies to Ferguson's police than to its African-American residents, and that making a complaint about officer misconduct is futile.

Despite the statement in FPD's employee misconduct investigation policy that "[t]he integrity of the police department depends on the personal integrity and discipline of each employee," FPD has done little to investigate external allegations that officers have not followed FPD policy or the law, or, with a few notable exceptions, to hold officers accountable when they have not. Ferguson Police Department makes it difficult to make complaints about officer conduct, and frequently assumes that the officer is telling the truth and the complainant is not, even where objective evidence indicates that the reverse is true.

It is difficult for individuals to make a misconduct complaint against an officer in Ferguson, in part because Ferguson both discourages individuals from making complaints and discourages City and police staff from accepting them. In a March 2014 email, for example, a lieutenant criticized a sergeant for taking a complaint from a man on behalf of his mother, who stayed in her vehicle outside the police station. Despite the fact that Ferguson policy requires that complaints be taken "from any source, identified or anonymous," the lieutenant stated "I would have had him bring her in, or leave." In another instance, a City employee took a complaint of misconduct from a Ferguson resident and relayed it to FPD. An FPD captain sent an email in response that the City employee viewed as being "lectured" for taking the complaint. The City Manager agreed, calling the captain's behavior "not only disrespectful and unacceptable, but it is dangerous in [that] it is inciteful [sic] and divisive." Nonetheless, there appeared to be no follow-up action regarding the captain, and the complaint was never logged as such or investigated.

While official FPD policy states clearly that officers must "never attempt to dissuade any citizen from lodging a complaint," FPD General Order 301.3, a contrary leadership message speaks louder than policy. This message is reflected in statements by officers that indicate a need to justify their actions when they do accept a civilian complaint. In one case, a sergeant explained: "Nothing I could say helped, he demanded the complaint forms which were provided." In another: "I spoke to [two people seeking to make a complaint] ... but after the conversation, neither had changed their mind and desired still to write out a complaint." We saw many instances in which people complained of being prevented from making a complaint, with no indication that FPD investigated those allegations. In one instance, for example, a man alleging significant excessive force reported the incident to a commander after being released from jail, stating that he was unable to make his complaint earlier because several different officers refused to let him speak to a sergeant to make a complaint about the incident and threatened to keep him in jail longer if he did not stop asking to make a complaint.

Some individuals also fear that they will suffer retaliation from officers if they report misconduct or even merely speak out as witnesses when approached by someone from FPD investigating a misconduct complaint. For instance, in one case FPD acknowledged that a witness to the misconduct was initially reluctant to complete a written statement supporting the complainant because he wanted no "repercussions" from the subject officer or other officers. In another case involving alleged misconduct at a retail store that we have already described, the store's district manager told the commander he did not want an investigation—despite how concerned he was by video footage showing an officer training his gun on two store employees as they took out the trash—because he wanted to "stay on the good side" of the police.

Even when individuals do report misconduct, there is a significant likelihood it will not be treated as a complaint and investigated. In one case, FPD failed to open an investigation of an allegation made by a caller who said an officer had kicked him in the side of the head and stepped on his head and back while he was face down with his hands cuffed behind his back, all the while talking about having blood on him from somebody else and "being tired of the B.S." The officer did not stop until the other officer on the scene said words to the effect of, "[h]ey, he's not fighting he's cuffed." The man alleged that the officer then ordered him to "get the f* * * up" and lifted him by the handcuffs, yanking his arms backward. The commander taking the call reported that the man stated that he supported the police and knew they had a tough job but was reporting the incident because it appeared the officer was under a lot of stress and needed counseling, and because he was hoping to prevent others from having the experience he did. The commander's email regarding the incident expressed no skepticism about the veracity of the caller's report and was able to identify the incident (and thus the involved officers). Yet FPD did not conduct an internal affairs investigation of this incident, based on our review of all of FPD's internal investigation files. There is not even an indication that a use-of-force report was completed.

In another case, an FPD commander wrote to a sergeant that despite a complainant being "pretty adamant that she was profiled and that the officer was rude," the commander "didn't even bother to send it to the chief for a control number" before hearing the sergeant's account of the officer's side of the story. Upon getting the officer's account second hand from the sergeant, the commander forwarded the information to the Police Chief so that it could be "filed in the non-complaint file." FPD officers and commanders also often seek to frame complaints as being entirely related to complainants' guilt or innocence, and therefore not subject to a misconduct investigation, even though the complaint clearly alleges officer misconduct.

In one instance, for example, commanders told the complainant to go to court to fight her arrest, ignoring the complainant's statement that the officer arrested her for Disorderly Conduct and Failure to Obey only after she asked for the officer's name. In another instance, a commander stated that the complainant made no allegations unrelated to the merits of the arrest, even though the complainant alleged rudeness and being "intimidated" during arrest, among a number of other non-guilt related allegations.

FPD appears to intentionally *not* treat allegations of misconduct as complaints even where it believes that the officer in fact committed the misconduct. In one incident, for example, a supervisor wrote an email directly to an officer about a complaint the Police Chief had received about an officer speeding through the park in a neighboring town. The supervisor informed the officer that the Chief tracked the car number given by the complainant back to the officer, but assured the officer that the supervisor's email was "[j]ust for your information. No need to reply and there is no record of this other than this email." In another instance referenced above, the district manager of a retail store called a commander to tell him that he had a video recording that showed an FPD officer pull up to the store at about midnight while two employees were taking out the trash, take out his weapon, and put it on top of a concrete wall, pointed at the two employees. When the employees said they were just taking out the trash and asked the officer if he needed them to take off their coats so that he could see their uniforms, the officer told the employees that he knew they were employees and that if he had not known "I would have put you on the ground." The commander related in an email to the sergeant and lieutenant that "there is no reason to doubt the Gen. Manager because he said he watched the video and he clearly saw a weapon—maybe the sidearm or the taser." Nonetheless, despite noting that "we don't need cowboy" and the "major concern" of the officer taking his weapon out of his holster and placing it on a wall, the commander concluded, "[n]othing for you to do with this other than make a mental note and for you to be on the lookout for that kind of behavior."[55]

In another case, an officer investigating a report of a theft at a dollar store interrogated a minister pumping gas into his church van about the theft. The man alleged that he provided his identification to the officer and offered to return to the store to prove he was not the thief. The officer instead handcuffed the man and drove him to the store. The store clerk reported that the detained man was not the thief, but the officer continued to keep the man cuffed, allegedly calling him "f*****g stupid" for asking to be released from the cuffs. The man went directly to FPD to file a complaint upon being released by the officer. FPD conducted an investigation but, because the complainant did not respond to a cell phone message left by the investigator within 13 days, reclassified the complaint as "withdrawn," even as the investigator noted that the complaint of improper detention would otherwise have been sustained, and noted that the "[e]mployee has been counseled and retraining is forthcoming." In still another case, a lieutenant of a neighboring agency called FPD to report that a pizza parlor owner had complained to him that an off-duty FPD officer had become angry upon being told that police discounts were only given to officers in uniform and said

---

55 This incident raises another concern regarding whether a second-hand informal account of a complaint, often the only record Ferguson retains, conveys the seriousness of the allegation of misconduct. In this illustrative instance, our conversation with a witness to this incident indicates that the officer pointed his weapon at each employee as he spoke to him, and threatened to shoot both, despite knowing that they were simply employees taking out the trash.

to the restaurant owner as he was leaving, "I hope you get robbed!" The allegation was not considered a complaint and instead, despite its seriousness, was handled through counseling at the squad level.[56]

Even where a complaint is actually investigated, unless the complaint is made by an FPD commander, and sometimes not even then, FPD consistently takes the word of the officer over the word of the complainant, frequently even where the officer's version of events is clearly at odds with the objective evidence. On the rare occasion that FPD does sustain an external complaint of officer misconduct, the discipline it imposes is generally too low to be an effective deterrent.[57]

---

56 We found additional examples of FPD officers behaving in public in a manner that reflects poorly on FPD and law enforcement more generally. In November 2010, an officer was arrested for DUI by an Illinois police officer who found his car crashed in a ditch off the highway. Earlier that night he and his squad mates—including his sergeant—were thrown out of a bar for bullying a customer. The officer received a thirty-day suspension for the DUI. Neither the sergeant nor any officers was disciplined for their behavior in the bar. In September 2012, an officer stood by eating a sandwich while a fight broke out at an annual street festival. After finally getting involved to break up the fight, he publically berated and cursed at his squad mates, screamed and cursed at the two female street vendors who were fighting, and pepper-sprayed a handcuffed female arrestee in the back of his patrol car. The officer received a written reprimand.

57 While the Chief's "log" of Internal Affairs ("IA") investigations contains many sustained allegations, most of these were internally generated; that is, the complaint was made by an FPD employee, usually a commander. In addition, we found that a majority of complaints are never investigated as IA cases, or even logged as complaints. The Chief's log, which he told us included all complaint investigations, includes 56 investigations from January 2010 through July 2014. Our review indicates that there were significantly more complaints of misconduct during this

Our investigation raised concerns in particular about how FPD responds to untruthfulness by officers. In many departments, a finding of untruthfulness pursuant to internal investigation results in an officer's termination because the officer's credibility on police reports and in providing testimony is subsequently subject to challenge. In FPD, untruthfulness appears not even to always result in a formal investigation, and even where sustained, has little effect. In one case we reviewed, FPD sustained a charge of untruthfulness against an officer after he was found to have lied to the investigator about whether he had engaged in an argument with a civilian over the loudspeaker of his police vehicle. FPD imposed only a 12-hour suspension on the officer. In addition, FPD appears not to have taken the officer's untruthfulness into sufficient account in several subsequent complaints, including in at least one case in which the complainant alleged conduct very similar to that alleged in the case in which FPD found the officer untruthful. Nor, as discussed above, has FPD or the City disclosed this information to defendants challenging charges brought by the officer. In another case a supervisor was sustained for false testimony during an internal affairs investigation and was given a written reprimand. In another case in which an officer was clearly untruthful, FPD did not sustain the charge.[58] In that case, an officer in another jurisdiction was assigned to monitor an intersection in that city because an FPD-marked vehicle allegedly had repeatedly been running the stop sign at that intersection. While at that intersection, and while receiving a complaint from

---

time period. Despite repeated requests, FPD provided us no other record of complaints received or investigated.

58 FPD may have initially accepted this as a formal complaint, but then informally withdrew it after completion of the investigation. No rationale is provided for doing so, but the case does not appear on the Chief's IA investigation log, and another case with this same IA number appears instead.

a person about the FPD vehicle, the officer saw that very vehicle "dr[iving] through the stop sign without tapping a brake," according to a sergeant with the other jurisdiction. When asked to respond to these allegations, the officer wrote, unequivocally, "I assure you I don't run stop signs." It is clear from the investigative file that FPD found that he did, in fact, run stop signs, as the officer was given counseling. Nonetheless, the officer received a counseling memo that made no mention of the officer's written denial of the misconduct observed by another law enforcement officer. This officer continues to write reports regarding significant uses of force, several of which our investigation found questionable.[59]

By failing to hold officers accountable, FPD leadership sends a message that FPD officers can behave as they like, regardless of law or policy, and even if caught, that punishment will be light. This message serves to condone officer misconduct and fuel community distrust.

4. FPD's Lack of Community Engagement Increases the Likelihood of Discriminatory Policing and Damages Public Trust

Alongside its divisive law enforcement practices and lack of meaningful response to community concerns about police conduct, FPD has made little effort in recent years to employ community policing or other community engagement strategies. This lack of community engagement has precluded the possibility of bridging the divide caused by Ferguson's law enforcement practices, and has increased the likelihood of discriminatory policing.

---

59 Our review of FPD's handling of misconduct complaints is just one source of our concern about FPD's efforts to ensure that officers are truthful in their reports and testimony, and to take appropriate measures when they are not. As discussed above, our review of FPD offense and force reports also raises this concern.

Community policing and related community engagement strategies provide the opportunity for officers and communities to work together to identify the causes of crime and disorder particular to their community, and to prioritize law enforcement efforts. *See Community Policing Defined* 1-16 (U.S. Dep't of Justice, Office of Community Oriented Policing Services, 2014). The focus of these strategies—in stark contrast to Ferguson's current law enforcement approach—is on crime prevention rather than on making arrests. *See Effective Policing and Crime Prevention: A Problem Oriented Guide for Mayors, City Managers, and County Executives* 1-62 (U.S. Dep't of Justice, Office of Community Oriented Policing Services, 2009). When implemented fully, community policing creates opportunities for officers and community members to have frequent, positive interactions with each other, and requires officers to partner with communities to solve particular public safety problems that, together, they have decided to address. Research and experience show that community policing can be more effective at crime prevention and at making people feel safer. *See* Gary Cordner, *Reducing Fear of Crime: Strategies for Police* 47 (U.S. Dep't of Justice, Office of Community Oriented Policing Services, Jan. 2010) ("Most studies of community policing have found that residents like community policing and feel safer when it is implemented where they live and work.") (citations omitted).

Further, research and law enforcement experience show that community policing and engagement can overcome many of the divisive dynamics that disconnected Ferguson residents and City leadership alike describe, from a dearth of positive interactions to racial stereotyping and racial violence. *See, e.g.,* Glaser, *supra,* at 207-11 (discussing research showing that community policing and similar approaches can help reduce racial bias and stereotypes and improve community relations); L. Song

Richardson & Phillip Atiba Goff, *Interrogating Racial Violence*, 12 Ohio St. J. of Crim. L. 115, 143-47 (2014) (describing how fully implemented and inclusive community policing can help avoid racial stereotyping and violence); *Strengthening the Relationship Between Law Enforcement and Communities of Color: Developing an Agenda for Action* 1-20 (U.S. Dep't of Justice, Office of Community Oriented Policing Services, 2014).

Ferguson's community policing efforts appear always to have been somewhat modest, but have dwindled to almost nothing in recent years. FPD has no community policing or community engagement plan. FPD currently designates a single officer the "Community Resource Officer." This officer attends community meetings, serves as FPD's public relations liaison, and is charged with collecting crime data. No other officers play any substantive role in community policing efforts. Officers we spoke with were fairly consistent in their acknowledgment of this, and of the fact that this move away from community policing has been due, at least in part, to an increased focus on code enforcement and revenue generation in recent years. As discussed above, our investigation found that FPD redeployed officers to 12-hour shifts, in part for revenue reasons. There is some evidence that community policing is more difficult to carry out when patrol officers are on 12-hour shifts, and this appears to be the case in Ferguson. While many officers in Ferguson support 12-hour shifts, several told us that the 12-hour shift has undermined community policing. One officer said that "FPD used to have a strong community policing ethic—then we went to a 12-hour day." Another officer told us that the 12-hour schedule, combined with a lack of any attempt to have officers remain within their assigned area, has resulted in a lack of any geographical familiarity by FPD officers. This same officer told us that it is viewed as more positive to write tickets than to "talk with your businesses." Another officer told us that FPD officers should put less energy into writing tickets and instead "get out of their cars" and get to know community members.

One officer told us that officers could spend more time engaging with community members and undertaking problem-solving projects if FPD officers were not so focused on activities that generate revenue. This officer told us, "everything's about the courts ... the court's enforcement priorities are money." Another officer told us that officers cannot "get out of the car and play basketball with the kids," because "we've removed all the basketball hoops—there's an ordinance against it." While one officer told us that there was a police substation in Canfield Green when FPD was more committed to community policing, another told us that now there is "nobody in there that anybody knows."

City and police officials note that there are several active neighborhood groups in Ferguson. We reached out to each of these during our investigation and met with each one that responded. Some areas of Ferguson are well-represented by these groups. But City and police officials acknowledge that, since August 2014, they have realized that there are entire segments of the Ferguson community that they have never made an effort to know, especially African Americans who live in Ferguson's large apartment complexes, including Canfield Green. While some City officials appear well-intentioned, they have also been too quick to presume that outreach to more disconnected segments of the Ferguson community will be futile. One City employee told us, "they think they do outreach, but they don't," and that some Ferguson residents do not even realize their homes are in Ferguson. Our investigation indicated that, while the City and police department may have to use different strategies for engagement in some parts of Ferguson than in others, true community policing efforts can have positive results. As an officer who has patrolled the area told us, "most of the people in Canfield are good people. They just don't have a lot of time to get involved."

5. Ferguson's Lack of a Diverse Police Force Further Undermines Community Trust

While approximately two-thirds of Ferguson's residents are African American, only four of Ferguson's 54 commissioned police officers are African American. Since August 2014, there has been widespread discussion about the impact this comparative lack of racial diversity within FPD has on community trust and police behavior. During this investigation we also heard repeated complaints about FPD's lack of racial diversity from members of the Ferguson community. Our investigation indicates that greater diversity within Ferguson Police Department has the potential to increase community confidence in the police department, but may only be successful as part of a broader police reform effort.

While it does appear that a lack of racial diversity among officers decreases African Americans' trust in a police department, this observation must be qualified. Increasing a police department's racial diversity does not necessarily increase community trust or improve officer conduct. There appear to be many reasons for this. One important reason is that African-American officers can abuse and violate the rights of African-American civilians, just as white officers can. And African-American officers who behave abusively can undermine community trust just as white officers can. Our investigation indicates that in Ferguson, individual officer behavior is largely driven by a police culture that focuses on revenue generation and is infected by race bias. While increased vertical and horizontal diversity, racial and otherwise, likely is necessary to change this culture, it probably cannot do so on its own.

Consistent with our findings in Ferguson and other departments, research more broadly shows that a racially

314

diverse police force does not guarantee community trust or lawful policing. *See Diversity in Law Enforcement: A Literature Review* 4 n.v. (U.S. Dep't of Justice, Civil Rights Division, Office of Justice Programs, & U.S. Equal Employment Opportunity Commission, Submission to President's Task Force on 21st Century Policing, Jan. 2015). The picture is far more complex. Some studies show that Africa-American officers are less prejudiced than white officers as a whole, are more familiar with African-American communities, are more likely to arrest white suspects and less likely to arrest black suspects, and receive more cooperation from African Americans with whom they interact on the job. *See* David A. Sklansky, *Not Your Father's Police Department: Making Sense of the New Demographics of Law Enforcement,* 96 J. Crim. L. & Criminology 1209, 1224-25 (2006). But studies also show that African Americans are equally likely to fire their weapons, arrest people, and have complaints made about their behavior, and sometimes harbor prejudice against African-American civilians themselves. *Id.*

While a diverse police department does not guarantee a constitutional one, it is nonetheless critically important for law enforcement agencies, and the Ferguson Police Department in particular, to strive for broad diversity among officers and civilian staff. In general, notwithstanding the above caveats, a more racially diverse police department has the potential to increase confidence in police among African Americans in particular. *See* Joshua C. Cochran & Patricia Y. Warren, *Racial, Ethnic, and Gender Differences in, Perceptions of the Police: The Salience of Officer Race Within the Context of Racial Profiling,* 28(2) J. Contemp. Crim. Just. 206, 206-27 (2012). In addition, diversity of all types—including race, ethnicity, sex, national origin, religion, sexual orientation and gender identity—can be beneficial both to police-community relationships and the culture of the law enforcement agency. Increasing gender and sexual orientation diversity in policing in particular may be critical in re-making internal police culture and creating new assumptions about what makes policing effective. *See, e.g.,* Sklansky, *supra,* at 1233-34; Richardson & Goff, *supra,* at 143-47; Susan L. Miller, Kay B. Forest, & Nancy C. Jurik, *Diversity in Blue, Lesbian and Gay Police Officers in a Masculine Occupation,* 5 Men and Masculinities 355, 355-85 (Apr. 2003).[60] Moreover, aside from the beneficial impact a diverse police force may have on the culture of the department and police-community relations, police departments are obligated under law to provide equal opportunity for employment. *See* Title VII of the Civil Rights Act of 1964, 42 U.S.C. § 2000e *et seq.*

Our investigation indicates that Ferguson can and should do more to attract and hire a more diverse group of qualified police officers.[61] However, for these efforts to be successful at increasing the diversity of its workforce, as well as effective at increasing community trust and improving officer behavior, they must be part of a broader reform effort within FPD. This reform effort must focus recruitment efforts on attracting qualified candidates of

---

60 While the emphasis in Ferguson has been on racial diversity, FPD also, like many police agencies, has strikingly disparate gender diversity: in Ferguson, approximately 55% of residents are female, but FPD has only four female officers. *See* 2010 *Census,* U.S. Census Bureau (2010), *available at* factfinder.census.gov/bkmk/table/1.0/en/DEC/10_DP/DPDP1/1600000US2923986 (last visited Feb. 26, 2015). During our investigation we received many complaints about FPD's lack of gender diversity as well.

61 While not the focus of our investigation, the information we reviewed indicated that Ferguson's efforts to retain qualified female and black officers may be compromised by the same biases we saw more broadly in the department. In particular, while the focus of our investigation did not permit us to reach a conclusive finding, we found evidence that FPD tolerates sexual harassment by male officers, and has responded poorly to allegations of sexual harassment that have been made by female officers.

all demographics with the skills and temperament to police respectfully and effectively, and must ensure that *all* officers—regardless of race—are required to police lawfully and with integrity.

V. CHANGES NECESSARY TO REMEDY FERGUSON'S UNLAWFUL LAW ENFORCEMENT PRACTICES AND REPAIR COMMUNITY TRUST

The problems identified within this letter reflect deeply entrenched practices and priorities that are incompatible with lawful and effective policing and that damage community trust. Addressing those problems and repairing the City's relationship with the community will require a fundamental redirection of Ferguson's approach to law enforcement, including the police and court practices that reflect and perpetuate this approach.

Below we set out broad recommendations for changes that Ferguson should make to its police and court practices to correct the constitutional violations our investigation identified. Ensuring meaningful, sustainable, and verifiable reform will require that these and other measures be part of a court-enforceable remedial process that includes involvement from community stakeholders as well as independent oversight. In the coming weeks, we will seek to work with the City of Ferguson toward developing and reaching agreement on an appropriate framework for reform.

A. Ferguson Police Practices

1. Implement a Robust System of True Community Policing

Many of the recommendations included below would require a shift from policing to raise revenue to policing in partnership with the entire Ferguson community.

317

Developing these relationships will take time and considerable effort. FPD should:

a. Develop and put into action a policy and detailed plan for comprehensive implementation of community policing and problem-solving principles. Conduct outreach and involve the entire community in developing and implementing this plan;

b. Increase opportunities for officers to have frequent, positive interactions with people outside of an enforcement context, especially groups that have expressed high levels of distrust of police. Such opportunities may include police athletic leagues and similar informal activities;

c. Develop community partnerships to identify crime prevention priorities, with a focus on disconnected areas, such as Ferguson's apartment complexes, and disconnected groups, such as much of Ferguson's African-American youth;

d. Modify officer deployment patterns and scheduling (such as moving away from the current 12-hour shift and assigning officers to patrol the same geographic areas consistently) to facilitate participating in crime prevention projects and familiarity with areas and people;

e. Train officers on crime-prevention, officer safety, and anti-discrimination advantages of community policing. Train officers on mechanics of community policing and their role in implementing it;

f. Measure and evaluate individual, supervisory, and agency police performance on community engagement, problem-oriented-policing projects, and crime prevention, rather than on arrest and citation productivity.

2. Focus Stop, Search, Ticketing and Arrest Practices on Community Protection

FPD must fundamentally change the way it conducts stops and searches, issues citations and summonses, and makes arrests. FPD officers must be trained and required to abide by the law. In addition, FPD enforcement efforts should be reoriented so that officers are required to take enforcement action because it promotes public safety, not simply because they have legal authority to act. To do this, FPD should:

a. Prohibit the use of ticketing and arrest quotas, whether formal or informal;

b. Require that officers report in writing all stops, searches and arrests, including pedestrian stops, and that their reports articulate the legal authority for the law enforcement action and sufficient description of facts to support that authority;

c. Require documented supervisory approval prior to:

    1. Issuing any citation/summons that includes more than two charges;

    2. Making an arrest on any of the following charges:

        i. Failure to Comply/Obey;

        ii. Resisting Arrest;

        iii. Disorderly Conduct/Disturbing the Peace;

        iv. Obstruction of Government Operations;

    3. Arresting or ticketing an individual who sought police aid, or who is cooperating with police in an investigation;

4. Arresting on a municipal warrant or wanted;

d. Revise Failure to Comply municipal code provision to bring within constitutional limits, and provide sufficient guidance so that all stops, citations, and arrests based on the provision comply with the Constitution;

e. Train officers on proper use of Failure to Comply charge, including elements of the offense and appropriateness of the charge for interference with police activity that threatens public safety;

f. Require that applicable legal standards are met before officers conduct pat-downs or vehicle searches. Prohibit searches based on consent for the foreseeable future;

g. Develop system of correctable violation, or "fix-it" tickets, and require officers to issue fix-it tickets wherever possible and absent contrary supervisory instruction;

h. Develop and implement policy and training regarding appropriate police response to activities protected by the First Amendment, including the right to observe, record, and protest police action;

i. Provide initial and regularly recurring training on Fourth Amendment constraints on police action, as well as responsibility within FPD to constrain action beyond what Fourth Amendment requires in interest of public safety and community trust;

j. Discontinue use of "wanteds" or "stop orders" and prohibit officers from conducting stops, searches, or arrests on the basis of "wanteds" or "stop orders" issued by other agencies.

3. Increase Tracking, Review, and Analysis of FPD Stop, Search, Ticketing and Arrest Practices

At the first level of supervision and as an agency, FPD must review more stringently officers' stop, search, ticketing, and arrest practices to ensure that officers are complying with the Constitution and department policy, and to evaluate the impact of officer activity on police legitimacy and community trust. FPD should:

    a. Develop and implement a plan for broader collection of stop, search, ticketing, and arrest data that includes pedestrian stops, enhances vehicle stop data collection, and requires collection of data on all stop and post-stop activity, as well as location and demographic information;

    b. Require supervisors to review all officer activity and review all officer reports before the supervisor leaves shift;

    c. Develop and implement system for regular review of stop, search, ticketing, and arrest data at supervisory and agency level to detect problematic trends and ensure consistency with public safety and community policing goals;

    d. Analyze race and other disparities shown in stop, search, ticketing, and arrest practices to determine whether disparities can be reduced consistent with public safety goals.

4. Change Force Use, Reporting, Review, and Response to Encourage De-Escalation and the Use of the Minimal Force Necessary in a Situation

FPD should reorient officers' approach to using force by ensuring that they are trained and skilled in using tools and tactics to de-escalate situations, and incentivized to avoid using force wherever possible. FPD also should implement a system of force review that ensures that improper force is detected and responded to effectively, and that policy, training, tactics, and officer safety concerns are identified. FPD should:

a. Train and require officers to use de-escalation techniques wherever possible both to avoid a situation escalating to where force becomes necessary, and to avoid unnecessary force even where it would be legally justified. Training should include tactics for slowing down a situation to increase available options;

b. Require onsite supervisory approval before deploying any canine, absent documented exigent circumstances; require and train canine officers to take into account the nature and severity of the alleged crime when deciding whether to deploy a canine to bite; require and train canine officers to avoid sending a canine to apprehend by biting a concealed suspect when the objective facts do not suggest the suspect is armed and a lower level of force reasonably can be expected to secure the suspect;

c. Place more stringent limits on use of ECWs, including limitations on multiple ECW cycles and detailed justification for using more than one cycle;

d. Retrain officers in use of ECWs to ensure they view and use ECWs as a tool of necessity, not convenience. Training should be consistent with principles set out in the *2011 ECW Guidelines*;

e. Develop and implement use-of-force reporting that requires the officer using force to complete a narrative, separate from the offense report,

describing the force used with particularity,
and describing with specificity the circumstances that required the level of force used,
including the reason for the initial stop or other
enforcement action. Some levels of force should
require all officers observing the use of force to
complete a separate force narrative;

f. Develop and implement supervisory review of
force that requires the supervisor to conduct a
complete review of each use of force, including
gathering and considering evidence necessary
to understand the circumstances of the force
incident and determine its consistency with law
and policy, including statements from individuals against whom force is used and civilian
witnesses;

g. Prohibit supervisors from reviewing or investigating a use of force in which they participated
or directed;

h. Ensure that complete use-of-force reporting
and review/investigation files—including all
offense reports, witness statements, and medical, audio/video, and other evidence—are kept
together in a centralized location;

i. Develop and implement a system for higher-
level, inter-disciplinary review of some types of
force, such as lethal force, canine deployment,
ECWs, and force resulting in any injury;

j. Improve collection, review, and response to use-
of-force data, including information regarding
ECW and canine use;

k. Implement system of zero tolerance for use of
force as punishment or retaliation rather than
as necessary, proportionate response to counter a threat;

l. Discipline officers who fail to report force and supervisors who fail to conduct adequate force investigations;

m. Identify race and other disparities in officer use of force and develop strategies to eliminate avoidable disparities;

n. Staff jail with at least two correctional officers at all times to ensure safety and minimize need for use of force in dealing with intoxicated or combative prisoners. Train correctional officers in de-escalation techniques with specific instruction and training on minimizing force when dealing with intoxicated and combative prisoners, as well as with passive resistance and noncompliance.

5. Implement Policies and Training to Improve Interactions with Vulnerable People

Providing officers with the tools and training to better respond to persons in physical or mental health crisis, and to those with intellectual disabilities, will help avoid unnecessary injuries, increase community trust, and make officers safer. FPD should:

a. Develop and implement policy and training for identifying and responding to individuals with known or suspected mental health conditions, including those observably in mental health crisis, and those with intellectual or other disabilities;

b. Provide enhanced crisis intervention training to a subset of officers to allow for ready availability of trained officers on the scenes of critical incidents involving individuals with mentally illness;

    c. Require that, wherever possible, at least one officer with enhanced crisis intervention training respond to any situation concerning individuals in mental health crisis or with intellectual disability, when force might be used;

    d. Provide training to officers regarding how to identify and respond to more commonly occurring medical emergencies that may at first appear to reflect a failure to comply with lawful orders. Such medical emergencies may include, for example, seizures and diabetic emergencies.

6. Change Response to Students to Avoid Criminalizing Youth While Maintaining a Learning Environment

FPD has the opportunity to profoundly impact students through its SRO program. This program can be used as a way to build positive relationships with youth from a young age and to support strategies to keep students in school and learning. FPD should:

    a. Work with school administrators, teachers, parents, and students to develop and implement policy and training consistent with law and best practices to more effectively address disciplinary issues in schools. This approach should be focused on SROs developing positive relationships with youth in support of maintaining a learning environment without unnecessarily treating disciplinary issues as criminal matters or resulting in the routine imposition of lengthy suspensions;

    b. Provide initial and regularly recurring training to SROs, including training in mental health, counseling, and the development of the teenage brain;

c. Evaluate SRO performance on student engagement and prevention of disturbances, rather
than on student arrests or removals;

d. Regularly review and evaluate incidents in
which SROs are involved to ensure they meet
the particular goals of the SRO program; to
identify any disparate impact or treatment by
race or other protected basis; and to identify
any policy, training, or equipment concerns.

7. Implement Measures to Reduce Bias and Its Impact on Police Behavior

Many of the recommendations listed elsewhere have
the potential to reduce the level and impact of bias on
police behavior (e.g., increasing positive interactions
between police and the community; increasing the collection and analysis of stop data; and increasing oversight
of the exercise of police discretion). Below are additional
measures that can assist in this effort. FPD should:

a. Provide initial and recurring training to all officers that sends a clear, consistent and emphatic
message that bias-based profiling and other
forms of discriminatory policing are prohibited.
Training should include:

1. Relevant legal and ethical standards;

2. Information on how stereotypes and implicit bias can infect police work;

3. The importance of procedural justice and
police legitimacy on community trust, police effectiveness, and officer safety;

4. The negative impacts of profiling on public
safety and crime prevention;

b. Provide training to supervisors and commanders on detecting and responding to bias-based profiling and other forms of discriminatory policing;

c. Include community members from groups that have expressed high levels of distrust of police in officer training;

d. Take steps to eliminate all forms of workplace bias from FPD and the City.

8. Improve and Increase Training Generally

FPD officers receive far too little training as recruits and after becoming officers. Officers need a better knowledge of what law, policy, and integrity require, and concrete training on how to carry out their police responsibilities. In addition to the training specified elsewhere in these recommendations, FPD should:

a. Significantly increase the quality and amount of all types of officer training, including recruit, field training (including for officers hired from other agencies), and in-service training;

b. Require that training cover, in depth, constitutional and other legal restrictions on officer action, as well as additional factors officers should consider before taking enforcement action (such as police legitimacy and procedural justice considerations);

c. Employ scenario-based and adult-learning methods.

9. Increase Civilian Involvement in Police Decision Making

In addition to engaging with all segments of Ferguson as part of implementing community policing, FPD should develop and implement a system that incorporates civilian input into all aspects of policing, including policy development, training, use-of-force review, and investigation of misconduct complaints.

10. Improve Officer Supervision

The recommendations set out here cannot be implemented without dedicated, skilled, and well-trained supervisors who police lawfully and without bias. FPD should:

    a. Provide all supervisors with specific supervisory training prior to assigning them to supervisory positions;

    b. Develop and require supervisors to use an "early intervention system" to objectively detect problematic patterns of officer misconduct, assist officers who need additional attention, and identify training and equipment needs;

    c. Support supervisors who encourage and guide respectful policing and implement community policing principles, and evaluate them on this basis. Remove supervisors who do not adequately review officer activity and reports or fail to support, through words or actions, unbiased policing;

    d. Ensure that an adequate number of qualified first-line supervisors are deployed in the field to allow supervisors to provide close and effective supervision to each officer under the supervisor's direct command, provide officers with the direction and guidance necessary to improve and develop as officers, and to identify, correct, and prevent misconduct.

11. Recruiting, Hiring, and Promotion

There are widespread concerns about the lack of diversity, especially race and gender diversity, among FPD officers. FPD should modify its systems for recruiting hiring and promotion to:

a. Ensure that the department's officer hiring and selection processes include an objective process for selection that employs reliable and valid selection devices that comport with best practices and federal anti-discrimination laws;

b. In the case of lateral hires, scrutinize prior training and qualification records as well as complaint and disciplinary history;

c. Implement validated pre-employment screening mechanisms to ensure temperamental and skill-set suitability for policing.

12. Develop Mechanisms to More Effectively Respond to Allegations of Officer Misconduct

Responding to allegations of officer misconduct is critical not only to correct officer behavior and identify policy, training, or tactical concerns, but also to build community confidence and police legitimacy. FPD should:

a. Modify procedures and practices for accepting complaints to make it easier and less intimidating for individuals to register formal complaints about police conduct, including providing complaint forms online and in various locations throughout the City and allowing for complaints to be submitted online and by third parties or anonymously;

b. Require that all complaints be logged and investigated;

c. Develop and implement a consistent, reliable, and fair process for investigating and responding to complaints of officer misconduct. As part of this process, FPD should:

    1. Investigate all misconduct complaints, even where the complainant indicates he or she does not want the complaint investigated, or wishes to remain anonymous;

    2. Not withdraw complaints without reaching a disposition;

d. Develop and implement a fair and consistent system for disciplining officers found to have committed misconduct;

e. Terminate officers found to have been materially untruthful in performance of their duties, including in completing reports or during internal affairs investigations;

f. Timely provide in writing to the Ferguson Prosecuting Attorney all impeachment information on officers who may testify or provide sworn reports, including findings of untruthfulness in internal affairs investigations, for disclosure to the defendant under *Brady v. Maryland*, 373 U.S. 83 (1963);

g. Document in a central location all misconduct complaints and investigations, including the nature of the complaint, the name of the officer, and the disposition of the investigation;

h. Maintain complete misconduct complaint investigative files in a central location;

i. Develop and implement a community-centered mediation program to resolve, as appropriate, allegations of officer misconduct.

13. Publically Share Information about the Nature and Impact of Police Activities

Transparency is a key component of good governance and community trust. Providing broad information to the public also facilitates constructive community engagement. FPD should:

a. Provide regular and specific public reports on police stop, search, arrest, ticketing, force, and community engagement activities, including particular problems and achievements, and describing the steps taken to address concerns;

b. Provide regular public reports on allegations of misconduct, including the nature of the complaint and its resolution;

c. Make available online and regularly update a complete set of police policies.

B. Ferguson Court Practices

1. Make Municipal Court Processes More Transparent

Restoring the legitimacy of the municipal justice system requires increased transparency regarding court operations to allow the public to assess whether the court is operating in a fair manner. The municipal court should:

a. Make public—through a variety of means, including prominent display on the City, police, and municipal court web pages—all court-related fines, fees, and bond amounts, and a description of the municipal court payment process, including court dates, payment options, and potential consequences for non-payment or missed court dates;

b. Create, adopt, and make public written procedures for all court operations;

c. Collect all orders currently in effect and make those orders accessible to the public, including by posting any such materials on the City, police, and municipal court web pages. Make public all new court orders and directives as they are issued;

d. Initiate a public education campaign to ensure individuals can have an accurate and complete understanding of how Ferguson's municipal court operates, including that appearance in court without ability to pay an owed fine will not result in arrest;

e. Provide broadly available information to individuals regarding low-cost or cost-free legal assistance;

f. Enhance public reporting by ensuring data provided to the Missouri Courts Administrator is accurate, and by making that and additional data available on City and court websites, including monthly reports indicating:

1. The number of warrants issued and currently outstanding;

2. The number of cases heard during the previous month;

3. The amount of fines imposed and collected, broken down by offense, including by race;

4. Data regarding the number of Missouri Department of Revenue license suspensions initiated by the court and the number of compliance letters enabling license reinstatement issued by the court.

g. Revise the municipal court website to enable these recommendations to be fully implemented.

2. Provide Complete and Accurate Information to a Person Charged with a Municipal Violation

In addition to making its processes more transparent to the public, the court should ensure that those with cases pending before the court are provided with adequate and reliable information about their case. The municipal court, in collaboration with the Patrol Division, should:

a. Ensure all FPD citations, summonses, and arrests are accompanied by sufficient, detailed information about the recipient's rights and responsibilities, including:

1. The specific municipal violation charged;

2. A person's options for addressing the charge, including whether in-person appearance is required or if alternative methods, including online payment, are available, and information regarding all pending deadlines;

3. A person's right to challenge the charge in court;

4. The exact date and time of the court session at which the person receiving the charge must or may appear;

5. Information about how to seek a continuance for a court date;

6. The specific fine imposed, if the offense has a preset fine;

7. The processes available to seek a fine reduction for financial incapacity, consistent with recommendation four set forth below;

8. The penalties for failing to meet court requirements.

b. Develop and implement a secure online system for individuals to be able to access specific details about their case, including fines owed, payments made, and pending requirements and deadlines.

3. Change Court Procedures for Tracking and Resolving Municipal Charges to Simplify Court Processes and Expand Available Payment Options

The municipal court should:

a. Strictly limit those offenses requiring in-person court appearance for resolution to those for which state law requires the defendant to make an initial appearance in court;

b. Establish a process by which a person may seek a continuance of a court date, whether or not represented by counsel;

c. Continue to implement its online payment system, and expand it to allow late payments, payment plan installments, bond payments, and other court payments to be made online;

d. Continue to develop and transition to an electronic records management system for court records to ensure all case information and events are tracked and accessible to court officials and FPD staff, as appropriate. Ensure electronic records management system has appropriate controls to limit user access and ability to alter case records;

e. Ensure that the municipal court office is consistently staffed during posted business hours to allow those appearing at the court window of the police department seeking to resolve municipal charges to do so;

f. Accept partial payments from individuals, and provide clear information to individuals about payment plan options.

4. Review Preset Fine Amounts and Implement System for Fine Reduction

The municipal court should:

a. Immediately undertake a review of current fine amounts and ensure that they are consistent not only with regional but also statewide fine averages, are not overly punitive, and take into account the income of Ferguson residents;

b. Develop and implement a process by which individuals can appear in court to seek proportioning of preset fines to their financial ability to pay.

5. Develop Effective Ability-to-Pay Assessment System and Improve Data Collection Regarding Imposed Fines

The municipal court should:

a. Develop and implement consistent written criteria for conducting an assessment of an individual's ability to pay prior to the assessment of any fine, and upon any increase in the fine or related court costs and fees. The ability-to-pay assessment should include not only a consideration of the financial resources of an individual, but also a consideration of any documented fines owed to other municipal courts;

b. Improve current procedures for collecting and tracking data regarding fine amounts imposed. Track initial fines imposed as an independent figure separate from any additional charges imposed during a case;

c. Regularly conduct internal reviews of data regarding fine assessments. This review should include an analysis of fines imposed for the same offenses, including by race of the defendant, to ensure fine assessments for like offenses are set appropriately.

6. Revise Payment Plan Procedures and Provide Alternatives to Fine Payments for Resolving Municipal Charges

The municipal court should:

a. Develop and implement a specific process by which a person can enroll in a payment plan that requires reasonable periodic payments.

That process should include an assessment of a person's ability to pay to determine an appropriate periodic payment amount, although a required payment shall not exceed $100. That process should also include a means for a person to seek a reduction in their monthly payment obligation in the event of a change in their financial circumstances;

b. Provide more opportunities for a person to seek leave to pay a lower amount in a given month beyond the court's current practice of requiring appearance the first Wednesday of the month at 11:00 a.m. Adopt procedures allowing individuals to seek their first request for a one-time reduction outside of court, and to have such requests be automatically granted. Such procedures should provide that subsequent requests shall be granted liberally by the Municipal Judge, and denials of requests for extensions or reduced monthly payments shall be accompanied by a written explanation of why the request was denied;

c. Cease practice of automatically issuing a warrant when a person on a payment plan misses a payment, and adopt procedures that provide for appropriate warnings following a missed payment, consistent with recommendation eight set forth below;

d. Work with community organizations and other regional groups to develop alternative penalty options besides fines, including expanding community service options. Make all individuals eligible for community service.

7. Reform Trial Procedures to Ensure Full Compliance with Due Process Requirements

The municipal court should take all necessary steps to ensure that the court's trial procedures fully comport with due process such that defendants are provided with a fair and impartial forum to challenge the charges brought against them. As part of this effort, the court shall ensure that defendants taking their case to trial are provided with all evidence relevant to guilt determinations consistent with the requirements of *Brady v. Maryland*, 373 U.S. 83 (1963), and other applicable law.

8. Stop Using Arrest Warrants as a Means of Collecting Owed Fines and Fees

As Ferguson's own Municipal Judge has recognized, municipal code violations should result in jail in only the rarest of circumstances. To begin to address these problems, Ferguson should only jail individuals for a failure to appear on or pay a municipal code violation penalty, if at all, if the following steps have been attempted in a particular case and have failed:

   a. a. Enforcement of fines through alternative means, including:

   1. Assessment of reasonable late fees;

   2. Expanding options for payment through community service;

   3. Modified payment plans with reasonable amounts due and payment procedures;

   4. A show cause hearing on why a warrant should not issue, including an assessment of ability to pay, where requested. At this hearing the individual has a right to counsel and, if the individual is indigent, the

court will assign counsel to represent the individual. *See* Mo. Sup. Ct. R. 37.65; Mo. Mun. Benchbook, Cir. Ct., Mun. Divs. § 13.8;

b. Personal service on the individual of the Order to Show Cause Motion that provides notice of the above information regarding right to counsel and the consequences of non-appearance; and

c. If the above mechanisms are unsuccessful at securing payment or otherwise resolving the case, the court should ensure that any arrest warrant issued has the instruction that it be executed only on days that the court is in session so that the individual can be brought immediately before the court to enable the above procedures to be implemented. *See* Mo. Mun. Benchbook, Cir. Ct., Mun. Divs. § 13.8 ("If a defendant fails to appear in court on the return date of the order to show cause or motion for contempt, *a warrant should be issued to get the defendant before the court for the hearing.*") (emphasis added)

9. Allow Warrants to be Recalled Without the Payment of Bond

Ferguson recently extended its warrant recall program, also called an "amnesty" program, which allows individuals to have municipal warrants recalled and to receive a new court date without paying a bond. This program should be made permanent. The municipal court should:

a. Allow all individuals to seek warrant recall in writing or via telephone, whether represented by an attorney or not;

b. Provide information to a participating individual at the time of the warrant recall, including the number of charges pending, the fine amount due if a charge has been assessed, the options available to pay assessed fines, the deadlines for doing so, and the requirements, if any, for appearing in court.

10. Modify Bond Amounts and Bond and Detention Procedures

Ferguson has two separate municipal code bond schedules and processes: one for warrantless arrests, and another for arrests pursuant to warrants issued by the municipal court. Ferguson's municipal court recently limited the number of municipal code violations for which officers can jail an individual without a warrant, and reduced the amount of time the jail may hold a defendant who is unable to post bond from 72 to 12 hours. These changes are a positive start, but further reforms are necessary. The City and municipal court should:

a. Limit the amount of time the jail may hold a defendant unable to post bond on *all* arrests for municipal code violations or municipal arrest warrants to 12 hours;

b. Establish procedures for setting bond amounts for warrantless and warrant-based detainees that are consistent with the Equal Protection Clause's prohibition on incarcerating individuals on the basis of indigency, and that ensure bond shall in no case exceed $100 for a person arrested pursuant to a municipal warrant, regardless of the number of pending charges;

c. At the time of bond payment, provide individuals with the option of applying a bond fee to underlying fines and costs, including in the event of forfeiture;

d. Take steps necessary, including the continued development of a computerized court records management system as discussed above, to enable court staff, FPD officers, and FPD correctional officers to access case information so that a person has the option of paying the full underlying fine owed in lieu of bond upon being arrested;

e. Increase options for making a bond payment, including allowing bond payment by credit card and through the online payment system, whether by a person in jail or outside of the jail;

f. Institute closer oversight and tracking of bond payment acceptance by FPD officers and FPD correctional officers;

g. Initiate practice of issuing bond refund checks immediately upon a defendant paying their fine in full and being owed a bond refund;

h. Ensure that all court staff, FPD officers, and FPD correctional officers understand Ferguson's bond rules and procedures.

11. Consistently Provide "Compliance Letters" Necessary for Driver's License Reinstatement After a Person Makes an Appearance Following a License Suspension

Per official policy, the municipal court provides people who have had their licenses suspended pursuant to Mo. Rev. Stat. § 302.341.1 with compliance letters enabling the suspension to be lifted only once the underlying fine has been paid in full. Court staff told us, however, that in "sympathetic cases," they provide compliance letters that enable people to have their licenses reinstated. The court should adopt and implement a policy of providing individuals with compliance letters immediately upon a person appearing in court following a license suspension pursuant to this statute.

12. Close Cases that Remain on the Court's Docket Solely Because of Failure to Appear Charges or Bond Forfeitures

In September 2014, the City of Ferguson repealed Ferguson Mun. Code § 13-58, which allowed the imposition of an additional "Failure to Appear" charge, fines, and fees in response to missed appearances and payments. Nonetheless, many cases remain pending on the court's docket solely on account of charges, fines, and fees issued pursuant to this statute or because of questionable bond forfeiture practices. The City and municipal court should:

    a. Close all municipal cases in which the individual has paid fines equal or greater to the amount of the fine assessed for the original municipal code violation—through Failure to Appear fines and fees or forfeited bond payments—and clear all associated warrants;

    b. Remove all Failure to Appear related charges, fines, and fees from current cases, and close all cases in which only a Failure to Appear charge, fine, or fee remains pending;

    c. Immediately provide compliance letters so that license suspensions are lifted for all individuals whose cases are closed pursuant to these reforms.

13. Collaborate with Other Municipalities and the State of Missouri to Implement Reforms

These recommendations should be closely evaluated and, as appropriate, implemented by other municipalities. We also recommend that the City and other municipalities work collaboratively with the state of Missouri on issues requiring statewide action, and further recommend:

a. Reform of Mo. Rev. Stat. § 302.341.1, which requires the suspension of individuals' driving licenses in certain cases where they do not appear or timely pay traffic charges involving moving violations;

b. Increased oversight of municipal courts in St. Louis County and throughout the state of Missouri to ensure that courts operate in a manner consistent with due process, equal protection, and other requirements of the Constitution and other laws.

VI. CONCLUSION

Our investigation indicates that Ferguson as a City has the capacity to reform its approach to law enforcement. A small municipal department may offer greater potential for officers to form partnerships and have frequent, positive interactions with Ferguson residents, repairing and maintaining police-community relationships. *See, e.g.,* Jim Burack, *Putting the "Local" Back in Local Law Enforcement, in, American Policing in 2022: Essays on the Future of the Profession* 79-83 (Debra R. Cohen McCullough & Deborah L. Spence, eds., 2012). These reform efforts will be well worth the considerable time and dedication they will require, as they have the potential to make Ferguson safer and more united.

seven

November 22, 2014, Cleveland, Ohio:

The Death of Tamir Rice

THE NOVEMBER 29, 2012 62-police vehicle chase covering 19-plus miles which resulted in the deaths of Timothy Russell and Malissa Williams in a hail of gunfire, may be considered one of the most egregious examples of police misconduct in recent history.

But the shooting death of Tamir Rice, a 12-year old, almost two years later, November 22, 2014, also in Cleveland, may be the absolute nadir in individual police incompetence and police departmental neglect.

The Tamir Rice case has become a *cause célèbre* in far more ways than one. Fortunately, the death of Tamir Rice was caught on a surveillance camera.

In a (recorded) 911 call, a citizen sitting in a park gazebo reported that someone, possibly a juvenile, was pointing "a pistol" at people at random in the Cudell Recreation Center. The caller not only said the person was a juvenile, but apparently twice said the gun was "probably a fake." It was not clear if the fake gun detail in that call was ever passed on to two officers Timothy Loehmann and Frank Garmback, responding to the call.

The caller then apparently left the gazebo and Tamir Rice subsequently entered it.

Loehmann and Garmback came to the scene and approached Rice, ordering him to put up his hands. Rice reached into his waistband, prompting one of the officers—Loehmann,—to fire two shots. One hit Rice in the torso. He was taken to MetroHealth Medical Center. He died the next day.

At no time did Rice brandish the "gun" at the officers or threaten to shoot them. It was later discovered the "gun" was an "airsoft" pistol, a pellet-gun type toy.

Videotape footage, released by police November 26, after demands from the Rice family, showed the following: Rice was pacing around the park, occasionally extending his right arm with what appears to be a gun in his hand, talking on a cellphone and sitting at a picnic table in the gazebo. The videotape shows the police patrol car pulling up beside the gazebo. Rice then appears to move his right hand toward his waistband, prompting Loehmann to get out of the patrol car and shoot him from a distance of less than 10 feet, within two seconds.

... shot him within two seconds of arriving on the scene.

Neither Loehmann nor Garmback administered first aid to Rice. (No Cleveland Police cars apparently carried first aid equipment.)

Almost four minutes later, a police detective and an FBI agent arrived; the FBI agent had been working on a bank robbery detail nearby. They treated Rice.

Three minutes later, paramedics took Rice to the MetroHealth Medical Center.

But Rice's mother said the police had put her 14-year old daughter in handcuffs and then threatened to arrest *her*, if she didn't calm down after being told of her son's death.

That too, was on videotape—the tape shows Rice's 14-year old sister being forced to the ground and handcuffed and placed in a patrol car after she ran toward

Rice. It also shows the police waiting four minutes before providing first aid to Rice.

... it was the absolute nadir in individual police incompetence and police departmental neglect ...

In the website *The Daily Kos*, (www.dailykos.com) for January 9, 2015, in an article "The outrageous and tragic hiring of officer Timothy Loehmann by the Cleveland police," Shaun King wrote of Loehmann's background, as an officer previously in the Independence Ohio, Police Department. (Independence is a southeast suburb of Cleveland.)

King wrote:

> The American public deserves better.
>
> Before Cleveland police department officer Timothy Loehmann tragically shot and killed 12-year-old Tamir Rice, he had accumulated a record of emotional instability, disregard for training, and ineptitude for the job so severe that he should never have been hired ... his previous supervisors in Independence, Ohio, said as much. As many as seven police departments and programs turned him down in the aftermath of his termination from Independence, but Cleveland, which claims they never checked his records, hired him. They should be held accountable for this mistake of fatal proportions.
>
> It's nearly impossible to find a documented case of someone less qualified to have a badge and a gun than Timothy Loehmann. It's frightening, when reviewing the evidence, to think that he was ever hired and makes one wonder how many other times police departments have completely ignored human resource files when making hires for those expected to protect and serve us.

Files from the Independence Police Department show that:

- At 23, Loehmann had never had a full-time job and previously had been working at a mainte-nance job part-time for eight dollars an hour:
- Supervisors reported he could not follow sim-ple directions, could not communicate clear thoughts nor recollections;
- * Supervisors reported severe emotional immaturity;
- His handgun performance(s) were dismal and he was apparently not prepared mentally for handgun training;
- He appeared to have no real commitment to the Independence Police Department.

The file on Loehmann was eventually 62 pages long.
The final statement, by a supervisor read:
"I do not believe time, nor training, will be able to change or correct these deficiencies."

After only five months on the job, Loehmann resigned from the Independence Police Department one step be-fore he would have been fired, Shaun King said.

King rightly observes if the Cleveland Police Human Resources department had read Loehmann's Independence Police Department file, he well might never have been hired in Cleveland.

He had applied, and had been rejected, by seven po-lice departments, including the police departments in Akron, Euclid and Parma Heights, in Ohio and the New York City Police Department.

Cleveland, com (www.Cleveland.com), the website of the *Cleveland Plain Dealer,* reported January 7, 2015, that Loehmann took tests for the Cuyahoga (Cleveland area) County Sheriff's Department. Loehmann passed the physical test: 27 push-ups in a minute, a mile and a half run in less than 10 minutes and other physical tests. But he failed the written tests, which included questions on problem solving, vocabulary, grammar, punctuation and spelling.

A passing grade is a 70; Loehmann scored 46 percent.

(At the public school, college and university level, a 70 is usually the lowest possible "C" score; a 46 is a clear "F" grade. A "D" begins at 60.)

At the time Loehmann shot Tamir Rice, Loehmann's partner was Frank Garmback. It wasn't exactly a case of the-blind-leading-the-blind; it was more of a case of the-corrupt-leading-the-incompetent.

The Wikipedia (www.wikipedia.com) entry "The Shooting of Tamir Rice," says:

> Garmback, who was driving the police cruiser, has been a police officer in Cleveland since 2008. In 2014, the City of Cleveland paid $100,000, to settle an excessive force lawsuit against him by a local woman; according to her lawsuit, Garmback "rushed and placed her in a chokehold, tackled her to the ground, twisted her wrist and began hitting her body" and "'such reckless, wanton and willful use of excessive force proximately caused bodily injury." The woman had called the police to report a car blocking her driveway. The settlement does not appear in Garmback's personnel file.

On December 5, 2014, the family of Tamir Rice filed a wrongful death lawsuit in federal court in Cleveland.

They named Timothy Loehmann, Frank Garmback and the City of Cleveland as defendants. The lawsuit claimed the officers "acted unreasonably, recklessly and with deliberate indifference to the safety and rights" of Tamir Rice, when the "confronted him in a surprise fashion and fired multiple shots at him without any adequate investigation."

The lawsuit claimed the officers were inadequately trained and supervised and that Loehmann should never have been hired after his history with the Independence Police. The lawsuit stated that compensatory and punitive charges would be determined at the trial.

What else could possibly go wrong with this abysmally tragic story?

After the death of Tamir Rice at the hands of the woefully—and criminally—inept policeman Timothy Loehmann?

What else could go wrong? Infighting then between the City of Cleveland, the Cleveland Police Department, the Cuyahoga County Sheriff's Office and the State of Ohio Attorney General's office.

In a follow-up article in *The Daily Kos,* Tuesday May 12, 2015, titled "The police killing of Tamir Rice and the rampant lie of cases being 'under investigation,'" Shaun King wrote:

Twelve-year-old Tamir Rice was shot by Officer Timothy Loehmann of the Cleveland Police Department on November 22, 2014, He fought to live until the next day, but died because of the gunshot to his torso.

November passed.
December passed.
January passed.
February passed.
March passed.
April passed.

Here we are in the middle of May, in 2015, and the family of Tamir Rice hasn't even seen a police report. From that tragic day where their beloved son and brother was shot and left to die, ignored by police, there on the pavement of his local park.

No officers have been charged, no reports have been released, no grand juries have been convened, nothing.

Winter and spring have passed in Cleveland and we are entering into the summer, yet still no answers have been given into what justice will look like for this devastated family. The entire incident was caught on film. It took place in broad daylight.

It doesn't take 165 days (3,960 hours or 237,600 minutes) to complete this investigation. Period.

Toward the end of May, 2015, nothing in the Tamir Rice case had been resolved; no charges have been filed and it took almost six months for the body to be returned to the family.

Shaun King continued to follow the Tamir Rice story, in a follow-up article in *The Daily Kos* May 20, 2015, under the headline:

Cleveland police charged 12-year-old
Tamir Rice with 'aggravated menacing'
and 'inducing panic'

Cleveland police had the paperwork done to file two charges against Tamir Rice:

Aggravated menacing

... and ...

Inducing panic

The police paperwork is reproduced in King's May 20, 2015, *Daily Kos* article.

Aggravated menacing ...

Inducing panic ...

Tamir Rice was 12 years old.

eight

April 2, 2015, Tulsa, Oklahoma:

The Death of Eric Courtney Harris

THE QUESTION IN THIS case—and, of course, in many others—is *WHY?*

WHY was this allowed to happen?

On April 2, 2015, Robert Bates, a volunteer Tulsa Reserve Deputy shot Eric Courtney Harris, a suspected drug dealer, during an undercover drug operation. Bates had apparently intended to shot Harris with a Taser. He grabbed his gun instead of his Taser. He shot Harris in the back, while Harris was running down a street.

Harris died an hour later.

He was not armed.

(Many will remember the name Eric Harris as one of two senior high school students—the other Dylan Klebold—who went to Columbine High School, Columbine, Colorado, which they attended, and killed 12 students and one teacher and injured 21 others. April 20, 1999. The two then committed suicide. That was one of the major national news stories of 1999.)

Robert Bates is, in fact, a 73-year old insurance broker.

He had worked as a police officer for one year in the 1960s.

Critics claimed he "paid to play a cop."

In a CNN article, "Deputy charged in Tulsa shooting" by Catherine E. Shoichet, Jason Morris and Ed Lavandera, April 14, 2015, claimed that Bates donated cars and video equipment to the Sheriff's office and had been a long-time friend, political supporter and contributed $2,500 to the reelection campaign of Tulsa County Sheriff Stanley Glanz.

Bates had been a volunteer Reserve Deputy since 2008.

Critics also questioned why he was involved at all, in such a high-stakes drug sting operation.

According to the CNN article, Eric Harris was the subject of an operation set up to catch him selling drugs and guns. The episode, like many others, was videotaped.

The video shows Harris getting out of a car and running from the police. There was a foot chase, and an officer wearing a body camera caught up to Harris and tackled him to the ground.

Footage from the video reveals the sound of a Taser and a gun and a voice saying, "I shot him. I'm sorry."

Harris is heard to say, "I'm losing my breath."

Another voice—apparently another deputy—says— "F* * * your breath."

Bates was subsequently charged with second-degree homicide. If convicted he would face four years in jail and a $1,000 fine.

The CNN article said that Sgt. Jim Clark, of the Tulsa Police department, who was brought in to review the case, excused the behavior of Robert Bates and another deputy heard cursing at Harris.

Clark said Bates was the "victim" of what he called "slip and capture," which occurred in a high stress situation, such as a drug sting, when a person intends to do one thing (Bates would use his Taser) but instead, inadvertently, does another thing (use his gun.)

That claim drew immediate criticism; it was called "junk science."

CNN quoted Phil Stinson, assistant professor of Criminal Justice at Bowling Green State University in Ohio: "It's not something that's supported by a testable theory. There's no peer-reviewed articles that would support this ... it's not generally accepted by the scientific community. So it's something that in most courts would not be admissible as evidence."

Scott Wood, an attorney representing Bates said the shooting was an "excusable homicide." And "we believe the video itself proves that it was an accident of misfortune that occurred while Deputy Bates was fulfilling his duties as a reserve deputy. He is not guilty of second-degree manslaughter."

Wood claimed that Bates had worked over 100 operations on search warrants where he was on the outer perimeter, but had never been on an arrest team or had been the point-man in an arrest situation. He worked largely in a support role.

But—but—

An MSNBC article by Michele Richinick, April 24, 2015, stated that colleagues questioned Bates' behavior as early as 2008:

A memo dated December 17, 2008 cited a sergeant telling a captain that Bates was using his personal vehicle to make unauthorized stops, which violated Tulsa County Sheriff's Office policies.

Attorney Wood, representing Bates, claimed that Bates had undergone all required training.

But, according to the MSNBC article, a 2009 internal review concluded that Bates had incomplete training, violated (Sheriff's Office) policies and received special treatment. But after the 2009 review, no action was taken.

An April 27, 2015 article headlined "Eric Harris Shooting: Sheriff's Official Tim Albin reigns," NBC News reported:

A top sheriff's official reigned on Monday in Tulsa, Oklahoma, where an unarmed man was shot and killed earlier this month by a volunteer reserve deputy who says he mistook his gun for a Taser.

Sheriff Stanley Glanz announced the resignation of Tim Albin, the undersheriff. A 2009 internal review obtained by NBC News found that Albin had asked employees to modify reviews and training documentation for the volunteer deputy Robert Bates.

The same review found that Albin told people who raised concerns about Bates to keep their mouths shut.

The CNN article by Shoichet, Morris and Lavandera said:

Authorities ... painted Harris as a dangerous, possibly PCP-addled illegal gun dealer. But Andre Harris, the brother of Eric Harris said that claims that his brother was violent and on PCP were false.

They also wrote:

Andre Harris, brother of Eric Harris told reporters that the sheriff's office tried to persuade him not to hire an attorney and quickly make the case "go away."

... and ...

Daniel Smolen, an attorney representing the (Eric) Harris family, said Bates paid big money to play a cop in his spare time.

"It's absolutely mind boggling that you have a wealthy businessman who's been essentially deputized to go play like he's some outlaw, like he's just cleaning up the streets."

nine |

April 12, 2015,
Baltimore, Maryland
The Death of Freddie Gray

THE INVESTIGATION AND PROSECUTION in the Freddie Gray case in Baltimore has proven to be significantly different than other similar cases nationwide. The prosecution, particularly, was far more prompt and positive than many expected.

The timeline of the case was:

April 12, 2015

8:39 a.m.—Four Baltimore officers on bicycle patrol at the corner of North Avenue and Mount Street in the west Baltimore areas make "eye contact" with Gray. They begin pursuing Gray after he fled. Later investigations are unclear about why the police chased Gray. They later claim he was arrested because he had an illegal switchblade knife, but the knife they discovered was legal under Baltimore law.

8:40-8:46 Gray gives up without a struggle. The scene is recorded on a cellphone video. Gray is on the ground and is half-carried, half-dragged to a police van after his legs seem to go limp. He is shown in a video screaming in pain as police drag-carry him to the van. He asks for an inhaler, but the request is refused.

A block away the van is stopped so Gray can be placed in leg irons. A video shows him at the back of the police van, stomach down, his legs protruding from the back of the van. Critics later claim that he was given a "rough ride," not placed in a seatbelt in the van, so he could be bounced around during transport.

8:47-9:23. The van makes a second stop. No reason has been given for the stop. On the way to the Baltimore Police Department's Western Division, the van makes a third stop to pick up another prisoner.

The van arrives as the police station. A normal 5-minute transport has taken 45 minutes. Paramedics are called and 21 minutes later, Gray is taken to the University of Maryland's Shock Trauma Center.

April 13, 2015

Baltimore police hold a press conference and deny any use of force in the arrest.

April 14, 2015

Gray undergoes surgery on his spine.

April 15-18, 2015

Gray remains in a coma.

April 18, 2015

Protests began. A crowd gathers at the Baltimore police Western headquarters, holding up their hands and turning their backs to the building. Gray's stepfather tells the crowd, "If this happens to him, it could happen to any of you."

("Freddie Gray: From Baltimore Arrest to Protests, a Timeline of the Case," NBC News website, May 21, 2915.)

April 19, 2015

Freddie Gray is pronounced dead in the hospital at 7:45 a.m. Reportedly, he had a severed spinal cord and crushed vocal cords.

May 6, 2015

Baltimore officials made two separate major announcements: Police Chief Anthony Batts admitted a lot of the tension between the public and the Baltimore Police came from a "distrust in law enforcement as a whole. We are part of the problem," he told CNN. "The community needs to hear that. The community needs to hear from us that we haven't been part of the solution, and now we have to evolve. Now we have to change."

Baltimore Mayor Stephanie Rawlings-Blake announced she is seeking help from the Department of Justice to reform the Baltimore city Police Department. We all know that Baltimore continues to have a fractured relationship between the police and the community," she said, "noting that the recent death of Freddie Gray while in police custody contributed to that fractured relationship. "We've got to get it right," she said, "Failure is not an option."

Marilyn Mosby then took over the case. Mosby, 35, is a black, fifth-generation member of her family to be involved in law enforcement. She holds a Jurist Doctor law degree from Boston College Law School and was elected State's Attorney for Baltimore in 2013.

When she was elected, she became the youngest top prosecutor in any major American city.

In late May, 2015—six months after Tamir Rice was

shot by Cleveland Police, no action had been taken; no one charged.

But Mosby moved quickly. On May 21, 2015, a Grand Jury indicted six Baltimore police officers.

The charges (and potential maximum sentences) were:

Officer Caesar Goodson:
- Second degree depraved heart murder (30 years)
- Involuntary manslaughter (10 years)
- Second degree negligent assault (10 years)
- Manslaughter by vehicle—gross negligence (10 years)
- Manslaughter by vehicle—criminal negligence (3 years)
- Misconduct in office for failure to perform a duty regarding the safety of a prisoner
- Reckless endangerment (5 years)

Officer William Porter:
- Involuntary manslaughter (10 years)
- Second degree negligent assault (10 years)
- Misconduct in office for failure to a perform a duty regarding the safety of a prisoner
- Reckless endangerment (5 years)

Lt. Brian Rice:
- Involuntary manslaughter (10 years)
- Second degree negligent assault (10 years)
- Misconduct in office for failure to perform a duty regarding the safety of a prisoner
- Reckless endangerment (5 years)

Officer Edward Nero:
- Second degree intentional assault (10 years)
- Misconduct in office for failure to perform a duty regarding the safety of a prisoner

- Misconduct in office
- Reckless endangerment (5 years)

Officer Garrett Miller:
- Second degree intentional assault (10 years)
- Misconduct in office for an illegal arrest
- Misconduct in office for failure to perform a duty regarding the safety of a prisoner
- Reckless endangerment (5 years)

Sgt. Alicia White:
- Involuntary manslaughter (10 years)
- Second degree negligent assault (10 years)
- Misconduct in office for failure to perform a duty regarding the safety of a prisoner
- Reckless endangerment (5 years)

Initially, False imprisonment charges were part of the charges, but were dropped. Misconduct in office/ Reckless endangerment charges for all six were added.

(Police subsequently admitted that Gray had not been secured in the back of the van with a seatbelt. Additionally, Gray was apparently in severe physical distress in the police van, but no officer aided him in any way.)

Since Goodson was driving the van, he faced the most charges, a possible 68 years in prison.

Many in Maryland, and surely those outside Maryland, may not understand "depraved heart murder." It is, in fact, callous disregard for the consequences of an individual's actions, as in: "he had a heart of stone." In Maryland, depraved heart murder carried a prison term of 30 years.

The prompt actions by Marilyn Mosby of the sweeping charges against the six was a rarity in law enforcement— and her actions kept Baltimore relatively calm.

How did the public react to the Freddie Gray arrest and death?

As an example, Julie Boswell, of Herndon, Virginia contributed her thoughts, in *The Huffington Post*, May 1, 2015:

> *They essentially kidnapped a random guy off the streets, assaulted him, shackled him and drove him around for 45 more minutes, denying him medical care as he was dying, then when he died, they waged a disinformation campaign to smear his name and slander him. Pretty horrific stuff.*

Many, many others have expressed the same sentiments on the internet, about this case and others....

In a lengthy and comprehensive article '"Why Baltimore Blew Up," in *Rolling Stone*, June 4, 2015, Matt Taibbi writes:

> Most Americans have never experienced this kind of policing. They haven't had to stare down the barrel of a service revolver drawn for no reason at a routine stop. They haven't had their wife and kids put on an ice-cold sidewalk curb while cops ran their license plate. They haven't ever been told to get the fuck back in their car right now, been accused of having too prominent a "bulge," had their dog shot and their kids handcuffed near its body during a wrong-door raid, watched their seven-year-old dragged to jail for sitting on a dirt bike, or dealt with any of a thousand other positively crazy things non-white America has come to expect from an interaction with law enforcement. "It's everywhere," says Christen Brown, who as a 24-year-old city parks employee was allegedly roughed up and arrested just for filming the police in a parking lot. "You can be somewhere minding your business and they will find their

best way to fuck with you, point blank. It's blatant disrespect."

This system, now standard in almost all of urban America, is Mayberry on one side and trending Moscow or 1980s South Africa on the other. Why? Because America loves to lie to itself about race. It's able to do so for many reasons, including the little-discussed fact that most people have literally no social interaction with black people, so they don't hear about this every day.

Police brutality is tough to talk about because white and black Americans see the issue so differently, with white Americans still overwhelmingly supportive and trustful of law enforcement. But the current controversy is as much about how modern law enforcement practices have ruined the job of policing as it is about racism. There are plenty of good cops out there, but the way policing works in cities like Baltimore, the bad ones can thrive. And disasters aren't just more likely, they're inevitable.

... and, Taibbi writes ...

In most cities, it's close to impossible to get a police officer removed for lies, abuse or other forms of misconduct.

(*Rolling Stone*, pp. 42, 46)

Epilogue:

A Narrative Without an End ...

This could very well be a narrative without an end ...
Sanford, Florida, Albuquerque, Cleveland, Staten Island, Ferguson, Missouri, Tulsa, Baltimore ...
... and more:

East Haven, Connecticut.

Latinos were subjected to far more stops, harsher treatment and retaliation against citizen complains, a 2011 Justice Department report found. Four police officers were arrested for allegedly targeting Latinos in more than 30 incidences. Since then, the Department has made "remarkable changes and not wavered once" in their commitment under a settlement agreement, the Justice report said.

Missoula County, Montana

Investigations here focused on allegations of gender bias against victims of sexual assault. The Justice Department had to threaten a lawsuit against authorities for not doing enough for rape victims. After a stand-off that lasted two years, local officials and the Justice Department reached an agreement to implement better sexual assault policies, better training for prosecutors and other measures. The University of Montana launched programs to address sensitivity in sexual assault cases.

New Orleans, Louisiana

Minorities were subjected to excessive force, illegal stops and searches, federal investigators said in a 2011 report. Even the dogs in the Police Department's K-9 unit were "uncontrollable" and even attacked their own handlers. More black residents were arrested than white and transgendered people were targeted.

"Hundreds" of officers resigned during the investigation and even some of the dogs in the K-9 unit were also "suspended." But even after the initial investigation, body cameras and in-car cameras were used in only 49 of 145 incidents. Interim Police Superintendent Michael Harrison told the *New Orleans Times-Picayune* that additional issues would be addressed on a "case-by-case basis."

Newark, New Jersey

Excessive force allegations, unwarranted stop and-search incidents, and discrimination against black residents were part of a 2011 report. In stops being made during that time, 75 percent were not warranted. Newark has a high crime rate and limited budgets for policing. Eventually, the Justice Department posted advertisements for a monitoring team for Newark police.

(Faith Karmini, "Ferguson's not the only city to get scathing federal report," CNN March 5, 2015.)

How much is police misconduct costing citizens of these—and other—American cities?

Nick Wing summarized the costs of wrongful death lawsuits—and other lawsuits—filed against the police, and year dates, in major U.S. cities:

> Boston, 2015-2015—$36 million;
> Chicago, 2004-214—$521 million;
> Cleveland, 2004-2014—$8.2 million;
> Dallas, 2011-2014—$6.6 million;
> Denver, since 2011—$12. million;

Los Angeles, 2002-2011—$101 million;
Minneapolis, 2011-2014—$9.3 million;
New York City, 2006-2011—$348 million;
Oakland, 1990-2014—$74 million;
Philadelphia, 2009-2014—$40 million.

Wing makes the obvious point that using all these millions of public funds for civic improvement projects—schools, parks, infrastructure projects, social programs—could make vast differences in all of these cities.

(Nick Wing: "We Pay a Shocking Price for Police Misconduct and Cops Wan Us to Just Accept It. We Shouldn't." *The Huffington Post,* May 29, 2015.)

Any major American city could be next on this list of sordid hypocrisy.

Only federal interventions and monitoring for the fore-seeable future—through the Department of Justice—can hope to rehabilitate—or even save—police departments in major U.S. cities.

Suggested Readings

Balko, Radley. *Overkill: The Rise of Paramilitary Raids in America*. Washington, D.C,; Cato Institute, 2006.

———. *Rise of the Warrior Cop: The Militarization of America's Police Forces*. New York: Public Affairs Press, 2013.

Diamond, Jeremy and Wesley Bruer. "Ferguson Police report: most shocking parts." CNN. March 4, 2015.

Dobuzinskis, Alex. "San Francisco Reviews Thousands of Arrests Following Officers' Racist Texts." Reuters, in *The Huffington Post*, May 8, 2015.

Fensch, Thomas. *At The Dangerous Edge of Social Justice: Race, Violence and Death in America*. N. Chesterfield, Va.: New Century Books, 2013.

Hazen, Dan, ed. *Inside the L.A. Riots—what really happened—and why it will happen again*. New York: Institute for Alterative Journalism, 1992.

"How Racism Doomed Baltimore." *The New York Times*, May 5, 2015.

King, Shaun. "Let's stop saying bad police officer are rare. Fact is they're plentiful from coast to coast." *The Daily Kos*, May 15, 2015.

Klein, Carol Swartout. "Why I Believe in the People of Ferguson." *The Huffington Post*, March 16, 2015.

Lewis, John. "Michael Brown, Eric Garner and the 'Other America.'" *The Atlantic Monthly*, Dec 15, 2014.

Taibbi, Matt. "Why Baltimore Blew Up." *Rolling Stone*, June 4, 2015.

Williams, Timothy. "Inquiry to Examine Racial Bias in the San Francisco Police." *The New York Times*, May 7, 2015.

About the Author

Thomas Fensch is the author or editor of over 30 books of nonfiction.

This book is a companion to *At the Dangerous Edge of Social Justice: Race, Violence and Death in America,* published in 2013.

He has a doctorate from Syracuse Univerity and lives outside Richmond, Virginia with his veteran literary advisors: Wolfie, a white German Shepherd, Sally, a Great Pyrenees, and Charlie, a Labradoodle.

www.ingramcontent.com/pod-product-compliance
Lightning Source LLC
Chambersburg PA
CBHW071623270326
41928CB00010B/1747